FamilyCircle®

Good Food

2001

FamilyCircle®

Good Food 2001

from the editors of Family Circle

FAMILY CIRCLE BOOKS, NEW YORK

Published by Random House Direct, Inc.
299 Park Avenue, New York, New York 10171
Family Circle Books Web address: www.Familycirclebooks.com

A Roundtable Press Book

Printed in the United Kingdom
First Edition

ISBN 0-002-41019-2

FOR ROUNDTABLE PRESS, INC.:

DIRECTORS: Marsha Melnick, Julie Merberg, Susan E. Meyer

SENIOR EDITOR: Carol Spier

BOOK DESIGN: pink design, inc. nyc

COPY EDITOR: Virginia Croft

EDITORIAL ASSISTANTS: Carrie Glidden, Sara Newberry

PRODUCTION: Bill Rose

FOR FAMILY CIRCLE BOOKS:

VICE-PRESIDENT AND GENERAL MANAGER: Lisa Faith Phillips

DIRECT MARKETING DIRECTOR: Tom Downing

ASSOCIATE OPERATIONS DIRECTOR: Deborah Williams

BUSINESS MANAGER: Peter Immediato

DIRECT MARKETING ASSOCIATE: Jennifer Zalewski

INVENTORY ASSISTANT: Eric Levy

DIRECT MARKETING ASSISTANT: Barbara Giordano

FOR FAMILY CIRCLE MAGAZINE:

EDITOR-IN-CHIEF: Susan Kelliher Ungaro

CREATIVE DIRECTOR: Diane Lamphron

EXECUTIVE EDITOR: Barbara Winkler

FOOD DIRECTOR: Peggy Katalinich

SENIOR FOOD EDITOR: Diane Mogelever

SENIOR ASSOCIATE FOOD EDITOR: Julie Miltenberger

EDITORIAL ASSISTANT: Keri Linas

TEST KITCHEN ASSISTANTS: Keisha Davis, Althea Needham

RECIPE EDITOR: David Ricketts

NUTRITIONIST: Patty Santelli

TEST KITCHEN: JoAnn Brett, Lauren Huber, Donna Meadow, Michael Tyrell, Robert Yamarone

FOR G+J PUBLISHING:

BOOKS & LICENSING DIRECTOR: Tammy Palazzo

BOOKS & LICENSING COORDINATOR: Sabeena Lalwani

BOOKS & LICENSING ASSISTANT: Carla Clark

Cover photographs: front, Brian Hagiwara; spine, Brian Hagiwara; back, Mark Thomas (top and middle), Brian Hagiwara (bottom).

The recipes shown on pages 2 through 7 appear as follows: Classic Ground Beef Tacos (page 2) on page 29. Carrot Salad (page 3, left) on page 124. Ribbons and Bows Cake (page 3, top) on page 184. Multigrain Bread (page 3, right) on page 110. Chocolate-Dipped Almond Biscotti (page 6) on page 220. Almond Pine-Nut Cookies (page 6) on page 219. Mock Guacamole (page 7, top) on page 16. Lisa's Fresh Salsa (page 7, top) on page 17. Seafood Skillet (page 7, left) on page 51. Pumpkin Parfaits (page 7, right) on page 140. Mediterranean Pork Skewers (page 7, bottom) on page 97.

Foreword

"There's a tasting!"

At least 5 times a day—and sometimes as often as 15!—these words summon me to the Family Circle Test Kitchen to sample our latest creation. (A tough job, yes, but someone's got to do it….) Gathered around the island in the center of the kitchen, the food editors and I nibble and critique. Too salty? Overcooked? Not sweet enough?

We're definitely what I'd call a tough audience and judge each recipe harshly. First and foremost, we want great taste. If and only if the dish passes that test, the evaluation continues: Are the steps simple and straightforward? Is the nutrition profile reasonable? Are the ingredients readily available and affordably priced? When the answers are all an enthusiastic yes, the recipe is ready for the pages of *Family Circle.*

In your hands are the results of all those tastings: a full year's worth of recipes collected in one handy reference and filled with lovely color photographs. You'll find sensational stir-fries *(Stir-Fried Shrimp with Honey Walnuts)* and terrific grilling options *(Basil Grilled Salmon* or *Sesame and Soy Grilled Steak Salad),* party-perfect starters *(Warm Cheddar-Thyme Vidalia Dip)* and goodies ready to wrap as gifts *(Banana-Coconut Loaf).* Plus soups, salads, vegetables and glorious desserts, from divinely decorated cakes to no-bake pies.

I've got to go now…to another tasting. Look for the results in **Good Food 2002!**

Peggy Katalinich
FAMILY CIRCLE FOOD DIRECTOR

Contents

FROM TOP: SHRIMP 'N' SAUSAGE
SKEWERS (PAGE 12); SPICY CHILI
CUPS (PAGE 12); ROASTED RED POTATOES
WITH CAVIAR (PAGE 14)

BRUSCHETTA (PAGE 17)

CURRIED SQUASH SOUP (PAGE 21)

Starters

Olive-Artichoke-Sausage Quiche

MAKES 6 servings PREP 10 minutes
REFRIGERATE 30 minutes COOK 6 minutes
BAKE at 400° for 30 to 33 minutes

1   refrigerated ready-to-use piecrust
3   eggs
½   pound sweet Italian sausage
1   can (14 ounces) artichoke hearts, drained, each heart cut into 6 pieces
½   cup chopped pimiento-stuffed olives
1   container (15 ounces) ricotta cheese
2   tablespoons grated Parmesan cheese

1. Fit piecrust into a 9-inch pie plate.

2. Beat eggs in a small bowl. Brush 1 tablespoon egg over piecrust; transfer remaining egg to a blender. Refrigerate crust 30 minutes.

3. Meanwhile, place sausage and artichoke hearts in a skillet; cover with water. Bring to simmering over high heat, lower heat and simmer 6 minutes. Drain. Place artichokes on paper toweling; pat dry. Set aside 12 pieces for garnish. Cut sausage into thin slices.

4. Place oven rack in lowest position. Heat oven to 400°.

5. Add olives, ricotta and Parmesan to egg in blender; whirl to blend.

6. Spoon sliced sausage and artichokes over crust. Pour in egg and cheese mixture. Arrange reserved artichoke pieces on top.

7. Bake in heated 400° oven 30 to 33 minutes or until a knife inserted in center comes out clean. Cool on a wire rack 10 minutes.

PER SERVING
399 calories, 27 g fat (9 g saturated), 17 g protein, 21 g carbohydrate, 1 g fiber, 864 mg sodium, 165 mg cholesterol.

Tuna Nachos

MAKES 6 servings PREP 5 minutes
BAKE at 350° for 12 minutes

2   cans (6 ounces each) water-packed solid white tuna, drained
½   cup sour cream
2   teaspoons chili powder
½   teaspoon ground cumin
¼   teaspoon salt
¼   teaspoon hot-pepper sauce
4½ ounces (half of 9-ounce bag) corn tortilla chips
1   cup salsa
¼   cup sliced pitted black olives
1   cup shredded pepper-Jack cheese (4 ounces)

1. Heat oven to 350°.

2. Mix tuna, sour cream, chili powder, cumin, salt and hot-pepper sauce in a small bowl. Line a large glass pie plate with tortilla chips. Distribute tuna mixture evenly on top. Spoon salsa over tuna. Top with olives and cheese.

3. Bake in heated 350° oven 12 minutes or until bubbly.

PER SERVING
318 calories, 17 g fat (8 g saturated), 18 g protein, 22 g carbohydrate, 1 g fiber, 1,141 mg sodium, 49 mg cholesterol.

Shredded Pork Nachos

MAKES 8 servings **PREP** 10 minutes
BAKE at 400° for 8 minutes

1   container (2 pounds) fully cooked shredded pork with BBQ sauce
1   can (7 ounces) Mexicali corn, drained
1   can (4½ ounces) chopped green chiles, drained
¼   cup chopped fresh cilantro
1   bag (9 ounces) corn tortilla chips
1   package (8 ounces) shredded cheddar cheese (2 cups)
2   scallions, chopped, including part of the green
1   can (2½ ounces) sliced pitted ripe black olives

1. Heat oven to 400°.

2. Spoon 2 cups pork with sauce into a medium-size bowl; reserve remainder for another use. Add corn, chiles and cilantro to pork in bowl.

3. Spread half of tortilla chips over a baking sheet. Spoon half of pork mixture over chips. Top with 1 cup cheese. Sprinkle with half of scallions and half of olives. Repeat with remaining chips, pork, cheese, scallions and olives.

4. Bake in heated 400° oven 8 minutes or until cheese is melted.

PER SERVING
468 calories, 21 g fat (8 g saturated), 26 g protein, 48 g carbohydrate, 3 g fiber, 1,238 mg sodium, 60 mg cholesterol.

Chorizo Quesadillas

The Mexican sausage chorizo, flavored with garlic and chili powder, is a spicy counterpart to black beans.

MAKES 4 servings **PREP** 5 minutes
COOK 3 minutes
BAKE at 400° for 5 to 6 minutes

½   cup chopped chorizo (3½ ounces)
1   can (19 ounces) black beans, drained and rinsed
6   tablespoons salsa
8   flour tortillas (7-inch)
1½   cups shredded pepper-Jack cheese (6 ounces)

1. Heat oven to 400°. Grease a large baking sheet.

2. Cook chorizo in a small skillet over medium-high heat 3 minutes. Transfer to a medium-size bowl. Stir in beans and salsa. Spread mixture over tortillas, dividing equally; divide cheese equally on top.

3. Fold each tortilla in half and transfer to prepared baking sheet. Bake in heated 400° oven 5 to 6 minutes or until cheese is melted. To serve, cut each tortilla in half.

PER SERVING
637 calories, 28 g fat (13 g saturated), 28 g protein, 69 g carbohydrate, 9 g fiber, 1,347 mg sodium, 60 mg cholesterol.

Shrimp 'n' Sausage Skewers

Shown on page 8.

MAKES about 5 dozen skewers
SOAK skewers in water 30 minutes
PREP 15 minutes **BROIL** 2 to 4 minutes

60 wooden skewers (6-inch)
½ cup apricot jam
2 tablespoons water
2 packages (3¼ ounces each) chorizo or other precooked spicy sausage, cut into ¼-inch-thick slices (about 60)
2 pounds large shrimp (about 60), peeled and deveined

1. Soak wooden skewers in a pan of water 30 minutes.

2. To make dipping sauce, heat jam and water in a small saucepan over medium-low heat, stirring to mix. Remove from heat.

3. Heat oven to broil.

4. Curve 1 shrimp around perimeter of 1 slice of chorizo; secure with a skewer. Place on a baking sheet. Repeat with remaining shrimp and chorizo.

5. Broil 1 to 2 minutes per side or until shrimp are cooked through. Serve with dipping sauce.

PER SKEWER
30 calories, 1 g fat (0 g saturated), 3 g protein, 2 g carbohydrate, 0 g fiber, 60 mg sodium, 21 mg cholesterol.

Spicy Chili Cups

Shown on page 8.

MAKES 45 mini chili cups
PREP 20 minutes **COOK** 40 to 45 minutes

1 tablespoon vegetable oil
¾ pound lean ground beef
1 medium onion, diced
½ sweet green pepper, cored, seeded and diced
2 large cloves garlic, chopped
1 can (14½ ounces) diced tomatoes, undrained
⅓ cup tomato paste
1 cup water
1 tablespoon chili powder
1½ teaspoons salt
¼ teaspoon ground red pepper (cayenne)
1 can (15 ounces) kidney beans, drained and rinsed
3 packages (2.1 ounces each) baked mini phyllo shells (45 shells total)
1 container (8 ounces) reduced-fat sour cream
½ cup shredded cheddar cheese

1. Heat oil in a large nonstick skillet over medium heat. Add beef, onion, green pepper and garlic; sauté, breaking up clumps of beef with a wooden spoon, 8 minutes.

2. Add tomatoes, tomato paste, water, chili powder, salt and ground red pepper. Bring to boiling. Reduce heat to low; simmer, uncovered, 30 to 35 minutes. Stir in beans; cook until warmed through, about 2 minutes.

3. Fill each phyllo shell with scant 1 tablespoon chili. Top with sour cream and cheddar cheese.

PER CHILI CUP
64 calories, 3 g fat (1 g saturated), 3 g protein, 5 g carbohydrate, 1 g fiber, 136 mg sodium, 9 mg cholesterol.

Sesame Chicken with Dipping Sauce

An appetizer that is equally appealing to children and adults. To vary the dish, use peeled, cleaned jumbo shrimp, cut into 1-inch pieces, instead of the chicken specified here. Why not make some of each version?

MAKES about 6 dozen pieces
PREP 20 minutes **STAND** 15 minutes
BAKE at 350° for 20 minutes

2 **pounds boneless, skinless chicken breasts, cut into 1-inch cubes**
¼ **cup teriyaki sauce**
½ **cup all-purpose flour**
1 **teaspoon salt**
½ **teaspoon black pepper**
4 **egg whites**
2 **bottles (2⅔ ounces each) sesame seeds (about 1½ cups), lightly toasted (see page 232)**

Dipping Sauce
1 **cup red currant jelly**
4 **teaspoons soy sauce**
2 **teaspoons grated fresh ginger**

1. Heat oven to 350°. Coat a baking sheet with nonstick cooking spray.

2. Combine chicken and teriyaki sauce in a medium-size bowl. Let stand 15 minutes.

3. Combine flour, salt and pepper in a large resealable plastic food-storage bag. Lightly beat egg whites in a medium-size bowl. Spread out sesame seeds in a shallow dish.

4. Add chicken cubes, a few at a time, to flour mixture. Seal bag; shake to coat chicken. Dip floured chicken cubes into egg white. Roll in sesame seeds to coat. Place on prepared baking sheet.

5. Bake in heated 350° oven about 20 minutes or until golden and chicken is cooked through.

6. Meanwhile, prepare sauce: Combine jelly, soy sauce and ginger in a small saucepan. Heat gently until warmed. Serve with chicken.

PER PIECE
41 calories, 1 g fat (0 g saturated), 3 g protein, 4 g carbohydrate, 0 g fiber, 69 mg sodium, 7 mg cholesterol.

1. Heat oven to 400°.

2. Place potatoes and oil in a roasting pan; toss until potatoes are well coated. Sprinkle with rosemary, garlic, salt and pepper; toss well.

3. Bake in heated 400° oven about 15 minutes. Lower oven temperature to 350°. Bake 20 minutes longer or until potatoes are cooked through but still somewhat firm; stir potatoes during baking.

4. Transfer roasting pan to a wire rack and let potatoes cool until warm.

5. Place potato halves, flat side up, on a serving platter. Dollop each potato half with a teaspoon of sour cream and a teaspoon of caviar. Serve at once.

PER POTATO HALF
21 calories, 10 g fat (0 g saturated), 1 g protein, 2 g carbohydrate, 0 g fiber, 35 mg sodium, 9 mg cholesterol.

Roasted Red Potatoes with Caviar

Shown on page 8.

MAKES about 42 potato halves
PREP 15 minutes
BAKE at 400° for 15 minutes; then at 350° for 20 minutes

1½ pounds very small red potatoes (about 21), scrubbed and cut in half
1 tablespoon olive oil
2 teaspoons dried rosemary, crushed
2 large cloves garlic, crushed through a press
¼ teaspoon salt
⅛ teaspoon black pepper
½ cup reduced-fat sour cream
1 small jar (2 ounces) black lumpfish caviar or caviar of your choice

Bacon and Cheese Deviled Eggs

MAKES 12 servings (2 halves each)
PREP 10 minutes

12 hard-cooked eggs, shelled
½ cup mayonnaise
1 tablespoon honey mustard
½ teaspoon salt
¼ teaspoon black pepper
4 slices bacon, cooked and crumbled
2 tablespoons shredded sharp cheddar cheese
Chopped fresh parsley for garnish (optional)

1. Halve eggs lengthwise. Remove yolks and place in a medium-size bowl. Set aside whites.

2. Mash egg yolks with a fork. Mix in mayonnaise, mustard, salt and pepper. Fold in bacon and cheese.

3. Fill each egg white half with egg yolk mixture. Cover and refrigerate until ready to serve. Garnish with parsley just before serving if desired.

PER SERVING
164 calories, 14 g fat (3 g saturated), 7 g protein, 2 g carbohydrate, 0 g fiber, 244 mg sodium, 220 mg cholesterol.

Caesar Dip

MAKES about 2½ cups **PREP** 5 minutes

1 **pound creamy cottage cheese**
½ **cup grated Parmesan cheese**
3 **tablespoons lemon juice**
1 **tablespoon Worcestershire sauce**
1½ **teaspoons garlic salt**
½ **teaspoon salt**
⅛ **teaspoon black pepper**
½ **teaspoon liquid hot-pepper sauce**
½ **teaspoon anchovy paste (optional)**
⅓ **cup olive oil**

Place cottage cheese, Parmesan, lemon juice, Worcestershire sauce, garlic salt, salt, black pepper, hot-pepper sauce, and, if desired, anchovy paste in a food processor; whirl about 2 minutes or until pureed. With machine running, gradually add oil through tube; whirl 1 minute.

PER TABLESPOON
34 calories, 3 g fat (1 g saturated), 2 g protein, 1 g carbohydrate, 0 g fiber, 157 mg sodium, 3 mg cholesterol.

Warm Cheddar-Thyme Vidalia Dip

MAKES 16 servings **PREP** 15 minutes
BAKE at 375° for 30 minutes

6 **ounces pepper-Jack cheese, shredded**
6 **ounces reduced-fat cheddar cheese, shredded**
4 **ounces light cream cheese**
½ **cup reduced-fat mayonnaise**
1 **teaspoon fresh thyme, chopped, or ¼ teaspoon dried thyme**
3 **cups finely chopped Vidalia or other sweet onion (one 1-pound onion)**

1. Heat oven to 375°.

2. Combine shredded cheeses, cream cheese, mayonnaise, thyme and 1 cup onion in a food processor. Whirl until fairly smooth. Spoon mixture into a shallow 6-cup baking dish. Stir in remaining 2 cups onion.

3. Bake in heated 375° oven 20 minutes. Stir. Bake 10 minutes longer. Cool slightly before serving.

PER SERVING
127 calories, 10 g fat (5 g saturated), 7 g protein, 4 g carbohydrate, 1 g fiber, 158 mg sodium, 23 mg cholesterol.

Cheese and Scallion Dip

MAKES 2 cups **PREP** 5 minutes
REFRIGERATE at least 1 hour

1   container (1 pound) nonfat
    sour cream
2   ounces blue cheese, crumbled
    (½ cup)
½   cup chopped scallions, including
    part of the green (about
    4 scallions)
¼   teaspoon salt
¼   teaspoon coarsely ground black
    pepper
    Assorted raw and/or blanched
    vegetables for serving

1. Place sour cream and blue cheese in
    a food processor; pulse with on-off
    motions until creamy (may be slightly
    lumpy). Transfer to a bowl. Stir in
    scallions, salt and pepper. Refrigerate
    at least 1 hour for flavors to develop.

2. Serve with a selection of raw and/or
    blanched vegetables.

PER ¼ CUP
63 calories, 2 g fat (1 g saturated), 6 g protein,
7 g carbohydrate, 0 g fiber, 206 mg sodium,
5 mg cholesterol.

Mock Guacamole

MAKES 1½ cups **PREP** 10 minutes
COOK about 15 minutes

1   pound sweet green peppers
2   tablespoons finely chopped onion
1   small clove garlic, finely chopped
1   teaspoon salt
½   teaspoon dried oregano
⅛   teaspoon black pepper
2   tablespoons fresh lime juice
    (1 lime)
6   sprigs fresh cilantro
¼   cup sour cream
    Chopped fresh cilantro for
    garnish (optional)
    Tortilla chips for serving (optional)

1. Roast green peppers over an open
    flame on stovetop or under broiler,
    turning occasionally, until charred all
    over, about 15 minutes. Place peppers
    in a brown paper bag; seal. Let cool.
    Remove peppers from bag. Halve
    peppers lengthwise; remove stems
    and seeds. Scrape off skins.

2. Place roasted peppers, onion, garlic,
    salt, oregano, black pepper, lime juice
    and cilantro sprigs in a blender or

small food processor and whirl until smooth. Scrape into a small bowl. Stir in sour cream. Garnish with chopped cilantro if desired. Serve with tortilla chips.

PER 2 TABLESPOONS
23 calories, 1 g fat (1 g saturated), 1 g protein,
3 g carbohydrate, 1 g fiber, 197 mg sodium,
2 mg cholesterol.

Lisa's Fresh Salsa

MAKES 4 cups **PREP** 20 minutes
REFRIGERATE 1 hour or overnight

1 pound fresh tomatoes, chopped (about 2 cups)
1 medium onion, chopped
½ medium sweet green pepper, cored, seeded and chopped (about ½ cup)
1 to 2 jalapeño chiles, cored, seeded and finely chopped
1 tablespoon sugar
½ teaspoon salt
½ teaspoon dried oregano
1 tablespoon vegetable oil
1 tablespoon fresh lime or lemon juice
1 tablespoon distilled white vinegar
1 can (8 ounces) tomato sauce
   Tortilla chips for serving (optional)

Mix together tomatoes, onion, green pepper, chiles, sugar, salt, oregano, oil, lime juice, vinegar and tomato sauce in a large bowl. Cover; refrigerate at least 1 hour or overnight. Serve with tortilla chips.

PER 2 TABLESPOONS
14 calories, 1 g fat (0 g saturated), 0 g protein,
2 g carbohydrate, 0 g fiber, 81 mg sodium,
0 mg cholesterol.

Bruschetta

Shown on page 9.

MAKES 16 servings **PREP** 20 minutes
BROIL 1 minute

2 cloves garlic, chopped
¼ teaspoon salt
¼ cup extra-virgin olive oil
1 loaf Italian bread, cut into sixteen 1-inch-thick slices
⅛ teaspoon black pepper
2 large ripe tomatoes (about ¾ pound), seeded and diced
1 teaspoon balsamic vinegar
1 tablespoon thinly sliced fresh basil
2 teaspoons minced red onion

1. Heat broiler.
2. Place chopped garlic on a cutting board; sprinkle with salt. Use side of a chef's knife to mash into a paste. Transfer to a small bowl; stir in oil.
3. Place bread slices on a baking sheet. Brush 1 side with some garlic-oil mixture. Reserve remaining oil mixture. Sprinkle bread with pepper.
4. Broil bread 1 minute or until slices start to brown slightly. Remove from broiler and set aside.
5. Mix tomatoes, vinegar, basil and onion in a medium-size bowl. Add remaining garlic-oil mixture.
6. Evenly spoon tomato mixture over bread slices. Serve at once.

PER SERVING
88 calories, 4 g fat (1 g saturated), 2 g protein,
11 g carbohydrate, 8 g fiber, 149 mg sodium,
0 mg cholesterol.

Speedy Cheese Sticks

MAKES 12 sticks **PREP** 15 minutes
BAKE at 375° for 12 to 15 minutes

6   **pieces string cheese (about
    1 ounce each)**
2   **packages (11 ounces each)
    refrigerated soft bread-stick dough**
2   **tablespoons pesto**
1   **egg white, lightly beaten**
2   **teaspoons grated Parmesan cheese**
1   **cup spaghetti sauce for dipping**

1. Heat oven to 375°.
2. Cut each piece of string cheese in half
    lengthwise.
3. Lightly flour a work surface and
    rolling pin. Separate each package
    of bread-stick dough into 12 strips.
    Lightly roll 2 strips until 1½ inches in
    width. Spread middle of 1 strip with
    scant ¼ teaspoon pesto. Place a string
    cheese half on top of pesto. Spread
    scant ¼ teaspoon pesto over middle
    of second strip of dough. Moisten
    edges with water and place, pesto side
    down, on top of cheese-topped strip;
    press edges together to seal. Transfer
    to an ungreased baking sheet.
4. Repeat with remaining dough, pesto
    and cheese. Lightly brush cheese
    sticks with beaten egg white; sprinkle
    with Parmesan. Using a sharp knife,
    cut three ½-inch-long slashes in top
    of each stick.
5. Bake in heated 375° oven 12 to
    15 minutes or until golden and
    puffed. Cool cheese sticks slightly on
    baking sheet on a wire rack.

6. Meanwhile, heat spaghetti sauce in a
    small saucepan. Transfer to a small
    bowl. Serve cheese sticks with sauce
    for dipping.

PER STICK
197 calories, 6 g fat (2 g saturated), 8 g protein,
26 g carbohydrate, 1 g fiber, 494 mg sodium,
9 mg cholesterol.

South-of-the-Border Snack Mix

MAKES about 12½ cups **PREP** 15 minutes
BAKE at 250° for 30 minutes

4   **cups broken tortilla chips (bite-size)**
3   **cups multi-bran cereal squares**
2   **cups mini cheese snack crackers**
2   **cups mini pretzel twists**
1½   **cups dry-roasted unsalted peanuts**
¼   **cup (½ stick) butter or margarine,
     melted**
2   **tablespoons Worcestershire sauce**
1   **tablespoon chili powder**
2   **teaspoons ground cumin**
1   **teaspoon garlic powder**
1   **teaspoon seasoned salt**
1   **teaspoon ground red pepper
     (cayenne), or to taste**

1. Position oven racks in second and
    third top levels in oven. Heat oven
    to 250°.
2. Combine tortilla chips, cereal,
    crackers, pretzels and peanuts in a
    large bowl.
3. Mix butter, Worcestershire sauce,
    chili powder, cumin, garlic powder,
    seasoned salt and red pepper in a
    small bowl. Pour over snack mixture;
    toss until mixture is lightly moistened.

Scrape mixture onto 2 ungreased 15 x 10 x 1-inch jelly-roll pans and spread evenly.

4. Bake in heated 250° oven 30 minutes or until coating on snack mixture begins to darken slightly, stirring every 10 minutes; after 15 minutes, switch pans between racks, rotating each pan front to back as you reposition it. Cool completely in pans on wire racks.

PER ¼ CUP SERVING
66 calories, 4 g fat (1 g saturated), 2 g protein, 7 g carbohydrate, 1 g fiber, 79 mg sodium, 3 mg cholesterol.

Caribbean Nuts

MAKES 4 cups **PREP** 15 minutes
BAKE at 300° for 30 minutes

- 2 tablespoons light-brown sugar
- 1 egg white
- 1 tablespoon onion powder
- 1 tablespoon dried thyme
- 2 teaspoons ground allspice
- 2 teaspoons black pepper
- 1 teaspoon salt
- ¾ teaspoon ground cinnamon
- ½ teaspoon ground nutmeg
- 4 cups dry-roasted unsalted peanuts

1. Heat oven to 300°.

2. Whisk together brown sugar, egg white, onion powder, thyme, allspice, pepper, salt, cinnamon and nutmeg in a large bowl. Add peanuts, 1 cup at a time, stirring well after each addition until peanuts are evenly coated with seasoning mixture. Scrape onto an ungreased 15 x 10 x 1-inch jelly-roll pan and spread evenly.

3. Bake in heated 300° oven 30 minutes or until nuts are lightly colored, stirring every 10 minutes. Cool completely in pan on a wire rack.

PER ¼ CUP
225 calories, 18 g fat (3 g saturated), 9 g protein, 10 g carbohydrate, 3 g fiber, 152 mg sodium, 0 mg cholesterol.

Almonds Italiano

MAKES 3 cups **PREP** 15 minutes
BAKE at 275° for 45 minutes

- 2 tablespoons olive oil
- 1 egg white
- 2 teaspoons dried basil
- 2 teaspoons dried oregano
- 2 teaspoons dried rosemary
- 2 teaspoons dried thyme
- 2 teaspoons garlic powder
- 2 teaspoons onion powder
- ½ teaspoon salt
- 3 cups whole unblanched almonds (about 14 ounces)

1. Heat oven to 275°.

2. Whisk together oil, egg white, basil, oregano, rosemary, thyme, garlic powder, onion powder and salt in a large bowl. Add almonds, 1 cup at a time, stirring well after each addition until almonds are evenly coated with herb mixture. Scrape onto an ungreased 15 x 10 x 1-inch jelly-roll pan and spread evenly.

3. Bake in heated 275° oven 45 minutes or until nuts are lightly toasted, stirring every 10 minutes. Cool completely in pan on a wire rack.

PER ¼ CUP
237 calories, 21 g fat (2 g saturated), 9 g protein, 9 g carbohydrate, 4 g fiber, 112 mg sodium, 0 mg cholesterol.

Gazpacho

MAKES 6 servings PREP 10 minutes
REFRIGERATE 2 hours

1 **seedless cucumber, coarsely chopped**
1 **sweet red pepper, cored, seeded and coarsely chopped**
1 **small onion, coarsely chopped**
1 **small clove garlic**
4 **cups spicy vegetable juice**
1 **tablespoon fresh lime juice**
¼ **teaspoon liquid hot-pepper sauce**
½ **teaspoon salt**

1. In a food processor, puree half of cucumber, half of red pepper, half of onion, garlic, 1 cup vegetable juice, lime juice, hot-pepper sauce and salt. Pour into a large bowl; add remaining 3 cups vegetable juice.

2. Cover bowl and refrigerate until gazpacho is chilled, about 2 hours. Serve garnished with remaining chopped cucumber, red pepper and onion.

PER SERVING
47 calories, 0 g fat (0 g saturated), 2 g protein, 10 g carbohydrate, 1 g fiber, 720 mg sodium, 0 mg cholesterol.

Springtime Soup

MAKES 8 servings PREP 10 minutes
COOK about 40 minutes

3 **vegetable bouillon cubes**
1 **cup boiling water**
1 **tablespoon vegetable oil**
2 **cups chopped leeks (white part only)**
5 **cups water**
1 **package (10 ounces) frozen peas**
1 **bag (10 ounces) romaine salad mix or romaine lettuce, leaves torn**
½ **cup heavy cream**
½ **teaspoon salt**
¼ **teaspoon black pepper**
¼ **teaspoon ground nutmeg**
½ **cup packaged dried mashed-potato flakes**
½ **cup sour cream**

1. Place bouillon cubes in a large heatproof bowl. Add boiling water. Stir to completely dissolve bouillon cubes.

2. Heat oil in a Dutch oven over low heat. Add leeks; cover and cook, stirring occasionally, until tender, about 20 minutes.

3. Increase heat to medium. Add bouillon liquid, 5 cups water and peas to leeks in pot; cook 10 minutes or until heated through. Add salad blend. Bring to boiling. Remove from heat. Let soup stand 5 minutes.

4. Working in batches, whirl soup in a food processor or blender to puree. Return to pot. Stir in cream, salt, pepper, nutmeg and potato flakes. Gently cook until heated through and slightly thickened, about 5 minutes. Serve soup dolloped with sour cream.

PER SERVING
162 calories, 12 g fat (6 g saturated), 4 g protein, 12 g carbohydrate, 3 g fiber, 829 mg sodium, 27 mg cholesterol.

Curried Squash Soup

Shown on page 9.

MAKES 4 servings (5½ cups)
PREP 15 minutes
COOK about 35 minutes

2½ pounds winter squash, such as butternut, acorn or hubbard, peeled, seeded and cut into ½-inch cubes
2½ cups water or chicken broth
½ cup orange juice
2 tablespoons butter
1 medium onion, chopped
1 clove garlic, finely chopped
1½ teaspoons curry powder
1¼ teaspoons salt
    Pinch ground red pepper (cayenne)
    Fresh lemon juice (optional)

1. Place squash in a medium-size saucepan. Add enough water to cover. Simmer until very tender, 12 to 15 minutes. Drain. Return squash to saucepan. Add 2½ cups water or broth and orange juice; mash.

2. Heat butter in a small skillet over medium heat. Add onion, garlic and curry powder; sauté until onion is softened, about 3 minutes. Lower heat; cover and cook until onion is very soft, about 12 minutes.

3. Add onion mixture to squash. Heat through.

4. Working in batches if necessary, whirl squash mixture in a food processor or blender until smooth. Return to saucepan. Add salt, red pepper and, if desired, a squeeze of lemon juice. Heat through.

PER SERVING
145 calories, 6 g fat (4 g saturated), 2 g protein, 24 g carbohydrate, 6 g fiber, 736 mg sodium, 16 mg cholesterol.

Broccoli Apple Bisque

MAKES 8 servings **PREP** 20 minutes
COOK about 20 minutes

1 large head broccoli (about 2 pounds)
2 tablespoons butter
1 small onion, finely chopped
2 large Red Delicious apples, peeled, cored and diced
2 cans (14½ ounces each) chicken broth
½ teaspoon salt
⅛ teaspoon black pepper
⅛ teaspoon ground nutmeg
1 tablespoon fresh lemon juice
⅛ teaspoon liquid hot-pepper sauce
⅓ cup sour cream
    Additional sliced or diced unpeeled apple for garnish (optional)

1. Cut off and discard most of broccoli stem. Chop remainder of broccoli; you should have about 8 cups.

2. Melt butter in a large heavy-bottomed saucepan. Add onion; sauté until softened, 2 minutes. Add apples, broccoli, broth, salt, pepper and nutmeg. Simmer until broccoli is tender, about 18 minutes.

3. Remove pan from heat. Stir in lemon juice and hot-pepper sauce. Let mixture cool slightly.

4. Working in batches, puree mixture in a blender. Return to pan; reheat to simmering. Just before serving, stir in sour cream. Garnish with apple if desired.

PER SERVING
119 calories, 7 g fat (4 g saturated), 3 g protein, 13 g carbohydrate, 4 g fiber, 604 mg sodium, 14 mg cholesterol.

STIR-FRIED SHRIMP WITH HONEY WALNUTS (PAGE 52)

BBQ BEEF AND VEGGIE FAJITAS (PAGE 92)

SAUSAGE AND POTATO SALAD (PAGE 100)

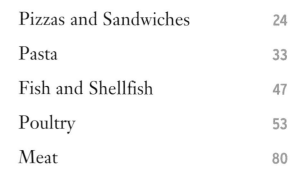

Main Courses

Individual Pizzas

MAKES 8 pizzas **PREP** 20 minutes
BAKE at 450° for 14 minutes

1 **package (2 pounds) frozen pizza dough, thawed**
1 **cup ricotta cheese**
2 **tablespoons pesto**
1 **package (3½ ounces) sliced pepperoni, chopped**
¼ **teaspoon salt**
⅛ **teaspoon black pepper**
1 **cup shredded mozzarella cheese (4 ounces)**

1. Heat oven to 450°. Grease 2 large baking sheets.

2. Using a sharp knife, cut each piece of dough into quarters. Roll out each quarter on a lightly floured surface into a 7-inch round. Transfer to prepared baking sheets.

3. Mix ricotta, pesto, pepperoni, salt and pepper in a small bowl. Spread each pizza with 3 tablespoons ricotta-pesto mixture, leaving a ½-inch border. Sprinkle mozzarella on top.

4. Bake in heated 450° oven 14 minutes or until cheese is melted.

PER PIZZA
476 calories, 19 g fat (7 g saturated), 19 g protein, 55 g carbohydrate, 2 g fiber, 1,168 mg sodium, 40 mg cholesterol.

Spinach Pizzas

Leaving pepperoni unchopped, assemble ingredients for Individual Pizzas, right, plus 1 package (10 ounces) frozen chopped spinach, thawed and squeezed dry. Assemble pizzas, adding spinach to ricotta-pesto mixture. Top pizzas with pepperoni slices before baking.

PER PIZZA
486 calories, 20 g fat (7 g saturated), 21 g protein, 57 g carbohydrate, 3 g fiber, 1,199 mg sodium, 40 mg cholesterol.

Quick Start Pizza

Using a sharp knife, cut each piece of pizza dough into quarters.

Taco Pan Pizza

MAKES 12 servings **PREP** 10 minutes
COOK 20 minutes
BAKE at 400° for 14 minutes

2   boxes (8½ ounces each) corn
    muffin mix
¼   cup milk
1   egg
1   pound ground beef
1   envelope (1¼ ounces) taco
    seasoning mix
1¼ cups mild chunky salsa
1   cup canned refried beans
1   cup shredded pepper-Jack cheese
1   container (8 ounces) sour cream
2   cups shredded iceberg lettuce
1   scallion, chopped, including part
    of the green

1. Heat oven to 400°. Grease a 15 x 10 x
    1-inch jelly-roll pan.

2. Stir together muffin mix, milk and
    egg in a medium-size bowl. Scrape
    dough into prepared pan; pat to an
    even thickness with damp fingers.

3. Bake in heated 400° oven 10 minutes
    or until edges are lightly browned.
    Transfer to a wire rack and set aside.
    Leave oven on.

4. Meanwhile, cook beef in a medium-
    size skillet over medium-high heat,
    breaking up clumps with a wooden
    spoon, 8 to 10 minutes or until no
    longer pink. Add seasoning mix and
    ¾ cup salsa. Lower heat; simmer,
    uncovered, 10 minutes.

5. Spread beans over corn bread in pan.
    Sprinkle with ½ cup cheese. Bake in
    heated 400° oven 2 minutes to melt
    cheese. Top with beef; sprinkle with
    remaining ½ cup cheese. Bake
    2 minutes to melt cheese.

6. Dollop sour cream over pizza. Top
    with lettuce, scallion and remaining
    ½ cup salsa.

PER SERVING
371 calories, 18 g fat (8 g saturated), 16 g protein,
37 g carbohydrate, 4 g fiber, 1,001 mg sodium,
64 mg cholesterol.

Clam Pizza

MAKES 4 servings **PREP** 5 minutes
COOK about 10 minutes
BAKE at 400° for 20 minutes

1   tablespoon olive oil
2   large cloves garlic, finely chopped
2   cans (6½ ounces each) chopped
    clams, drained
1   ready-to-use pizza shell
    (16 ounces)
⅓   cup ricotta cheese
1   cup shredded mozzarella cheese

1. Heat oven to 400°.

2. Heat oil in a small skillet over low
    heat. Add garlic; sauté 7 minutes.
    Add clams; cook 2 minutes.

3. Spread clams evenly over pizza shell.
    Arrange ricotta and mozzarella evenly
    on top.

4. Place pizza shell on a baking sheet.
    Bake in 400° oven 20 minutes or
    until melted.

PER SERVING
528 calories, 19 g fat (6 g saturated), 33 g protein,
54 g carbohydrate, 0 g fiber, 767 mg sodium,
71 mg cholesterol.

Shrimp and Rice Tacos

MAKES 12 soft tacos **PREP** 15 minutes
REFRIGERATE 30 to 45 minutes
COOK 5 minutes **STAND** 10 minutes

4	tablespoons olive oil
2	cloves garlic, finely chopped
2	tablespoons lime juice (1 lime)
1	teaspoon salt
½	teaspoon dried oregano
¼	teaspoon black pepper
1½	pounds small shrimp, peeled and deveined
½	cup mayonnaise
½	cup salsa
1	cup instant rice
12	corn tortillas (6-inch)
1	lime, cut into wedges
1	cup shredded Bibb lettuce

1. Mix together 3 tablespoons oil, garlic, lime juice, salt, oregano and pepper in a shallow glass baking dish. Add shrimp; stir to coat evenly with marinade. Cover dish; refrigerate 30 to 45 minutes.

2. Mix together mayonnaise and salsa in a small bowl. Cover and refrigerate.

3. Heat remaining tablespoon oil in a large nonstick skillet over medium-high heat. Remove shrimp from marinade with a slotted spoon; reserve marinade. Add shrimp to skillet in an even layer; cook about 2 minutes on each side, until just cooked.

4. Add reserved marinade to shrimp in skillet. Bring to simmering over medium-high heat. Remove skillet from heat. Stir in rice until well blended. Cover skillet; let stand 10 minutes or until rice is tender.

5. Warm tortillas according to package directions.

6. Place about ⅓ cup shrimp and rice mixture on one half of each tortilla. Season with a squeeze of fresh lime juice; top with shredded lettuce and mayonnaise-salsa mixture. Roll up.

PER TACO
220 calories, 13 g fat (1 g saturated), 9 g protein, 17 g carbohydrate, 2 g fiber, 449 mg sodium, 73 mg cholesterol.

Grilled Turkey Tacos

MAKES 12 soft tacos **PREP** 20 minutes
REFRIGERATE at least 1 hour
COOK about 16 minutes

¼	cup olive oil
2	cloves garlic, finely chopped
½	bunch fresh cilantro, finely chopped (about ⅓ cup)
2	tablespoons lime juice (1 lime)
½	teaspoon salt
½	teaspoon dried oregano
1	jalapeño chile, cored, seeded and diced
1½	pounds turkey cutlets
1	large sweet green pepper, cored, seeded and cut into ½-inch-wide strips
1	large red onion, cut into ¾-inch-wide wedges
12	flour tortillas (8-inch)
1	ripe avocado, peeled, pitted and diced
½	cup sour cream

Garnishes (optional)

¼	cup coarsely chopped fresh cilantro
1	lime, cut into small wedges

1. Mix together oil, garlic, cilantro, lime juice, salt, oregano and jalapeño in a large shallow glass dish. Add turkey cutlets, turning to coat with marinade. Cover dish and refrigerate at least 1 hour, turning cutlets occasionally.

2. Prepare a charcoal grill with hot coals, setting rack 6 inches from coals; or heat a gas grill to high; or heat broiler. Alternatively, grease a stovetop grill pan; heat over medium-high heat.

3. Place turkey cutlets on outdoor grill, under broiler or in grill pan; grill or broil about 3 minutes on each side or until internal temperature registers 170° on an instant-read thermometer. Remove turkey cutlets; keep warm.

4. Grill or broil green pepper and red onion on same rack or in grill pan until tender, about 5 minutes on each side.

5. Meanwhile, slice turkey cutlets into ½-inch-wide strips.

6. Warm tortillas according to package directions.

7. Divide turkey and vegetables among tortillas, top with avocado and sour cream, and roll up. Serve garnished with cilantro and lime wedges if desired.

PER TACO
246 calories, 12 g fat (2 g saturated), 17 g protein, 19 g carbohydrate, 1 g fiber, 279 mg sodium, 43 mg cholesterol.

Barbecue Chicken Tacos

MAKES 12 soft tacos **PREP** 15 minutes
BROIL 8 to 10 minutes

¾ **cup bottled barbecue sauce**
1½ **pounds boneless, skinless chicken breast halves**
1 **package (10 ounces) frozen corn kernels, cooked**
¼ **teaspoon salt**
12 **corn tortillas (6-inch)**
1 **small head lettuce, shredded**
1 **cup shredded Monterey Jack cheese (4 ounces)**
2 **scallions, chopped, including part of the green**

1. Position broiler-pan rack 6 inches from heat. Heat broiler.

2. Measure out ½ cup barbecue sauce. Brush onto chicken breast halves. Place chicken on broiler-pan rack; broil 4 to 5 minutes on each side.

3. Slice chicken into long ½-inch-thick strips. Mix with remaining ¼ cup barbecue sauce, corn and salt. Keep warm.

4. Warm tortillas according to package directions.

5. To serve, place lettuce on tortillas. Top with chicken. Sprinkle with cheese and scallions. Fold in half.

PER TACO
177 calories, 5 g fat (2 g saturated), 16 g protein, 17 g carbohydrate, 2 g fiber, 287 mg sodium, 40 mg cholesterol.

Three-Bean Tacos

MAKES 10 soft tacos PREP 15 minutes
COOK about 16 minutes

1   tablespoon olive oil
1   medium onion, finely chopped
1   sweet green pepper, cored,
    seeded and chopped
1   tablespoon chili powder
½   teaspoon salt
¼   teaspoon ground cumin
¼   teaspoon garlic powder
1   can (8 ounces) tomato sauce
1   can (19 ounces) kidney beans,
    drained and rinsed
1   can (15½ ounces) pinto beans,
    drained and rinsed
1   can (15½ ounces) cannellini beans,
    drained and rinsed
10 flavored flour tortillas (10-inch),
    such as spinach or roasted
    red pepper
1   cup shredded iceberg lettuce
1   pint cherry tomatoes, each cut
    into quarters
1   cup shredded pepper-Jack cheese
    (4 ounces)

1. Heat oil in a large nonstick skillet
    over medium-high heat. Add
    onion and green pepper; cook until
    softened, about 10 minutes.

2. Add chili powder, salt, cumin and
    garlic powder; cook 1 minute. Stir in
    tomato sauce. Bring to simmering.
    Add kidney, pinto and cannellini
    beans; cook 5 minutes or until heated
    through. Lightly mash bean mixture.

3. Warm tortillas according to package
    directions.

4. Mix lettuce, tomatoes and cheese in a
    medium-size bowl.

5. Spoon bean mixture on one half of
    each tortilla, dividing equally; roll up.
    Serve with lettuce mixture on the side.

PER TACO
307 calories, 10 g fat (2 g saturated), 14 g protein,
47 g carbohydrate, 8 g fiber, 864 mg sodium,
10 mg cholesterol.

Pork Picadillo Tacos

MAKES 10 hard tacos PREP 15 minutes
COOK about 18 minutes WARM taco shells
at 375° for about 5 minutes

1   tablespoon vegetable oil
1   medium onion, finely chopped
2   cloves garlic, finely chopped
1½   pounds ground pork
½   teaspoon salt
½   teaspoon ground cinnamon
¼   teaspoon ground cumin
¼   teaspoon ground cloves
¼   teaspoon black pepper
1   can (8 ounces) tomato sauce
1   can (11 ounces) Mexicali corn,
     drained
10   large taco shells
1   cup shredded green cabbage
1   cup sour cream
     Chopped fresh cilantro for garnish
     (optional)

1. Heat oven to 375°.

2. Heat oil in a large skillet over
    medium-high heat. Add onion and
    garlic; sauté until softened, about
    3 minutes. Add pork; sauté until meat
    is no longer pink, 5 to 7 minutes.

3. Add salt, cinnamon, cumin, cloves
    and pepper; cook 1 minute. Add
    tomato sauce. Bring to simmering;
    simmer, stirring, about 5 minutes.

4. Add corn; cook until heated through, about 2 minutes.

5. Warm taco shells in heated 375° oven about 5 minutes. Spoon about ½ cup pork mixture into each taco shell. Top filling with cabbage; drizzle with sour cream. Garnish with cilantro if desired.

PER TACO
324 calories, 21 g fat (8 g saturated), 15 g protein, 21 g carbohydrate, 3 g fiber, 557 mg sodium, 56 mg cholesterol.

Classic Ground Beef Tacos

MAKES 16 hard tacos **PREP** 15 minutes
COOK about 15 minutes **WARM** taco shells at 375° for about 5 minutes

1 tablespoon olive oil
1 medium onion, thinly sliced
1½ pounds ground beef
1 tablespoon chili powder
¾ teaspoon salt
¼ teaspoon ground cumin
⅛ teaspoon ground red pepper (cayenne)
1 can (8 ounces) tomato sauce
16 regular-size taco shells
1½ cups shredded iceberg lettuce
½ pint cherry tomatoes, each cut into quarters
½ cup shredded cheddar cheese (4 ounces)
1 small onion, chopped
½ cup bottled taco sauce

1. Heat oven to 375°.

2. Heat oil in a large nonstick skillet over medium-high heat. Add sliced onion; cook until softened, about 3 minutes. Add beef; cook, breaking up clumps with a wooden spoon, until beef is no longer pink, 5 to 7 minutes.

3. Add chili powder, salt, cumin and red pepper; cook, stirring, 1 minute. Stir in tomato sauce. Bring to boiling. Lower heat to medium. Cook about 5 minutes, stirring occasionally.

4. Warm taco shells in heated 375° oven about 5 minutes. Spoon about ¼ cup meat mixture into each shell. Top filling with lettuce, tomatoes, cheese, onion and taco sauce.

PER TACO
171 calories, 11 g fat (4 g saturated), 9 g protein, 10 g carbohydrate, 2 g fiber, 209 mg sodium, 30 mg cholesterol.

PANTRY PLUS: TACO TALK

For starters, choose between soft tortillas and crispy shells.

- Tortillas come in flour and corn varieties. Flour tortillas are available in many sizes; 8- and 10-inch diameters are most common. Each 8-inch tortilla has 160 calories and 3.5 grams fat; each 10-inch has 185 calories and 4 grams fat. Corn tortillas are generally 6 inches across; each contains about 58 calories and 0.7 grams of fat.

- Flour tortillas come flavored with everything from spinach and herbs to tomato and basil— even smoked chiles.

- Crispy taco shells, always made of corn tortillas, come in two sizes—regular and large. Each regular-size shell has 70 calories and 3.5 grams fat; each large size, 95 calories and 6 grams fat.

Philly Steak Pockets

MAKES 4 servings **PREP** 10 minutes
BAKE at 375° for 15 minutes

1   package (8 ounces) crescent
    roll dough
4   teaspoons yellow mustard
4   slices deli roast beef
4   slices American cheese
1   can (4 ounces) diced green
    chiles, drained

1. Heat oven to 375°.
2. On a work surface, unroll dough into
    4 rectangles. Spread each rectangle
    with 1 teaspoon mustard. Top each
    with 1 slice roast beef, 1 slice cheese
    and one-quarter of chiles.

3. Beginning at a short end, roll up each
    rectangle. Pinch seam closed. Place,
    seam side down, on an ungreased
    baking sheet. Slash tops diagonally
    with a sharp knife.
4. Bake in heated 375° oven 15 minutes
    or until golden and crisp. Serve warm.

PER SERVING
305 calories, 16 g fat (6 g saturated), 16 g protein,
23 g carbohydrate, 0 g fiber, 1,286 mg sodium,
30 mg cholesterol.

Italian Sandwiches

MAKES 4 servings **PREP** 5 minutes

2   small ready-to-use thin-crust pizza
    shells (one 8-ounce package)
4   teaspoons Italian salad dressing
1   jar (7 ounces) roasted red
    peppers, drained
¼   pound salami, sliced
¼   pound provolone cheese, sliced
4   lettuce leaves

1. Cut each pizza shell in half
    horizontally; lift off top halves.
2. Drizzle each bottom half with
    1 teaspoon dressing. Top with
    peppers, salami, cheese and lettuce,
    dividing equally. Drizzle with
    remaining 2 teaspoons dressing.
    Cover with top halves of bread.
    Cut into wedges for serving.

PER SERVING
404 calories, 23 g fat (10 g saturated), 19 g protein,
27 g carbohydrate, 1 g fiber, 1,155 mg sodium,
55 mg cholesterol.

Monte Cristo Strata

MAKES 6 servings **PREP** 5 minutes
REFRIGERATE 2 to 24 hours
BAKE at 350° for 45 minutes

8   slices deli ham
9   slices deli Swiss cheese
8   slices sandwich bread
4   eggs
1   cup milk
2   teaspoons Dijon mustard
½   teaspoon salt
¼   teaspoon black pepper

1.   Coat a 12 x 7 x 2-inch baking dish with nonstick cooking spray. Place 4 slices ham over bottom of dish. Top with 3 slices cheese, 4 slices bread, 4 slices ham, 3 slices cheese, 4 slices bread and 3 slices cheese.

2.   Whisk eggs, milk, mustard, salt and pepper in a small bowl. Pour over strata in baking dish. Cover with plastic wrap. Refrigerate at least 2 hours or up to 24 hours.

3.   Heat oven to 350°. Remove plastic wrap from baking dish; replace with aluminum foil.

4.   Bake in heated 350° oven 20 minutes. Uncover. Bake 25 minutes longer. Broil to crisp top if desired. Cut into 6 pieces and serve warm.

PER SERVING
330 calories, 15 g fat (7 g saturated), 25 g protein, 24 g carbohydrate, 1 g fiber, 1,695 mg sodium, 198 mg cholesterol.

Reuben Roll

MAKES 4 servings **PREP** 10 minutes
BAKE at 400° for 20 to 23 minutes

1   package (10 ounces) refrigerated pizza dough
3   ounces sliced pastrami
2   tablespoons Russian dressing
½   cup drained sauerkraut
3   ounces shredded Swiss cheese

1.   Position oven rack in bottom third of oven. Heat oven to 400°. Grease a baking sheet.

2.   Unroll dough. Lay pastrami over top of dough, leaving a ½-inch border around edges. Spread dressing over pastrami. Spread sauerkraut over top; sprinkle with cheese.

3.   Roll up from a long side; pinch seam to seal. Tuck ends under; pinch to seal. Place, seam side down, on prepared baking sheet.

4.   Bake in heated 400° oven 20 to 23 minutes or until golden brown. Slice crosswise into quarters.

PER SERVING
377 calories, 18 g fat (7 g saturated), 16 g protein, 35 g carbohydrate, 0 g fiber, 817 mg sodium, 40 mg cholesterol.

1. Unfold bread on a work surface. Spread with cheese. Arrange peppers in a band down center, parallel to short sides of bread. Arrange ham slices over entire surface; spread salad dressing on top of ham. Arrange scallions parallel to peppers from center to one short side of bread.

2. Beginning with opposite short side, without scallions, roll up bread. Trim ends. Slice into 1½- to 2-inch-thick pinwheels.

PER SERVING
219 calories, 13 g fat (7 g saturated), 7 g protein, 20 g carbohydrate, 2 g fiber, 566 mg sodium, 53 mg cholesterol.

Greek Roll

MAKES 6 servings **PREP** 15 minutes

1   piece flat shepherd's bread (lavash), not whole wheat (about 10 x 14 inches)
1   container (8 ounces) hummus
1   package (about 4 ounces) crumbled feta cheese
1   can (about 2¼ ounces) sliced ripe olives, drained
2   tomatoes, thinly sliced

1. Unfold bread on a work surface. Spread with hummus; top with feta, olives and tomatoes.

2. Beginning with a short side, roll up bread. Trim ends. Slice into 1½- to 2-inch-thick pinwheels.

PER SERVING
195 calories, 9 g fat (3 g saturated), 9 g protein, 22 g carbohydrate, 4 g fiber, 525 mg sodium, 17 mg cholesterol.

Ham and Scallion Roll

MAKES 6 servings **PREP** 15 minutes

1   piece flat shepherd's bread (lavash), not whole wheat (about 10 x 14 inches)
1   container (about 6½ ounces) spreadable herb cheese
1   sweet red pepper, cored, seeded and cut into matchstick strips
4   ounces thinly sliced deli ham
3   tablespoons mayonnaise-style salad dressing
3   scallions, trimmed and sliced lengthwise, including most of the green

32

Turkey-Bacon Roll

MAKES 6 servings **PREP** 15 minutes

1   piece flat shepherd's bread (lavash), not whole wheat (about 10 x 14 inches)
⅓   cup Thousand Island dressing
¼   cup crumbled cooked bacon (4 slices)
8   ounces sliced deli turkey
4   ounces sliced Muenster cheese
1   cup shredded lettuce

1. Unfold bread on a work surface. Top with dressing, bacon, turkey, cheese and lettuce.

2. Beginning with a short side, roll up bread. Trim ends. Slice into 1½- to 2-inch-thick pinwheels.

PER SERVING
318 calories, 19 g fat (9 g saturated), 19 g protein, 19 g carbohydrate, 1 g fiber, 924 mg sodium, 59 mg cholesterol.

PANTRY PLUS: ROLL IT UP

Sandwich rolls, so easy to make ahead, are great choices for family parties.

• The Ham and Scallion Roll, Turkey-Bacon Roll and Greek Roll can be prepared several hours in advance. Wrap unsliced rolls in plastic wrap; refrigerate. To serve, remove plastic wrap from rolls and slice as directed.

• Large (10-inch) flour tortillas may be substituted for the flat shepherd's bread (lavash). Use two flour tortillas for each piece of flat shepherd's bread, dividing the filling evenly between the two.

• For variety, try using large tortillas flavored with spinach or carrot.

Noodle Toss

MAKES 6 servings **PREP** 5 minutes
COOK 15 minutes

1½   pounds chicken tenders
½   cup teriyaki sauce
¼   teaspoon red-pepper flakes
4   cups plus 2 tablespoons water
1   package (about ½ pound) carrot sticks, large pieces cut in half
2½   cups broccoli flowerets
3   packages (3 ounces each) ramen noodles
4   teaspoons cornstarch
⅓   cup peanuts, coarsely chopped

1. Combine chicken, teriyaki sauce and red-pepper flakes in a plastic bag.

2. Meanwhile, bring 4 cups water to boiling in a large saucepan. Add carrots; cover and cook 3 minutes.

3. Add broccoli, chicken with teriyaki sauce and noodles (omit seasoning packets); cook, covered, 4 minutes, stirring once to break apart noodles and turn chicken.

4. Mix remaining 2 tablespoons water with cornstarch in a cup. Add to pot; stir until sauce is thickened and chicken is cooked through, 1 to 2 minutes.

5. Transfer to a large bowl. Top with peanuts. Serve warm.

PER SERVING
418 calories, 14 g fat (3 g saturated), 32 g protein, 41 g carbohydrate, 4 g fiber, 1,030 mg sodium, 63 mg cholesterol.

Tortellini Combo

MAKES 6 servings **PREP** about 15 minutes
COOK 12 minutes

1	**pound cheese tortellini**
2	**jars (6½ ounces each) marinated artichoke hearts, drained, marinade reserved**
½	**pound tomatoes, seeded and diced**
8	**ounces smoked mozzarella, cubed**
½	**cup fresh basil, chopped**
½	**teaspoon salt**
¼	**teaspoon black pepper**
	Fresh parsley sprigs for garnish (optional)

1. Cook tortellini in a large pot of lightly salted boiling water until al dente, firm but tender. Drain well.

2. Meanwhile, halve artichoke hearts; mix with tomatoes and mozzarella in a large serving bowl.

3. Combine reserved marinade, basil, salt and pepper in a small bowl. Add to artichoke mixture along with tortellini. Toss to combine. Garnish with parsley if desired.

PER SERVING
406 calories, 18 g fat (8 g saturated), 22 g protein, 43 g carbohydrate, 4 g fiber, 792 mg sodium, 72 mg cholesterol.

Rigatoni with Broccoli

MAKES 6 servings **PREP** 10 minutes
COOK 15 minutes

1	**pound rigatoni**
¾	**pound Italian-style chicken sausage, casings removed**
3	**cloves garlic, sliced**
¾	**cup fat-free chicken broth**
¼	**teaspoon red-pepper flakes**
8	**cups broccoli flowerets**
1	**tablespoon garlic olive oil**
1	**tablespoon fresh lemon juice**
1	**teaspoon salt**
¼	**teaspoon black pepper**
3	**tablespoons grated Parmesan cheese**

1. Cook rigatoni in a large pot of lightly salted boiling water until al dente, firm but tender. Drain; keep warm.

2. Meanwhile, crumble sausage into a large nonstick skillet. Add garlic; sauté over medium-high heat 5 minutes.

3. Add broth, red-pepper flakes and broccoli to skillet. Cover; cook 5 minutes. Uncover; stir in oil, lemon juice, salt, pepper and Parmesan. Remove from heat.

4. Toss rigatoni and sauce in a serving bowl. Cover; let stand 2 minutes.

PER SERVING
417 calories, 9 g fat (2 g saturated), 25 g protein, 62 g carbohydrate, 9 g fiber, 679 mg sodium, 46 mg cholesterol.

Cheesy Penne, Bacon and Broccoli

MAKES 6 servings **PREP** 10 minutes
COOK about 30 minutes

4	slices bacon
1	small onion, finely chopped
3	tablespoons all-purpose flour
2	cups milk
1	pound penne
1	small head broccoli (1 pound), cut into flowerets (about 3½ cups)
¼	teaspoon salt
⅛	teaspoon black pepper
4	ounces ⅓-less-fat cream cheese
4	ounces blue cheese or Gorgonzola cheese
	Pinch ground red pepper (cayenne)
3	tablespoons grated Parmesan cheese

1. Fry bacon in a large skillet over medium-low heat until crisp, about 7 minutes. Transfer to paper toweling to drain.

2. Drain all but 3 tablespoons drippings from skillet. Add onion to skillet; increase heat to medium-high and cook until softened, 8 to 10 minutes. Reduce heat to medium. Sprinkle onion with flour; stir in, scraping up any browned bits. Whisk in milk, ½ cup at a time, until smooth. Cook, stirring, 2 minutes or until thickened.

3. Meanwhile, cook penne in a large pot of lightly salted boiling water until al dente, firm but tender; add broccoli during last 4 minutes of cooking. Drain penne and broccoli; transfer to a serving bowl; keep warm.

4. Add salt, pepper, cream cheese and blue cheese to thickened milk in skillet; whisk until smooth. Remove from heat. Stir in red pepper and 2 tablespoons Parmesan. Crumble bacon; stir into sauce. Pour sauce over penne and broccoli; toss to combine. Top with remaining 1 tablespoon Parmesan.

PER SERVING
556 calories, 24 g fat (13 g saturated), 22 g protein, 63 g carbohydrate, 4 g fiber, 657 mg sodium, 55 mg cholesterol.

Farfalle Fresca

MAKES 6 servings **PREP** about 5 minutes
COOK 10 minutes

1	pound bow-tie pasta (farfalle)
1	can (11 ounces) Mandarin orange segments, drained, ⅓ cup syrup reserved
1	small red onion, halved lengthwise and sliced crosswise (about ½ cup)
1	cup diced sweet red pepper
1	bag (6 ounces) fresh baby spinach
⅔	cup Italian salad dressing
⅓	cup sliced almonds

1. Cook bow-ties in a large pot of lightly salted boiling water until al dente, firm but tender. Drain well.

2. Meanwhile, combine orange segments, onion, pepper, spinach and salad dressing in a large serving bowl. Add bow-ties; toss. Sprinkle almonds on top.

PER SERVING
523 calories, 17 g fat (2 g saturated), 13 g protein, 80 g carbohydrate, 5 g fiber, 237 mg sodium, 0 mg cholesterol.

1. Heat a medium-size skillet over medium-high heat. Add oil and garlic; cook 1 to 2 minutes. Add carrots; cook 4 minutes.

2. Cook pasta in a large pot of lightly salted boiling water until al dente, firm but tender.

3. Meanwhile, reduce heat under skillet to medium. Add asparagus; cover. Cook 8 minutes or until vegetables are tender. Uncover; add sweet peppers. Cook 5 minutes, stirring occasionally. Add cherry tomatoes, salt, black pepper and half-and-half. Stir in ¼ cup pasta cooking water.

4. Drain pasta; transfer to a serving bowl. Add vegetables with sauce; sprinkle with Parmesan. Toss to mix.

PER SERVING
389 calories, 10 g fat (3 g saturated), 13 g protein, 63 g carbohydrate, 6 g fiber, 355 mg sodium, 12 mg cholesterol.

Pasta Primavera

MAKES 6 servings **PREP** 15 minutes
COOK 20 minutes

2   tablespoons olive oil
3   cloves garlic, sliced
3   carrots, peeled and sliced
1   pound bow-tie pasta (farfalle)
1   bunch asparagus (about 1 pound), tough ends trimmed and spears cut into 1½-inch pieces
1   sweet red pepper, cored, seeded and cut into 1½-inch strips
1   sweet yellow pepper, cored, seeded and cut into 1½-inch strips
1   cup cherry tomatoes (about 24), halved
¾   teaspoon salt
¼   teaspoon black pepper
⅔   cup half-and-half
2   tablespoons grated Parmesan cheese

PANTRY PLUS: SAUCY GIFTS

Looking for a thoughtful hostess gift? Many pasta sauces can be made ahead; stored properly, they'll keep for a couple of weeks.

• To store sauce, spoon while hot into sterilized canning jars; seal. Cool slightly on wire racks. Refrigerate up to 2 weeks.

• To take along as a hostess gift, arrange a jar of sauce, a suitable pasta, Parmesan cheese and a grater in a colander. (Keep sauce in the refrigerator until the last minute, then add to the cache.) Wrap with clean plastic wrap and fasten with a bow. Be sure to add a tag with instructions to refrigerate perishables immediately.

Orecchiette Arrabbiata

MAKES 6 servings **PREP** 5 minutes
COOK 27 minutes

1   tablespoon olive oil
1   medium onion, finely chopped
3   large cloves garlic, finely chopped
1   tablespoon water
2   cans (14½ ounces each) zesty diced
     tomatoes or diced tomatoes with
     green chiles
1   can (8 ounces) tomato sauce
½   teaspoon red-pepper flakes
     Pinch ground red pepper (cayenne)
½   teaspoon dried oregano
1   pound orecchiette (ear-shaped) or
     any tubular pasta
1   bag (6 ounces) fresh baby spinach
¼   teaspoon salt
¼   teaspoon black pepper
2   tablespoons grated Parmesan cheese

1. Heat oil in a medium-size saucepan
    over medium-low heat. Add onion;
    cook 5 minutes, being careful not to
    let it brown. Add garlic and water;
    cook 2 minutes.

2. Stir diced tomatoes, tomato sauce,
    red-pepper flakes, ground red pepper
    and oregano into saucepan. Simmer,
    uncovered, stirring occasionally,
    15 minutes.

3. Meanwhile, cook orecchiette in a
    large pot of lightly salted boiling
    water until al dente, firm but tender.

4. Coarsely slice spinach. Add to sauce;
    cook 5 minutes. Add salt and pepper.

5. Drain orecchiette; transfer to a large
    serving bowl. Add sauce; toss to mix.
    Sprinkle with Parmesan cheese.

PER SERVING
393 calories, 5 g fat (1 g saturated), 14 g protein,
74 g carbohydrate, 5 g fiber, 971 mg sodium,
2 mg cholesterol.

Chunky Tomato Sauce

*This sauce is good on virtually any pasta—and
it makes a great gift.*

MAKES 2 quarts **PREP** 20 minutes
COOK about 50 minutes

2   tablespoons olive oil
1   cup chopped onion (1 large onion)
2   cloves garlic, finely chopped
1   cup chopped sweet green pepper
     (1 medium pepper)
1   cup chopped zucchini (1 medium
     zucchini)
1   cup chopped mushrooms (about
     2 ounces)
3   canned flat anchovies, chopped
2   cans (28 ounces each) chopped
     tomatoes
1   can (6 ounces) tomato paste
½   teaspoon sugar
¼   cup chopped fresh parsley
1   tablespoon balsamic vinegar
1   tablespoon salt
½   teaspoon black pepper

1. Heat oil in a 4-quart saucepan over
    medium-high heat. Add onion and
    garlic; sauté 8 minutes or until almost
    tender. Add green pepper, zucchini,
    mushrooms and anchovies; sauté
    8 to 10 minutes or until vegetables
    are almost tender.

2. Stir in tomatoes, tomato paste and
    sugar. Bring to boiling over medium-
    high heat. Reduce heat to low;
    simmer, uncovered, 30 minutes or
    until sauce is thickened, stirring
    occasionally. Stir in parsley, vinegar,
    salt and black pepper.

PER ½ CUP
55 calories, 2 g fat (0 g saturated), 2 g protein,
9 g carbohydrate, 2 g fiber, 598 mg sodium,
1 mg cholesterol.

1. Heat oil in a large skillet over medium-high heat. Add onion; cook 10 minutes or until softened (add 1 to 2 tablespoons water if needed to prevent sticking). Add Canadian bacon and vodka; cook 3 minutes.

2. Cook penne in a large pot of lightly salted boiling water until al dente, firm but tender.

3. Meanwhile, reduce heat under skillet to medium. Add tomatoes, tomato sauce, olives, sugar, salt and pepper; cook over medium heat, stirring occasionally, 12 minutes.

4. Drain penne; transfer to a serving bowl.

5. Stir Parmesan, half-and-half and basil into sauce in skillet; heat through. Add sauce to pasta in bowl; toss to mix.

PER SERVING
397 calories, 7 g fat (2 g saturated), 17 g protein, 63 g carbohydrate, 3 g fiber, 919 mg sodium, 13 mg cholesterol.

Penne with Vodka Sauce

MAKES 6 servings **PREP** 10 minutes
COOK 25 minutes

2	teaspoons olive oil
1	medium onion, chopped
6	ounces lean Canadian bacon, diced
¼	cup vodka
1	pound penne
1	can (15 ounces) diced tomatoes
1	can (8 ounces) tomato sauce
12	Kalamata olives, pitted and quartered
½	teaspoon sugar
¼	teaspoon salt
¼	teaspoon black pepper
3	tablespoons grated Parmesan cheese
½	cup fat-free half-and-half
¼	cup loosely packed fresh basil leaves, shredded

Fettuccine Carbonara

Surprise—this version of the creamy classic stars fat-free half-and-half and turkey bacon!

MAKES 6 servings **PREP** 5 minutes
COOK 15 minutes

1	pound fettuccine
1½	cups fat-free half-and-half
½	cup cholesterol-free egg replacement (not frozen)
1	tablespoon all-purpose flour
½	teaspoon salt
½	teaspoon black pepper
¼	teaspoon ground nutmeg
6	slices turkey bacon, chopped
1	cup frozen peas
½	cup grated Parmesan cheese
2	tablespoons chopped fresh parsley

1. Cook fettuccine in a large pot of lightly salted boiling water until al dente, firm but tender.

2. Whisk together half-and-half, egg substitute, flour, salt, pepper and nutmeg in a small bowl.

3. Meanwhile, cook bacon in a medium-size skillet over medium heat 5 minutes or until crisp.

4. Add half-and-half mixture and peas to bacon in skillet. Cook over medium-low heat, whisking, until slightly thickened, 5 minutes (do not heat quickly or sauce will separate).

5. Drain fettuccine; transfer to a serving bowl. Add sauce, Parmesan and parsley; toss to mix.

PER SERVING
437 calories, 7 g fat (2 g saturated), 21 g protein, 70 g carbohydrate, 5 g fiber, 641 mg sodium, 7 mg cholesterol.

Pasta with Mushroom Sauce

MAKES 6 servings **PREP** 5 minutes
COOK about 20 minutes

1   envelope (0.9 ounce) garlic-mushroom recipe soup mix
2   cups water
1   pound penne
2   tablespoons olive oil
1   small sweet red pepper, cored, seeded and sliced
1½   pounds assorted sliced mushrooms
½   cup grated Parmesan cheese
½   cup chopped fresh parsley
¼   cup heavy cream
     Fresh parsley sprigs for garnish (optional)

1. Whisk together soup mix and water in a medium-size bowl; set aside.

2. Cook penne in a large pot of lightly salted boiling water until al dente, firm but tender. Drain well; transfer to a large serving bowl and keep warm.

3. Meanwhile, heat oil in a large skillet. Add pepper and mushrooms; sauté until partially tender, about 10 minutes. Stir in reserved soup mixture. Increase heat to medium-high; cook, uncovered, until slightly thickened, about 8 minutes. Stir in ¼ cup Parmesan, parsley and cream; cook another 1 minute or until heated through.

4. Add mushroom sauce and remaining ¼ cup Parmesan to penne in bowl; toss to mix well. Garnish with parsley sprigs if desired.

PER SERVING
413 calories, 13 g fat (5 g saturated), 15 g protein, 60 g carbohydrate, 5 g fiber, 438 mg sodium, 20 mg cholesterol.

Mushroom Ravioli with Roasted-Garlic Cream Sauce

MAKES 6 servings **PREP** 10 minutes
BAKE at 350° for 1 hour
COOK about 15 minutes

1	**whole head garlic**
2	**teaspoons olive oil**
1	**pound mushroom-stuffed ravioli**
2	**cups heavy cream**
½	**teaspoon salt**
⅛	**teaspoon black pepper**
¼	**cup thinly sliced fresh basil leaves**

1. Heat oven to 350°.
2. Slice off and discard top of garlic head. Place head in middle of a 9-inch square of aluminum foil. Drizzle oil over cut surface of garlic cloves. Lift foil up around garlic; fold edges together to seal.

Garlic Roasting Prep

Place garlic head, cut end up, in center of foil square. Drizzle oil over cut surface of cloves.

Lift foil up around garlic; fold edges together to seal securely.

3. Bake in heated 350° oven 1 hour or until garlic is knife-tender. Set aside until cool enough to handle.
4. Cook ravioli in a large pot of lightly salted boiling water until al dente, firm but tender. Drain well; transfer to a serving bowl and keep warm.
5. Meanwhile, squeeze each garlic clove out of its skin into a medium-size skillet. Stir cream into skillet. Bring to simmering over medium-high heat; simmer 10 minutes or until reduced by one-third. Add salt and pepper. Transfer sauce to a blender; whirl 1 to 2 minutes to puree. Stir basil into sauce in blender. Pour sauce over ravioli; toss to coat ravioli.

PER SERVING
481 calories, 37 g fat (22 g saturated), 11 g protein, 30 g carbohydrate, 1 g fiber, 477 mg sodium, 120 mg cholesterol.

Pasta with Cheese and Mushroom Sauce

MAKES 6 servings **PREP** 5 minutes
COOK 25 minutes

1	**pint fat-free half-and-half**
½	**cup skim milk**
3	**tablespoons all-purpose flour**
	Pinch ground nutmeg
	Pinch ground red pepper (cayenne)
2	**packages (10 ounces each) sliced mushrooms**
¾	**teaspoon salt**
¼	**teaspoon black pepper**
¼	**cup dry white wine**
1	**pound cavatappi or elbow pasta**
1½	**cups shredded light Jarlsberg cheese (6 ounces)**
2	**tablespoons grated Parmesan cheese**
1	**scallion, chopped, including part of the green**

1. Whisk together half-and-half, milk, flour, nutmeg and red pepper in a medium-size bowl.

2. Cook mushrooms with salt and pepper in a large saucepan over medium heat 15 minutes or until moisture from mushrooms is evaporated. Add wine; cook, stirring, 2 minutes.

3. Meanwhile, cook cavatappi in a large pot of lightly salted boiling water until al dente, firm but tender. Drain well; transfer to a serving bowl.

4. Add half-and-half mixture to mushrooms in saucepan; cook until mixture starts to thicken and bubble, 5 to 8 minutes. Whisk in cheeses until sauce is fairly smooth.

5. Pour sauce over pasta; stir well to coat. Top with scallion.

PER SERVING
441 calories, 8 g fat (5 g saturated), 23 g protein, 66 g carbohydrate, 4 g fiber, 459 mg sodium, 22 mg cholesterol.

Chicken and Fettuccine Alfredo

MAKES 6 servings **PREP** 15 minutes
COOK 20 minutes

¾   **pound fettuccine**
3   **cups broccoli flowerets**
1¼ **pounds boneless, skinless chicken breasts, sliced into 2 x 1-inch pieces**
2   **tablespoons all-purpose flour**
3   **tablespoons butter**
1½ **cups half-and-half**
½   **cup grated Parmesan cheese**
1   **teaspoon Dijon mustard**
     Pinch ground nutmeg

½   **teaspoon salt**
½   **teaspoon dried tarragon**
⅛   **teaspoon black pepper**
⅛   **teaspoon ground red pepper (cayenne)**
1   **egg**

1. Cook fettuccine in a large pot of lightly salted boiling water 8 minutes. Add broccoli; cook 4 minutes. Drain; transfer to a large bowl. Keep warm.

2. Toss chicken with flour to coat lightly. Heat butter in a large skillet over medium-high heat. Add chicken; sauté 5 minutes or until lightly browned and cooked through. Remove chicken from skillet; keep warm.

3. Add half-and-half, Parmesan and mustard to same skillet; simmer, stirring occasionally, 4 minutes to thicken. Add nutmeg, salt, tarragon, black pepper and red pepper. Remove from heat.

4. Whisk egg in a small bowl, whisk in ½ cup cheese sauce from skillet, then whisk mixture into skillet. Add chicken. Heat until thickened; do not boil. Add to bowl with pasta and broccoli; toss to coat.

PER SERVING
526 calories, 20 g fat (11 g saturated), 35 g protein, 52 g carbohydrate, 4 g fiber, 437 mg sodium, 132 mg cholesterol.

Skillet Lasagna

MAKES 6 servings PREP 5 minutes
COOK about 25 minutes

1   pound ground turkey
1   large onion, chopped (1 cup)
1   clove garlic, finely chopped
2   cups pasta sauce
¼   cup chopped fresh parsley
1   teaspoon dried oregano
¾   teaspoon dried basil
1   container (16 ounces) large-curd
     cottage cheese
1   cup shredded mozzarella cheese
     (4 ounces)
½   cup grated Parmesan cheese
3   to 6 no-boil lasagna noodles

1.   Cook turkey, onion and garlic in a
     10-inch nonstick skillet over medium
     heat, breaking up clumps with a
     wooden spoon, 8 minutes or until
     turkey is no longer pink. Stir in
     1 cup pasta sauce, parsley, oregano
     and basil, spreading evenly in skillet.

2.   Remove skillet from heat. Spoon
     cottage cheese evenly over top. Sprinkle
     with ½ cup mozzarella and ¼ cup
     Parmesan. Arrange whole noodles
     over top, then break a noodle and fill
     any gaps with pieces. Pour remaining
     1 cup pasta sauce over top; gently
     press noodles to moisten.

3.   Cover skillet; bring to simmering
     over medium heat, reduce heat and
     simmer 15 minutes or until noodles
     are tender. Sprinkle lasagna top with
     remaining ½ cup mozzarella and
     remaining ¼ cup Parmesan.

4.   Simmer, covered, 2 minutes or until
     cheese is melted. Remove skillet from
     heat; let stand, covered, 15 minutes.

PER SERVING
529 calories, 21 g fat (9 g saturated), 39 g protein,
44 g carbohydrate, 3 g fiber, 953 mg sodium,
93 mg cholesterol.

Ravioli with Sausage

MAKES 6 servings PREP 7 minutes
COOK about 15 minutes

3   links hot or sweet Italian sausage
     (¾ pound), casings removed
1   jar (32 ounces) pasta sauce
2   tablespoons sliced fresh basil
1   pound cheese ravioli
¼   cup heavy cream

1.   Heat a large skillet over medium-high
     heat. Add sausage; sauté 8 minutes,
     breaking up clumps with a wooden
     spoon. Stir in 1½ cups pasta sauce and
     basil; cook 5 minutes.

2.   Meanwhile, cook ravioli in a large pot
     of lightly salted boiling water until
     al dente, firm but tender. Drain well.
     Transfer to a serving bowl.

3.   Transfer sausage mixture to a food
     processor or blender; whirl to puree.
     Return to skillet. Add remaining
     pasta sauce and cream; heat through.
     Add sauce to bowl with ravioli.
     Toss to mix.

PER SERVING
315 calories, 15 g fat (7 g saturated), 15 g protein,
31 g carbohydrate, 2 g fiber, 644 mg sodium,
75 mg cholesterol.

Spaghetti
with Meatballs

To time this right, have the water boiling so you can cook the spaghetti while the sauce is simmering and the meatballs are baking.

MAKES 8 servings **PREP** 15 minutes
BAKE at 400° for 15 minutes
COOK 20 minutes

Meatballs

2   slices white bread
2   tablespoons skim milk
8   ounces sliced mushrooms
1   jar (12 ounces) roasted red
    peppers, drained and chopped
1   pound ground turkey
1   teaspoon salt
½   teaspoon dried Italian seasoning
¼   teaspoon black pepper
1   tablespoon minced dried onion
1   egg, lightly beaten

Sauce

1   tablespoon olive oil
1   medium onion, chopped
1   can (28 ounces) crushed tomatoes
3   tablespoons tomato paste
2   teaspoons sugar
1   teaspoon garlic salt
½   teaspoon red-pepper flakes

1   pound thin spaghetti

1. Heat oven to 400°. Grease a
    15½ x 10½ x 1-inch jelly-roll pan.

2. Prepare meatballs: Finely crumble
    bread into a small bowl. Add milk;
    set aside to soak.

3. Meanwhile, measure out 1 cup
    mushrooms; chop. Place in a
    medium-size bowl; add ½ cup roasted
    peppers, turkey, salt, Italian
    seasoning, black pepper, dried onion
    and soaked bread. Add egg. Mix well
    until ingredients are evenly blended.
    Reserve remainder of mushrooms
    and roasted peppers for sauce.

4. With moistened fingers and using
    1 slightly rounded tablespoon for
    each, shape mixture into about
    32 meatballs. Place on prepared pan.

5. Bake in heated 400° oven about
    15 minutes or until an instant-read
    thermometer inserted in center of a
    meatball registers 165°. Remove from
    oven; cover and keep warm.

6. Meanwhile, prepare sauce: Heat oil
    in a large straight-sided skillet over
    medium-high heat. Add onion; cook
    6 minutes. Add reserved mushrooms
    and roasted peppers; cook 4 minutes,
    stirring. Stir in tomatoes, tomato
    paste, sugar, garlic salt and red-pepper
    flakes. Cover; simmer 10 minutes.

7. Meanwhile, cook spaghetti in a large
    pot of lightly salted boiling water
    until al dente, firm but tender. Drain
    well; transfer to a serving bowl.

8. Transfer meatballs to tomato sauce in
    skillet; gently stir to coat meatballs
    with sauce. Spoon sauce with meatballs
    over spaghetti; toss to mix.

PER SERVING
419 calories, 10 g fat (2 g saturated), 22 g protein,
61 g carbohydrate, 4 g fiber, 1,048 mg sodium,
68 mg cholesterol.

Tri-Color Lasagna

MAKES 12 servings **PREP** 25 minutes
BAKE at 350° for 30 minutes

1   **container (15 ounces) ricotta cheese**
½   **cup grated Parmesan cheese**
¼   **cup pesto sauce**
1   **egg**
2⅔ **cups Alfredo sauce**
2   **cups marinara sauce**
12   **no-boil lasagna noodles**
3   **cups shredded mozzarella cheese**

1. Beat together ricotta, ¼ cup Parmesan, 1 tablespoon pesto and egg in a small bowl. Divide Alfredo sauce evenly between 2 small bowls; stir remaining 3 tablespoons pesto into one of them.

2. Heat oven to 350°.

3. Position a 13 x 9 x 2-inch glass baking dish with a long side facing you. Spread ½ cup marinara sauce in bottom. Top with 3 noodles, placing them side by side across width of dish. Spread ⅓ cup plain Alfredo sauce on middle noodle. Spread ⅓ cup marinara sauce on left noodle. Spread ⅓ cup pesto-Alfredo sauce on right noodle. Spoon one-third of ricotta mixture evenly on top of sauces. Sprinkle 1 cup mozzarella on top.

4. Repeat layering of noodles, sauces, ricotta and mozzarella, spreading marinara sauce over middle noodle, plain Alfredo sauce over right noodle and pesto-Alfredo sauce over left noodle.

5. Repeat layering again, spreading pesto-Alfredo sauce over middle noodle, marinara sauce over right noodle and plain Alfredo sauce over left noodle.

6. Place remaining 3 noodles on top. Spread remaining marinara on left noodle, plain Alfredo on middle noodle and remaining pesto-Alfredo on right noodle. Sprinkle with remaining ¼ cup Parmesan.

7. Cover baking dish with aluminum foil. Bake in heated 350° oven 30 minutes or until hot and bubbly.

Note: Lasagna can be prepared ahead through step 6 and frozen, unbaked, up to 2 months. Tightly cover baking dish with plastic wrap, then heavy-duty aluminum foil. Thaw in refrigerator overnight. Remove foil and plastic wrap; re-cover baking dish with foil. Bake as directed in step 7.

PER SERVING
420 calories, 29 g fat (16 g saturated), 19 g protein, 23 g carbohydrate, 1 g fiber, 812 mg sodium, 92 mg cholesterol.

Four-Cheese Baked Macaroni

The key to eliminating the flour taste from a white sauce, the base for this cheese sauce, lies in cooking the flour-butter mixture 2 minutes before adding the milk.

MAKES 12 servings **PREP** 20 minutes
COOK about 8 minutes
BAKE at 350° for 45 minutes

1	pound rotelle pasta
2	cups shredded sharp cheddar cheese (8 ounces)
1	cup shredded mozzarella cheese (4 ounces)
½	cup shredded Jarlsberg cheese (2 ounces)
½	cup grated Parmesan cheese
¼	cup (½ stick) unsalted butter
¼	cup all-purpose flour
4	cups milk
1	teaspoon salt
¼	teaspoon ground nutmeg
⅛	teaspoon ground red pepper (cayenne)
2	large ripe tomatoes, cored and thinly sliced

1. Heat oven to 350°. Coat bottom and sides of a 13 x 9 x 2-inch baking dish (or other shallow 4-quart casserole) with nonstick cooking spray.

2. Cook rotelle in a large pot of lightly salted boiling water until al dente, firm but tender.

3. Meanwhile, mix together cheddar, mozzarella, Jarlsberg and Parmesan cheeses in a large bowl.

4. Drain pasta well. Add butter to pasta cooking pot; melt over medium heat. Whisk in flour until well blended; continue to cook, whisking constantly, 2 minutes. Whisk in 1 cup milk until well blended. Gradually whisk in remaining 3 cups milk, 1 cup at a time, whisking after each addition until well blended. Stir in salt, nutmeg and red pepper. Bring mixture to simmering, stirring; cook, whisking constantly, until thickened and smooth, about 2 minutes.

5. Remove pot from heat. Gradually add 2 cups cheese mixture, whisking until sauce is very smooth. Add pasta to sauce in pot; toss until well coated.

6. Sprinkle ½ cup remaining cheese mixture evenly in bottom of prepared baking dish. Spoon half of pasta mixture into baking dish, spreading evenly. Sprinkle 1 cup remaining cheese mixture over pasta. Spoon in remaining pasta mixture. Sprinkle with remaining ½ cup cheese mixture. Arrange sliced tomatoes on top.

7. Bake macaroni and cheese in heated 350° oven 45 minutes or until top of macaroni is lightly golden. Remove dish from oven; let stand at least 10 minutes before serving.

Note: Recipe can be prepared through step 6, omitting tomato slices, a day ahead. Cover and refrigerate until ready to bake. Then add tomato; allow extra baking time.

PER SERVING
361 calories, 18 g fat (11 g saturated), 17 g protein, 33 g carbohydrate, 2 g fiber, 463 mg sodium, 56 mg cholesterol.

2. Add apricots, prunes and cherries; cook 1 minute or until onion and celery are lightly golden.

3. Stir in couscous; cook 1 minute. Add broth, salt and pepper. Bring to boiling. Immediately remove skillet from heat; cover and let stand 10 minutes. Fluff couscous with a fork.

PER SERVING
260 calories, 4 g fat (1 g saturated), 8 g protein, 52 g carbohydrate, 4 g fiber, 487 mg sodium, 3 mg cholesterol.

Confetti Couscous

MAKES 6 servings **PREP** 5 minutes
COOK 2 minutes

1   can (14 ounces) nonfat chicken broth
1   teaspoon grated lemon rind
2   tablespoons lemon juice (1 lemon)
½   teaspoon salt
1   box (10 ounces) couscous
1   jar (4 ounces) chopped pimientos, drained
1   package (10 ounces) frozen peas, thawed
½   cup slivered almonds, toasted (see page 232)

1. Bring broth, lemon rind, lemon juice and salt to boiling in a medium-size saucepan. Stir in couscous. Remove from heat. Cover and let stand 5 minutes. Fluff with a fork.

2. Mix couscous, pimientos, peas and almonds in a large serving bowl.

PER SERVING
210 calories, 4 g fat (0 g saturated), 9 g protein, 35 g carbohydrate, 4 g fiber, 226 mg sodium, 0 mg cholesterol.

Fruited Couscous

MAKES 6 servings **PREP** 10 minutes
COOK 15 minutes

1   teaspoon butter
1   medium onion, chopped
2   cloves garlic, finely chopped
1   rib celery, finely chopped
2   tablespoons pine nuts
4   dried apricots, cut into ¼-inch pieces
4   pitted prunes, cut into ¼-inch pieces
½   cup dried cherries or raisins
1   box (10 ounces) couscous
1   can (14½ ounces) chicken broth
½   teaspoon salt
¼   teaspoon black pepper

1. Melt butter in a large nonstick skillet over medium heat. Add onion, garlic and celery and cook 2 minutes. Add pine nuts; cook another 2 minutes.

Basil Grilled Salmon

MAKES 4 servings **PREP** 20 minutes
REFRIGERATE 30 minutes
GRILL OR BROIL 8 to 10 minutes

1   bunch fresh basil, stemmed
4   cloves garlic, peeled
1   teaspoon extra-virgin olive oil
2   teaspoons grated lemon rind
¼   cup fresh lemon juice
½   teaspoon salt
½   teaspoon black pepper
4   salmon fillets or steaks
    (1½ pounds total)
    **Spicy Corn Relish (right) for
    serving (optional)**

1. Combine basil, garlic, oil, lemon
    rind, lemon juice, salt and pepper in
    a blender. Whirl until you have a
    smooth paste.

2. Place salmon in a baking dish. Spread
    half of basil mixture over salmon,
    turning salmon to coat well. Refrigerate
    salmon 30 minutes, turning after
    15 minutes. Reserve remaining half of
    basil mixture for basting.

3. Meanwhile, prepare a charcoal grill
    with hot coals, setting rack 6 inches
    from coals; or heat a gas grill to high;
    or heat broiler.

4. Grill salmon, basting with reserved
    marinade, 4 to 5 minutes per side
    or until opaque in center. Transfer
    fish to plates. Serve with Spicy Corn
    Relish if desired.

PER SERVING
197 calories, 6 g fat (1 g saturated), 32 g protein,
2 g carbohydrate, 0 g fiber, 241 mg sodium,
83 mg cholesterol.

Spicy Corn Relish

Prepare a charcoal grill with hot
coals, setting rack 6 inches from
coals; or heat a gas grill to high;
or heat broiler. Shuck 2 ears corn.
Brush with a little olive oil.
Grill or broil about 8 minutes or
until golden brown on all sides.

Meanwhile, peel, pit and chop
1 avocado. Core, seed and dice
1 small tomato. Seed and mince
2 jalapeño chiles.

Let corn cool to room temperature.
Cut kernels from cobs. Stir
together corn kernels, 1 teaspoon
olive oil, ¼ teaspoon salt and
¼ teaspoon black pepper in a
medium-size bowl. Add avocado,
tomato, jalapeño, ½ cup chopped
fresh cilantro and 2 tablespoons
fresh lime juice; gently stir to
mix well.

MAKES 3 cups

*Note: 1 cup cooked canned or frozen
corn kernels may be substituted for the
roasted fresh corn.*

PER ¼ CUP
45 calories, 3 g fat (0 g saturated), 1 g protein,
4 g carbohydrate, 1 g fiber, 49 mg sodium,
0 mg cholesterol.

Mixed Seafood Newburg

MAKES 12 servings **PREP** 10 minutes
COOK about 15 minutes
BAKE at 400° for 30 minutes

¾ pound fettuccine
1   can (6½ ounces) minced clams, drained and juice reserved
3   tablespoons all-purpose flour
2   cups half-and-half
1   cup milk
1   teaspoon salt
¼   teaspoon ground nutmeg
⅛   teaspoon ground red pepper (cayenne)
2   tablespoons butter, melted
½   cup dry plain bread crumbs
¾   pound sea scallops
¾   pound medium shrimp, peeled and deveined
1   package (10 ounces) frozen sliced carrots, thawed

1. Heat oven to 400°. Grease a 4-quart casserole.

2. Cook fettuccine in a large pot of lightly salted boiling water until al dente, firm but tender. Drain well.

3. Meanwhile, heat clam juice in a large skillet over medium heat. Sprinkle in flour and whisk to combine; cook, stirring frequently, 2 minutes. Gradually whisk in half-and-half and milk; simmer, whisking constantly, 5 to 7 minutes or until mixture thickens. Stir in salt, nutmeg and red pepper.

4. Meanwhile, stir melted butter into bread crumbs in a small bowl.

5. Add scallops and drained clams to skillet; simmer gently 2 minutes. Add shrimp; simmer 2 to 3 minutes or until cooked through.

6. Remove skillet from heat. Stir in carrots and fettuccine. Transfer to prepared casserole. Top with bread crumb mixture. Bake in heated 400° oven 30 minutes or until heated through.

PER SERVING
232 calories, 9 g fat (5 g saturated), 13 g protein, 26 g carbohydrate, 2 g fiber, 453 mg sodium, 64 mg cholesterol.

Cleaning Shrimp

Peel off shell from head end to tail. Then remove tail.

Using a paring knife, slice back side along dark vein.

Scrape out vein with tip of knife and discard.

Rosemary Grilled Shrimp with Tuscan Bean Salad

MAKES 6 servings **PREP** 15 minutes
REFRIGERATE 30 minutes
GRILL OR BROIL 6 minutes

Vinaigrette
- ⅓ **cup extra-virgin olive oil**
- ⅓ **cup fresh lemon juice**
- 4 **cloves garlic, finely chopped**
- 1 **tablespoon finely chopped fresh rosemary**
- ½ **teaspoon salt**
- ¼ **teaspoon black pepper**

- 1½ **to 1¾ pounds extra-large shrimp (about 30 shrimp), peeled and deveined**
- ¼ **teaspoon red-pepper flakes**
- 2 **cans (19 ounces each) cannellini beans, drained**
- 1 **large ripe tomato, seeded and diced (about 1 cup)**
- 1 **small red onion, chopped (about ½ cup)**
- 3 **tablespoons chopped fresh parsley**

1. Prepare vinaigrette: Combine oil, lemon juice, garlic, rosemary, salt and black pepper in a 1-cup glass measure.

2. Place shrimp in a plastic food-storage bag. Add 3 tablespoons vinaigrette and red-pepper flakes; seal. Turn to coat shrimp. Refrigerate 30 minutes, turning once.

3. Meanwhile, prepare a charcoal grill with medium-hot coals, setting rack 5 inches from coals; or heat a gas grill to medium-high; or heat broiler. Oil grill rack or broiler-pan rack.

4. Combine beans, tomato, onion, remaining vinaigrette and parsley in a large bowl. Cover and refrigerate until ready to serve.

5. Remove shrimp from vinaigrette marinade; thread onto 6 metal skewers or fresh rosemary branches, dividing equally. Discard remaining marinade.

6. Grill or broil skewers 6 minutes or until opaque, turning once. Serve shrimp with bean salad.

PER SERVING
274 calories, 13 g fat (2 g saturated), 24 g protein, 25 g carbohydrate, 8 g fiber, 575 mg sodium, 135 mg cholesterol.

Festive Shrimp and Artichokes

MAKES 4 servings **PREP** 5 minutes
COOK 15 minutes

1   box (6.3 ounces) wild mushroom
    pilaf
3   tablespoons butter
3   large cloves garlic, chopped
1   package (10 ounces) sliced
    mushrooms
1   pound shrimp, peeled and
    deveined
½   teaspoon dried tarragon
⅓   cup dry white wine
1   can (14 ounces) artichoke hearts,
    drained and quartered
¼   teaspoon black pepper
¼   cup water
1   tablespoon chicken bouillon
    granules

1. Cook pilaf according to package
   directions.

2. Meanwhile, melt butter in a large
   nonstick skillet over medium heat.
   Add garlic and mushrooms; sauté
   6 minutes.

3. Add shrimp and tarragon; cook
   4 minutes. Add wine, artichoke
   hearts, pepper, water and chicken
   bouillon granules; cook, stirring,
   4 minutes or until shrimp are cooked
   through. Serve with pilaf.

PER SERVING
388 calories, 13 g fat (7 g saturated), 26 g protein,
44 g carbohydrate, 3 g fiber, 1,628 mg sodium,
193 mg cholesterol.

Grilled Shrimp on Brown Rice

MAKES 6 servings **PREP** 10 minutes
COOK 10 minutes
GRILL OR BROIL 3 to 4 minutes

2   cups instant brown rice
1   pound large shrimp, peeled and
    deveined
1   tablespoon apricot preserves
1   can (15¼ ounces) mixed tropical
    fruit, drained and ¾ cup juice
    reserved
1   tablespoon rice-wine vinegar
1   teaspoon dark Asian sesame oil
1   tablespoon vegetable oil
1   teaspoon grated fresh ginger
¼   teaspoon salt
⅛   teaspoon black pepper
1   cup grape tomatoes or halved
    cherry tomatoes
1   can (8 ounces) whole water
    chestnuts, drained and sliced

1. Prepare a charcoal grill with hot coals,
   setting rack 6 inches from coals; or
   heat a gas grill to high; or heat broiler.

2. Prepare instant brown rice according
   to package directions, omitting butter
   and salt. Set aside and let cool.

3. Thread shrimp onto 6 metal skewers,
   dividing equally. Brush with apricot
   preserves. Grill or broil shrimp,
   turning once, 3 to 4 minutes or until
   cooked through.

4. Meanwhile, to make dressing, whisk
   together reserved fruit juice, vinegar,
   sesame oil, vegetable oil, ginger, salt
   and pepper in a small bowl until
   well blended.

5. Combine rice, fruit, tomatoes and water chestnuts in a large bowl. Add half of dressing; toss until ingredients are well coated.

6. To serve, place 1 cup rice mixture on each plate. Top each with a skewer of grilled shrimp. Drizzle each serving with remaining dressing, dividing equally.

PER SERVING
233 calories, 5 g fat (0 g saturated), 13 g protein, 35 g carbohydrate, 4 g fiber, 215 mg sodium, 90 mg cholesterol.

Seafood Skillet

Coconut water (not the same as coconut milk) provides a surprising flavor boost here. Look for it in grocery aisles devoted to Mexican or Caribbean products.

MAKES 6 servings **PREP** 10 minutes
COOK about 15 minutes

3	slices bacon, chopped
2	cloves garlic, finely chopped
1	pound bay scallops
¼	pound medium shrimp, peeled and deveined
1	can (11.8 ounces) coconut water
¼	cup water
2	teaspoons chicken bouillon granules
½	teaspoon salt
¼	teaspoon red-pepper flakes
1	package (1 pound) frozen sweet pepper strips, thawed
2	cups instant rice

1. Cook bacon in a large nonstick skillet over medium heat 4 minutes. Add garlic, scallops and shrimp; cook over medium-high heat 4 minutes.

2. Add coconut water, water, bouillon granules, salt and red-pepper flakes. Bring to boiling. Add peppers; simmer 3 minutes.

3. Stir in rice; cover and remove from heat. Let stand, stirring occasionally, 5 minutes or until liquid is absorbed.

PER SERVING
267 calories, 7 g fat (2 g saturated), 15 g protein, 34 g carbohydrate, 4 g fiber, 843 mg sodium, 43 mg cholesterol.

Stir-Fried Shrimp with Honey Walnuts

Shown on page 22.

MAKES 6 servings **PREP** 45 minutes
REFRIGERATE 1 hour **COOK** 20 minutes

Honey Walnuts

⅔ cup walnut halves
½ cup water
1 tablespoon honey

Shrimp

1 pound large shrimp, peeled and deveined
¼ cup dry sherry
1 tablespoon grated fresh ginger
¾ cup chicken broth
3 tablespoons soy sauce
2 tablespoons ketchup
2 tablespoons sugar
2 tablespoons rice-wine vinegar or distilled white vinegar
1½ tablespoons cornstarch
1 teaspoon dark Asian sesame oil
⅛ teaspoon ground red pepper (cayenne)
3 tablespoons vegetable oil
8 scallions, cut diagonally into 1½-inch pieces
1 large sweet red pepper, cored, seeded and cut into 1-inch pieces
2 cloves garlic, finely chopped
1 pound snow peas, trimmed
Cooked rice for serving (optional)

1. Prepare walnuts: Bring nuts, water and honey to boiling in a small saucepan over medium heat; cook 5 to 8 minutes or until water boils away and nuts begin to sizzle. Continue to cook, shaking pan to coat nuts. Arrange nuts in a single layer on a heatproof plate to dry.

2. Prepare shrimp: Mix shrimp, 2 tablespoons sherry and ginger in a bowl; refrigerate at least 1 hour.

3. Combine remaining 2 tablespoons sherry, broth, soy sauce, ketchup, sugar, vinegar, cornstarch, sesame oil and ground red pepper in a small bowl.

4. Heat 1 tablespoon vegetable oil in a large skillet over high heat. Add honey walnuts to skillet; stir-fry until crisp and brown, about 2 or 3 minutes. Turn out onto heatproof plate.

5. Heat another 1 tablespoon vegetable oil in same skillet. Drain shrimp. Add shrimp, scallions, sweet red pepper and garlic to skillet; stir-fry 3 to 5 minutes or until vegetables are crisp-tender and shrimp are pink and curled. Transfer to a large platter; keep warm.

6. Wipe out skillet. Heat remaining 1 tablespoon vegetable oil in skillet. Add snow peas; stir-fry 1 minute or just until tender. Return shrimp and vegetables to skillet. Stir in ketchup-broth mixture. Bring to boiling; cook, stirring frequently, until thickened, 2 to 3 minutes.

7. Serve shrimp over hot rice if desired, topped with honey walnuts.

Note: Honey walnuts can be prepared several days in advance. Store in an airtight container.

PER SERVING
279 calories, 16 g fat (2 g saturated), 15 g protein, 21 g carbohydrate, 3 g fiber, 810 mg sodium, 90 mg cholesterol.

Roasted Chicken with 20 Cloves of Garlic

Traditionally, this dish is served with toasted French bread onto which the garlic is squeezed from the skins by each diner.

MAKES 6 servings **PREP** 15 minutes
BAKE at 375° for 25 minutes; then at 450° for 45 minutes

2	teaspoons olive oil
1	teaspoon black pepper
½	teaspoon dried rosemary
¼	teaspoon dried thyme
1	whole chicken (3½ pounds)
1	small onion, peeled and cut in half
1	small lemon, cut in half
20	cloves garlic, unpeeled (about 2 whole heads, separated)
¾	cup dry white wine
1	can (14½ ounces) chicken broth
2	tablespoons chopped fresh parsley
½	teaspoon salt

1. Heat oven to 375°.

2. Mix oil, pepper, rosemary and thyme in a small bowl. Rub over outside of chicken. Place onion and lemon in cavity of chicken. Truss chicken if desired.

3. Place chicken, breast side up, in a Dutch oven. Scatter garlic around chicken. Pour in wine and broth. Place on stovetop. Cover; bring to boiling.

4. Transfer to heated 375° oven. Bake, covered, 25 minutes. Increase oven temperature to 450°. Uncover; bake 45 minutes or until an instant-read thermometer inserted in thigh registers 180°.

5. Transfer chicken and garlic to a platter; cover with aluminum foil. Skim as much fat as possible from pot. Squeeze out 6 cloves cooked garlic into a small bowl. Mash, stirring in a few tablespoons of cooking liquid, and then whisk back into cooking liquid in pot. Stir in parsley and salt.

6. Carve chicken. Spoon broth over each serving and garnish with a few cloves garlic. (To eat garlic, gently press with a fork to squeeze out pulp from skin.)

PER SERVING
344 calories, 20 g fat (5 g saturated), 35 g protein,
4 g carbohydrate, 0 g fiber, 574 mg sodium,
112 mg cholesterol.

Baked Chicken on Pecan Stuffing

MAKES 4 servings **PREP** 10 minutes
COOK 5 minutes
BAKE at 400° for 45 minutes

3	tablespoons butter
1	small onion, chopped
2	ribs celery, chopped
1	apple, peeled, cored and diced
1	teaspoon salt
½	teaspoon plus ⅛ teaspoon dried sage
½	teaspoon black pepper
¾	pound stale Italian bread, cubed
¾	cup chicken broth
1	egg, lightly beaten
½	cup plus 3 tablespoons chopped pecans
½	cup raisins
4	chicken breast halves (1½ pounds)
¼	cup apple jelly
⅛	teaspoon ground cinnamon

1. Heat oven to 400°.

2. Heat butter in a medium-size skillet over medium heat. Add onion, celery and apple; cook 5 minutes. Stir in ½ teaspoon salt, ½ teaspoon sage and pepper.

3. Place bread cubes in a large bowl; add onion mixture. Drizzle with broth and egg. Stir in ½ cup pecans and raisins. Spread in a 13 x 9 x 2-inch baking dish. Top with chicken, skin side up, and sprinkle with remaining ½ teaspoon salt.

4. Bake in heated 400° oven 30 minutes.

5. Meanwhile, melt jelly with cinnamon and remaining ⅛ teaspoon sage in a small saucepan over low heat.

6. Brush mixture on chicken; top with remaining 3 tablespoons pecans. Bake 15 minutes longer.

PER SERVING
828 calories, 36 g fat (10 g saturated), 43 g protein, 88 g carbohydrate, 43 g fiber, 1,389 mg sodium, 161 mg cholesterol.

Crispy Oven-Baked Chicken

MAKES 12 servings **PREP** 20 minutes
BAKE at 350° for 1 hour

2	cups crushed cornflakes
½	cup grated Parmesan cheese
2	teaspoons salt
½	teaspoon ground red pepper (cayenne)
3	eggs
24	chicken drumsticks (about 6 pounds total), skin removed

1. Heat oven to 350°. Line 2 shallow roasting pans with aluminum foil. Coat with nonstick cooking spray.

2. Mix together cornflakes, Parmesan, salt and red pepper in a large bowl.

3. Lightly beat eggs in a shallow dish. Dip each drumstick in egg; roll in cornflake mixture to coat. Place on prepared pans. Lightly coat chicken with nonstick cooking spray.

4. Bake in heated 350° oven, without turning, 1 hour or until internal temperature registers 180° on an instant-read thermometer. Serve hot or chilled.

PER SERVING
256 calories, 7 g fat (3 g saturated), 30 g protein, 16 g carbohydrate, 1 g fiber, 725 mg sodium, 138 mg cholesterol.

Cheese and Chicken Enchiladas

MAKES 6 servings **PREP** 25 minutes
BAKE at 350° for 25 minutes

2   cups shredded cooked chicken
    (about ½ roasted chicken)
1   package (8 ounces) shredded
    Mexican cheese blend (2 cups)
1   cup shredded cheddar cheese
    (4 ounces)
1   package (1 pound) frozen sweet
    pepper strips, thawed (about
    2½ cups)
½   teaspoon chili powder
¼   teaspoon salt
⅛   teaspoon ground cumin
12 corn tortillas (6-inch)
1   can (19 ounces) enchilada sauce
¾   cup fat-free half-and-half

1. Heat oven to 350°.

2. Place chicken in a large bowl. Add
    1 cup Mexican cheese, all the cheddar
    cheese, 2 cups peppers, chili powder,
    salt and cumin; toss to combine.

3. Wrap tortillas in damp paper
    toweling; place in a microwave oven
    and warm at 100% power 2 minutes.
    Alternatively, wrap tortillas in
    aluminum foil and warm in heated
    350° oven 10 minutes.

4. Whisk together enchilada sauce and
    half-and-half in a small bowl. Spread
    ½ cup evenly in bottom of a 13 x 9 x
    2-inch baking dish.

5. Dip one side of a tortilla into sauce
    mixture in bowl; place, dipped side
    up, on a work surface. Spoon ¼ cup
    chicken mixture across center of
    tortilla; roll up, enclosing filling.
    Place, seam side down, in sauce in
    baking dish.

6. Repeat with remaining tortillas and
    filling. Pour remaining sauce mixture
    in bowl over enchiladas in dish.

7. Chop remaining ½ cup peppers.
    Sprinkle remaining 1 cup Mexican
    cheese over enchiladas in dish. Top
    with chopped peppers. Cover baking
    dish with aluminum foil.

8. Bake enchiladas in heated 350° oven
    15 minutes. Remove foil. Bake
    enchiladas, uncovered, 10 minutes
    longer or until sauce is bubbly and
    cheese on top is melted.

PER SERVING
570 calories, 35 g fat (19 g saturated), 33 g protein,
33 g carbohydrate, 5 g fiber, 734 mg sodium,
131 mg cholesterol.

Chunky Chicken Dijon

MAKES 12 servings **PREP** 15 minutes
COOK 12 to 13 minutes
BAKE at 400° for 30 minutes

3   **tablespoons butter**
1   **pound mushrooms, thinly sliced**
2   **tablespoons all-purpose flour**
1   **can (14½ ounces) chicken broth**
½   **teaspoon salt**
¼   **teaspoon garlic powder**
⅛   **teaspoon ground nutmeg**
⅛   **teaspoon black pepper**
1   **tablespoon Dijon mustard**
2¼ **pounds cooked chicken, cut into ½-inch cubes (4 to 4½ cups)**
2   **packages (10 ounces each) frozen chopped broccoli, thawed**
2   **cups shredded cheddar cheese (8 ounces)**
3   **cups cooked white rice**

1. Heat oven to 400°. Grease a 13 x 9 x 2-inch baking dish.

2. Melt butter in a large skillet over medium heat. Add mushrooms; cook until softened, 6 to 7 minutes, stirring occasionally. Sprinkle flour over mushrooms; cook, stirring, 1 minute.

3. Gradually add broth, stirring constantly and scraping any browned bits from bottom of skillet. Bring to boiling. Lower heat; simmer until sauce is thickened, about 5 minutes.

4. Add salt, garlic powder, nutmeg and pepper. Remove from heat. Stir in mustard. Add chicken.

5. Mix broccoli and cheddar in a large bowl. Spread rice in bottom of prepared baking dish; top with

broccoli mixture. Spread chicken mixture evenly on top. Bake in heated 400° oven 30 minutes or until heated through.

PER SERVING
337 calories, 16 g fat (8 g saturated), 33 g protein, 14 g carbohydrate, 2 g fiber, 477 mg sodium, 104 mg cholesterol.

Soy-Glazed Chicken with Couscous

MAKES 6 servings **PREP** 10 minutes
COOK 5 minutes **BAKE** at 350° for 45 minutes **BROIL** 5 minutes

½   **cup reduced-sodium soy sauce**
¼   **cup packed dark-brown sugar**
½   **teaspoon ground ginger**
2   **tablespoons rice-wine vinegar**
2   **tablespoons dark Asian sesame oil**
2   **teaspoons cornstarch**
1   **whole chicken (4 pounds), cut into 8 pieces**
1   **box (10 ounces) couscous**
3   **ounces snow peas, trimmed**
1   **can (8 ounces) sliced water chestnuts, drained**
     Sesame seeds for garnish (optional)

1. Heat oven to 350°.

2. Whisk soy sauce, brown sugar, ginger, vinegar, sesame oil and cornstarch in a small saucepan; cook, stirring, until glaze thickens, 2 minutes.

3. Place chicken, skin side up, on a rack in a broiler pan. Brush with glaze.

4. Bake in heated 350° oven 45 minutes or until internal temperature of chicken breasts registers 170° on an instant-read thermometer; brush with

glaze every 10 minutes. Increase oven temperature to broil; broil chicken 5 minutes to crisp skin.

5. Meanwhile, prepare couscous following package directions, adding peas and water chestnuts along with water indicated on package.

6. Arrange chicken on a platter with couscous; sprinkle with sesame seeds if desired.

PER SERVING
592 calories, 25 g fat (6 g saturated), 46 g protein, 47 g carbohydrate, 1 g fiber, 1,295 mg sodium, 127 mg cholesterol.

Chicken Cutlet Parmigiana

MAKES 4 servings **PREP** 10 minutes
COOK about 8 minutes
BAKE at 375° for 4 to 5 minutes

2 eggs, lightly beaten
½ teaspoon salt
⅛ teaspoon black pepper
2 tablespoons all-purpose flour
¾ cup dry Italian-seasoned bread crumbs
4 boneless, skinless chicken breast halves (1½ pounds total), slightly flattened
3 tablespoons vegetable oil
2 tablespoons butter
1 can (8 ounces) tomato sauce
1½ cups shredded mozzarella cheese (6 ounces)
2 tablespoons chopped fresh parsley Cooked spaghetti tossed with tomato sauce for serving (optional)

1. Mix eggs, salt and pepper in a shallow dish. Place flour in a second dish. Place bread crumbs in a third dish.

2. Dip chicken breast halves in flour to coat lightly, shaking off excess. Dip in egg mixture. Coat both sides with crumbs. Place on a sheet of waxed paper.

3. Heat oven to 375°.

4. Heat oil and butter in a large nonstick skillet over medium heat. Add chicken; cook 3 to 4 minutes per side or until golden and internal temperature registers 170° on an instant-read thermometer. Transfer chicken to a rimmed baking sheet. Spoon tomato sauce over each piece, dividing equally. Top with mozzarella.

5. Bake in heated 375° oven 4 to 5 minutes or until cheese is melted. Sprinkle with parsley and serve with spaghetti if desired.

PER SERVING
583 calories, 33 g fat (13 g saturated), 50 g protein, 19 g carbohydrate, 2 g fiber, 1,322 mg sodium, 254 mg cholesterol.

PANTRY PLUS: COOK TO THE SAFE DEGREE
Always cook poultry thoroughly, as indicated here. Use an instant-read thermometer to ascertain the internal temperature; make sure thermometer doesn't touch any bones.

Ground	165°
Whole (measure in thigh)	180°
Thigh or drumstick	180°
Breast	170°
Stuffing	165°

Chicken Sausage and Apples

MAKES 4 servings **PREP** 5 minutes
COOK 30 minutes

1   package (10 to 12 ounces)
    precooked chicken sausage with
    apple, sliced into ½-inch-thick
    pieces
1   teaspoon unsalted butter
1   large red onion, sliced
1   large Golden Delicious apple,
    peeled, cored and sliced
½   cup apple cider or chicken broth
½   cup bottled chutney, chopped
    Mashed Potatoes (page 129) for
    serving (optional)

1. Heat a skillet over medium-high heat.
   Add sausage; sauté until golden
   brown, about 5 minutes. Transfer to
   a plate; keep warm.

2. Heat butter in same skillet over
   medium heat. Add onion; sauté
   8 minutes or until slightly softened.
   Add apple; cook 5 minutes or until
   slightly softened.

3. Stir in cider, chutney and sausage;
   cook, stirring occasionally, 10 minutes
   or until onion is softened and sauce is
   slightly thickened. If too thick, add a
   little more cider. Serve with Mashed
   Potatoes if desired.

PER SERVING
382 calories, 12 g fat (3 g saturated), 17 g protein,
55 g carbohydrate, 4 g fiber, 743 mg sodium,
83 mg cholesterol.

Chicken with Mushrooms

MAKES 4 servings **PREP** 15 minutes
REFRIGERATE 1 hour
COOK about 40 minutes

⅓   cup plain low-fat yogurt
1   tablespoon lemon juice
1   tablespoon plus 1 teaspoon
    snipped fresh dill
4   boneless, skinless chicken breast
    halves (1¼ pounds total)
3   slices bacon
½   cup all-purpose flour
1½ teaspoons salt
¼   teaspoon black pepper
2   teaspoons olive oil
1   medium onion, chopped
1   can (14½ ounces) chicken broth
¼   cup dry white wine
½   pound green beans, trimmed and
    cut into 1-inch lengths
½   pound small mushrooms, halved
½   cup heavy cream

1. Combine yogurt, lemon juice and
   1 tablespoon dill in a large bowl.
   Add chicken; turn to coat. Refrigerate
   1 hour to marinate.

2. Cook bacon in a large nonstick skillet
   over medium heat until crisp.
   Transfer with a slotted spoon to paper
   toweling to drain; reserve. Drain and
   discard all but 1 tablespoon drippings
   from skillet.

3. Combine flour with 1 teaspoon salt
   and pepper in a shallow dish. Remove
   chicken from marinade; dip in flour
   mixture to coat lightly, shaking off
   excess flour.

4. Heat skillet with remaining bacon
   drippings over medium-high heat.

Add chicken; cook 2 minutes per side or until golden. Transfer chicken to a platter.

5. Heat oil in same skillet over medium-high heat. Add onion; sauté 8 minutes. Pour in broth and wine; bring to boiling, scraping up any browned bits from bottom of skillet with a wooden spoon. Add beans and mushrooms; simmer, uncovered, 5 minutes.

6. Crumble bacon. Add cream and remaining ½ teaspoon salt to skillet. Return chicken and crumbled bacon to skillet; cook, uncovered, over low heat until internal temperature of chicken registers 170° on an instant-read thermometer, about 15 minutes. Stir in remaining 1 teaspoon dill.

PER SERVING
421 calories, 15 g fat (5 g saturated), 47 g protein, 22 g carbohydrate, 4 g fiber, 1,443 mg sodium, 121 mg cholesterol.

Sweet-and-Sour Stuffed Peppers

MAKES 4 servings **PREP** 10 minutes
COOK about 30 minutes

2   sweet red peppers
2   sweet green peppers
1   tablespoon olive oil
1   pound ground chicken
1   teaspoon salt
½   teaspoon ground ginger
¼   teaspoon black pepper
1   cup instant rice
¾   cup bottled sweet-and-sour sauce
¾   cup boiling water
¼   cup chopped water chestnuts

Sweet-and-Sour Stuffed Peppers

1. Slice one-quarter off stem end of each pepper. Remove membranes, seeds and stems; reserve tops. Invert peppers on waxed paper. Chop enough of reserved tops to equal ½ cup; save or discard remainder.

2. Heat oil in a large saucepan. Add chicken, chopped peppers, salt, ginger and black pepper; sauté 8 minutes or until chicken is no longer pink. Sprinkle in rice; add sauce and boiling water, stirring. Bring mixture to boiling, then cover. Remove from heat and let stand 5 minutes. Stir in water chestnuts.

3. Transfer chicken mixture to a large bowl. Wipe out pan. Add ½ cup water. Place a steamer basket in pan.

4. Spoon chicken mixture into peppers, dividing equally. Place peppers upright in basket. Cover and bring water to boiling. Lower heat and steam 10 to 15 minutes or until tender.

PER SERVING
361 calories, 11 g fat (1 g saturated), 23 g protein, 42 g carbohydrate, 3 g fiber, 1,032 mg sodium, 72 mg cholesterol.

Creamy Chicken Thighs and Rice

MAKES 4 servings **PREP** 15 minutes
REFRIGERATE 30 minutes **COOK** 25 minutes

1   container (8 ounces) plain low-fat yogurt
1   tablespoon lemon juice
1¼   teaspoons sugar
1¼   teaspoons salt
1   teaspoon paprika
½   teaspoon ground coriander
¼   teaspoon curry powder
1½   pounds boneless, skinless chicken thighs, cut into 2-inch chunks
1   sweet red pepper, cored, seeded and cut into ½-inch diamonds
1½   cups converted white rice
¼   teaspoon cumin seeds
1   cup frozen peas
2   teaspoons cornstarch
2   tablespoons water
½   cup sour cream
     Chopped fresh parsley for garnish (optional)

1. Mix yogurt, lemon juice, sugar, salt, paprika, coriander and curry powder in a medium-size bowl. Mix in chicken and red pepper. Cover; refrigerate 30 minutes.

2. Meanwhile, cook rice according to package directions, using 3 cups water and adding cumin seeds along with water; add peas during last 5 minutes. Keep warm.

3. Transfer chicken with marinade to a large skillet. Bring to simmering and simmer 12 minutes.

4. Dissolve cornstarch in water in a small bowl; add to pan. Cook until sauce thickens, 2 minutes.

5. Stir in sour cream; heat through but do not allow sauce to boil. Serve chicken over rice, garnished with parsley if desired.

PER SERVING
571 calories, 15 g fat (7 g saturated), 31 g protein, 75 g carbohydrate, 4 g fiber, 811 mg sodium, 85 mg cholesterol.

"Scalloped" Chicken and Potatoes

MAKES 6 servings **PREP** 15 minutes
COOK 30 minutes

2½   pounds medium red new potatoes (about 8), sliced ¼ inch thick
1   can (14½ ounces) chicken broth
1   package (8 ounces) cream cheese
1   cup milk
3   tablespoons all-purpose flour
1   teaspoon chicken bouillon granules
½   teaspoon dried thyme
¼   teaspoon dried sage
¼   teaspoon garlic powder
¼   teaspoon salt
¼   teaspoon black pepper
4   scallions, chopped, including part of the green
1¼   pounds boneless, skinless chicken breasts, cut into ¾-inch cubes
1   package (10 ounces) frozen cut green beans
1½   cups shredded Havarti or Swiss cheese
     Fresh sage sprigs for garnish (optional)

1. Place potatoes and 1 cup broth in a Dutch oven. Bring to boiling; cook over medium-high heat 15 minutes or until almost tender.

2. Meanwhile, whisk cream cheese with milk and remaining broth in a medium-size bowl until blended. Beat in flour, bouillon granules, thyme, sage, garlic powder, salt, pepper and scallions.

3. Add chicken and cream cheese mixture to potatoes in pot. Cover; lower heat and simmer 5 minutes, stirring occasionally. Stir in green beans and Havarti; cook 10 minutes longer or until chicken is cooked through. Serve garnished with sage sprigs if desired.

PER SERVING
522 calories, 26 g fat (15 g saturated), 37 g protein, 35 g carbohydrate, 5 g fiber, 714 mg sodium, 125 mg cholesterol.

One-Pot Chicken and Sausage

MAKES 4 servings **PREP** 10 minutes
COOK about 1 hour 10 minutes

½ **pound Italian sausages, each cut diagonally into thirds**
4 **skinless chicken breast halves, bone-in (2½ pounds total)**
2 **teaspoons olive oil**
3 **cloves garlic, chopped**
1 **teaspoon dried rosemary**
1 **pound small red new potatoes with skin, quartered**
3 **tablespoons water**
¼ **cup dry white wine**
3 **tablespoons balsamic vinegar**
2 **small sweet red peppers, cored, seeded and cut into 1-inch squares**
½ **teaspoon salt**
¼ **teaspoon black pepper**
  Fresh rosemary sprigs for garnish (optional)

1. Cook sausage in a large nonstick skillet over medium-low heat until browned on all sides, about 8 minutes. Transfer to a large plate.

2. Add chicken, meaty side down, to skillet; cook, turning once, 5 minutes. Transfer to plate; set aside.

3. Heat oil in same skillet. Add garlic and rosemary; sauté 1 minute. Add potatoes and 3 tablespoons water; cover and cook 15 minutes.

4. Push potatoes to side of skillet. Stir in wine, vinegar, red peppers, salt and black pepper. Return chicken and sausage to skillet. Cover; cook over medium-low heat 35 minutes or until internal temperature of chicken registers 170° on an instant-read thermometer. Transfer chicken and sausage to a platter; cover and keep warm.

5. Cover skillet; cook potatoes in sauce 8 minutes longer or until tender. Spoon potatoes and sauce over chicken. Garnish with rosemary sprigs if desired.

PER SERVING
427 calories, 15 g fat (4 g saturated), 50 g protein, 20 g carbohydrate, 3 g fiber, 663 mg sodium, 135 mg cholesterol.

Cajun Chicken with Citrus Salsa

MAKES 4 servings **PREP** 15 minutes
COOK about 6 minutes

3　tablespoons Cajun seasoning
¾　teaspoon onion powder
⅛　teaspoon black pepper
⅛　teaspoon ground red pepper (cayenne)
4　boneless, skinless chicken breast halves (1¼ pounds total), slightly flattened
2　tablespoons vegetable oil
1　can (11 ounces) Mandarin orange segments, drained and chopped
1　can (8 ounces) crushed pineapple, drained
2　tablespoons lime juice
1　jalapeño chile, seeded and minced
2　tablespoons chopped fresh cilantro
¼　teaspoon salt
　　Mashed Potatoes (page 129) for serving (optional)

1. Stir together Cajun seasoning, onion powder, black pepper and red pepper in a shallow dish. Rub over chicken breast halves.

2. Heat oil in a large nonstick skillet over medium-high heat. Add chicken; cook 2 to 3 minutes per side or until lightly browned and internal temperature registers 170° on an instant-read thermometer.

3. Combine Mandarin oranges, pineapple, lime juice, jalapeño, cilantro and salt in a small bowl. Serve salsa with chicken and, if desired, Mashed Potatoes.

PER SERVING
272 calories, 10 g fat (1 g saturated), 30 g protein, 15 g carbohydrate, 0 g fiber, 307 mg sodium, 78 mg cholesterol.

Chicken Sausage Stir-Fry

MAKES 6 servings **PREP** 10 minutes
MARINATE 10 minutes
COOK about 25 minutes

Marinade
¼　cup hoisin sauce
2　tablespoons reduced-sodium soy sauce
2　tablespoons rice-wine vinegar
1　clove garlic, finely chopped
1　tablespoon grated fresh ginger
⅛　teaspoon ground red pepper (cayenne)

Stir-Fry
½　pound green beans, trimmed and cut in half crosswise
1　can (15 ounces) baby corn, drained
1　large sweet red pepper, cored, seeded and cut into ¼-inch-wide strips
1　teaspoon vegetable oil
1　package (10 to 12 ounces) precooked jalapeño-flavored chicken sausage, cut diagonally into ½-inch-thick slices
½　teaspoon cornstarch
⅓　cup chicken broth

　　Cooked rice for serving (optional)
　　Chopped scallions for garnish (optional)

1. Prepare marinade: Stir together hoisin, soy sauce, vinegar, garlic, ginger and red pepper in a bowl.

2. Prepare stir-fry: Cook green beans in a medium-size saucepan of boiling water until tender, about 12 minutes. Drain.

3. Place corn, sweet red pepper and green beans in a medium-size bowl. Add ¼ cup marinade; stir to combine. Let stand 10 minutes.

4. Meanwhile, heat oil in a large nonstick skillet over high heat. Add sausage; sauté until golden brown, 5 minutes. Transfer to a plate; keep warm.

5. Lower heat to medium-high. Add vegetables and remaining marinade to skillet; sauté 4 minutes.

6. Dissolve cornstarch in broth in a small bowl; add to skillet. Cook until vegetables are crisp-tender and sauce is thickened, 2 to 3 minutes. Add sausage; heat through. If desired, serve over hot cooked rice, garnished with chopped scallions.

PER SERVING
243 calories, 5 g fat (1 g saturated), 12 g protein, 37 g carbohydrate, 2 g fiber, 770 mg sodium, 45 mg cholesterol.

Chicken Teriyaki over Asian Noodles

MAKES 4 servings **PREP** 5 minutes
COOK 10 minutes

¼	cup dry sherry
2	tablespoons soy sauce
2	tablespoons teriyaki sauce
2	tablespoons sugar
3	teaspoons dark Asian sesame oil
1	teaspoon ground ginger
1	package (8 ounces) lo mein noodles or egg noodles
2	tablespoons vegetable oil
2	cloves garlic, finely chopped

2	scallions, white and green parts separated and chopped
1	package (1 pound) teriyaki-seasoned boneless, skinless chicken breasts, cut into ½-inch pieces
1	package (1 pound) frozen Asian stir-fry vegetables, thawed
1	tablespoon cornstarch
1	tablespoon water

1. Mix sherry, soy sauce, teriyaki sauce, sugar, 2 teaspoons sesame oil and ginger in a small bowl.

2. Cook noodles according to package directions. Drain; toss with remaining 1 teaspoon sesame oil.

3. Meanwhile, heat vegetable oil in a large nonstick skillet over high heat. Add garlic and white part of scallions; stir-fry 30 seconds or until fragrant. Add chicken to skillet; stir-fry 2 to 3 minutes or until partially cooked.

4. Add vegetables and teriyaki sauce mixture to skillet; stir-fry 3 to 4 minutes or until heated through.

5. Stir cornstarch and water in a small bowl until smooth; stir into skillet. Cook until mixture is thickened, about 1 minute.

6. Place noodles on a serving platter. Top with chicken and vegetables; sprinkle with remaining scallions.

PER SERVING
479 calories, 12 g fat (1 g saturated), 27 g protein, 70 g carbohydrate, 4 g fiber, 1,524 mg sodium, 50 mg cholesterol.

Chicken with Green Beans and Cashews

MAKES 4 servings **PREP** 15 minutes
COOK about 45 minutes

¾   **cup unsalted roasted cashews**
1   **pound green beans, trimmed**
4   **slices bacon, chopped**
5   **tablespoons all-purpose flour**
1   **teaspoon salt**
½   **teaspoon dried thyme**
¼   **teaspoon black pepper**
1   **egg**
1   **teaspoon water**
4   **boneless, skinless chicken breast halves (1 pound total)**
1   **medium onion, chopped**
½   **pound mushrooms, sliced**
1   **can (14½ ounces) chicken broth**
½   **cup sour cream**
    Cooked pasta or Mashed Potatoes (page 129) for serving (optional)

1. Finely chop ¼ cup cashews.
2. Cook green beans in a large pot of lightly salted boiling water just until tender, about 5 minutes. Drain; rinse under cold water to stop cooking.
3. Cook bacon in a large nonstick skillet until crisp, about 6 minutes. Drain on paper toweling. Pour off and reserve drippings.
4. Combine 2 tablespoons flour, ½ teaspoon salt, thyme and pepper on waxed paper. Place chopped cashews on another sheet of waxed paper. Whisk egg with water in a shallow dish.
5. Heat 1 tablespoon bacon drippings in same skillet over medium heat.
6. Dip chicken breasts in flour mixture to coat lightly, dip in egg, then press chopped cashews onto top of each.
7. Add chicken to skillet; sauté, nut side down, about 4 minutes or until golden. Turn; sauté until browned, about 2 minutes. Transfer to paper toweling.
8. Heat another 1 tablespoon bacon drippings in same skillet. Add onion; sauté 2 to 3 minutes or until softened. Add mushrooms and bacon; cook, stirring, 3 to 5 minutes or until mushrooms are lightly browned. Sprinkle remaining 3 tablespoons flour and remaining ½ teaspoon salt over mushrooms; stir until flour is moistened. Gradually pour in broth, stirring constantly; cook, stirring, until sauce comes to boiling and thickens.
9. Arrange chicken on sauce in skillet. Reduce heat to low; cover. Simmer 10 minutes or until internal temperature of chicken registers 170° on an instant-read thermometer.
10. Add green beans to skillet; cover and heat through. Stir in sour cream; do not let boil. Top with remaining cashews. Serve with pasta or Mashed Potatoes if desired.

PER SERVING
575 calories, 34 g fat (11 g saturated), 40 g protein, 31 g carbohydrate, 6 g fiber, 1,635 mg sodium, 147 mg cholesterol.

Chicken Stir-Fry

MAKES 6 servings **PREP** 5 minutes
COOK 10 minutes

1   tablespoon dark Asian sesame oil
1¼ pounds boneless, skinless chicken
     breast halves, cut into thin strips
1   tablespoon vegetable oil
½   pound sliced mushrooms
1   bunch scallions, cut into 1-inch
     pieces, including part of the green
2   cups shredded carrots (two-thirds
     of 10-ounce package shredded
     carrots)
1   cup bottled stir-fry sauce
⅔   cup salted dry-roasted cashews
     Cooked rice for serving (optional)

1. Heat sesame oil in a large nonstick
    skillet over high heat. Add chicken;
    stir-fry 3 minutes. Transfer chicken
    to a plate; keep warm.

2. Heat vegetable oil in same skillet over
    high heat. Add mushrooms, scallions
    and carrots; stir-fry 5 minutes. Add
    stir-fry sauce and chicken to skillet;
    stir-fry until chicken is cooked
    through, 1 to 2 minutes. Top with
    cashews and serve with rice if desired.

PER SERVING
333 calories, 18 g fat (3 g saturated), 23 g protein,
20 g carbohydrate, 2 g fiber, 527 mg sodium,
52 mg cholesterol.

Salsa-Style Drumsticks

MAKES 4 servings **PREP** 10 minutes
REFRIGERATE 4 hours or overnight
BROIL 15 to 20 minutes
COOK 25 to 30 minutes

1   small onion, halved and thinly sliced
     Juice of 2 limes
2   tablespoons vegetable oil
½   teaspoon liquid hot-pepper sauce
1   can (14 ounces) stewed tomatoes
1   jalapeño chile, seeded and diced
8   chicken drumsticks (2½ pounds)
1¼ cups water
1   package (10 ounces) yellow rice

1. Mix onion, lime juice, oil, hot-pepper
    sauce, tomatoes, jalapeño and
    drumsticks in a medium-size bowl.
    Cover and refrigerate 4 hours or
    overnight.

2. Heat broiler, positioning oven rack
    6 to 8 inches from heat.

3. Leaving drumsticks in bowl, transfer
    salsa marinade to a small skillet;
    return drumsticks to refrigerator.
    Add water to skillet. Bring to boiling.
    Lower heat; simmer 25 to 30 minutes
    or until onion is tender.

4. Prepare rice according to package
    directions.

5. Meanwhile, after salsa has simmered
    10 minutes, place drumsticks in a
    single layer, skin side up, on broiler-
    pan rack. Broil 15 to 20 minutes,
    turning once. Serve chicken with
    salsa and rice.

PER SERVING
673 calories, 28 g fat (5 g saturated), 42 g protein,
64 g carbohydrate, 3 g fiber, 1,291 mg sodium,
115 mg cholesterol.

2 sweet yellow peppers, cored, seeded and quartered
1 pound Italian-style chicken sausage links

1. Mix vinegar, thyme, sugar, mustard, salt, pepper and garlic in a small bowl. Whisk in oil. Reserve ⅓ cup in a serving bowl for dressing. Divide remaining marinade between 2 plastic bags. Add chicken to one and zucchini, tomatoes, scallions and sweet peppers to the other. Marinate 20 minutes.

2. Meanwhile, prepare a charcoal grill with hot coals, setting rack 6 inches from coals; or heat a gas grill to high; or heat broiler.

3. Grill or broil chicken and sausage 20 to 25 minutes, turning once; add vegetables after 10 minutes. Cook vegetables 8 to 10 minutes, turning once. Discard marinade in bags. Cut vegetables and sausage into bite-size pieces. Add to bowl with reserved dressing; mix. Serve chicken with vegetables.

PER SERVING
415 calories, 24 g fat (5 g saturated), 40 g protein, 11 g carbohydrate, 3 g fiber, 437 mg sodium, 154 mg cholesterol.

Grilled Chicken Legs with Vegetables

MAKES 6 servings **PREP** 15 minutes
MARINATE 20 minutes
GRILL OR BROIL about 25 minutes

½ cup red-wine vinegar
1 teaspoon dried thyme
½ teaspoon sugar
½ teaspoon Dijon mustard
½ teaspoon salt
¼ teaspoon black pepper
2 cloves garlic, minced
½ cup olive oil
6 whole chicken legs (about 3 pounds total), skin removed
2 small zucchini, halved lengthwise
6 plum tomatoes, halved
4 scallions, trimmed

Apricot-Glazed Chicken

MAKES 4 servings **PREP** 10 minutes
COOK 10 minutes
GRILL OR BROIL about 8 minutes

2 teaspoons vegetable oil
¼ teaspoon curry powder
¼ teaspoon salt
⅛ teaspoon black pepper
4 boneless, skinless chicken breast halves (1½ pounds total)

Glaze

⅓ cup apricot preserves
¼ cup orange juice
1 tablespoon rice-wine vinegar
1 teaspoon brown sugar
¼ teaspoon curry powder
⅛ teaspoon red-pepper flakes

Cooked green beans for serving (optional)
Mashed Potatoes (page 129) for serving (optional)

1. Mix oil, curry powder, salt and pepper in a shallow dish. Add chicken; turn to coat.

2. Prepare a charcoal grill with medium-hot coals, setting rack 6 inches from coals; or heat a gas grill to medium-high; or heat broiler.

3. Prepare glaze: Cook preserves, orange juice, vinegar, brown sugar, curry powder and red-pepper flakes in a small saucepan over medium-low heat until thickened, 10 minutes. Divide in half; reserve half for basting and half for serving as a sauce.

4. Grill or broil chicken 3 to 4 minutes per side or until internal temperature registers 170° on an instant-read thermometer; baste with half of glaze during last few minutes. Serve with remaining half of glaze and green beans and Mashed Potatoes if desired.

PER SERVING
288 calories, 6 g fat (1 g saturated), 36 g protein, 21 g carbohydrate, 0 fiber, 237 mg sodium, 94 mg cholesterol.

Chicken Italiano

MAKES 6 servings **PREP** 5 minutes
GRILL OR BROIL 6 minutes

¼ cup plus 1 teaspoon garlic-flavored oil
1 teaspoon dried oregano
¼ teaspoon cracked black pepper
¼ teaspoon garlic powder
6 boneless, skinless chicken breast halves (2 pounds total)
½ teaspoon salt
1 jar (4 ounces) chopped pimientos, drained
½ teaspoon balsamic vinegar
Cooked rice for serving (optional)

1. Prepare a charcoal grill with medium-hot coals; or heat a gas grill to medium-high; or heat broiler. Brush grill rack or broiler-pan rack with oil and position 6 inches from heat.

2. Whisk together ¼ cup oil, oregano, pepper and garlic powder in a small bowl.

3. Place chicken breast halves between sheets of plastic wrap. Lightly pound until ¼ inch thick. Brush both sides of chicken with oil mixture; sprinkle with salt. Grill 3 minutes per side or until internal temperature of chicken registers 170° on an instant-read thermometer.

4. Meanwhile, mix pimientos, vinegar and remaining 1 teaspoon oil in a small bowl. Serve chicken over rice if desired; top with pimiento sauce.

PER SERVING
253 calories, 13 g fat (2 g saturated), 31 g protein, 1 g carbohydrate, 0 g fiber, 269 mg sodium, 84 mg cholesterol.

Cheesy Chicken Burgers

Grilled Chicken with Spicy Sweet Potatoes

Time this right—prepare the rub first, then cook the sweet potatoes. When they are done, you'll need just minutes to cook the chicken.

MAKES 4 servings **PREP** 10 minutes
GRILL OR BAKE potatoes at 450° for 45 to 50 minutes
GRILL OR BROIL chicken 6 to 8 minutes

Herb Rub

¼	**cup chili powder**
1	**tablespoon brown sugar**
2	**teaspoons dried oregano**
1	**teaspoon dried thyme**
½	**teaspoon salt**
½	**teaspoon black pepper**

1¼ **pounds boneless, skinless chicken breasts**
Spicy Sweet Potatoes (left) for serving (optional)

1. Prepare a charcoal grill with medium-hot coals; or heat a gas grill to medium-high; or heat broiler. Brush grill rack or broiler-pan rack with oil and position 6 inches from heat.

2. Prepare rub: Whisk together chili powder, brown sugar, oregano, thyme, salt and pepper in a cup. Pour into a shallow dish, reserving 1½ tablespoons for Spicy Sweet Potatoes.

3. Place chicken breast halves between sheets of plastic wrap. Lightly pound until ¼ inch thick. Add to dish with rub, turning to coat. Grill or broil 3 to 4 minutes per side or until cooked through. Serve with Spicy Sweet Potatoes if desired.

PER SERVING
186 calories, 6 g fat (1 g saturated), 29 g protein, 5 g carbohydrate, 2 g fiber, 344 mg sodium, 78 mg cholesterol.

Spicy Sweet Potatoes

Prepare a medium-hot grill or heat oven to 450°. Coat four 12-inch squares heavy-duty foil with nonstick cooking spray. Cut 1½ pounds unpeeled sweet potatoes into 1-inch cubes; place in a medium-size bowl. Add 1½ tablespoons herb rub (reserved from Grilled Chicken recipe, right), 1 tablespoon oil and ½ teaspoon salt. Toss to coat. Place in middle of foil squares, dividing equally. Fold up foil and seal with double folds. Grill, covered, or roast in oven until tender, 45 to 50 minutes.

MAKES 4 servings

PER SERVING
162 calories, 4 g fat (0 g saturated), 3 g protein, 31 g carbohydrate, 4 g fiber, 566 mg sodium, 0 mg cholesterol.

Cheesy Chicken Burgers

MAKES 6 servings **PREP** 15 minutes
GRILL OR BROIL 8 minutes

1¼ pounds ground chicken
4 ounces light cream cheese
½ cup shredded cheddar cheese
(2 ounces)
3 tablespoons dry plain bread crumbs
1 small onion, grated
2 tablespoons chopped fresh parsley
1 teaspoon dried rosemary or
snipped fresh chives
1 teaspoon salt
¼ teaspoon black pepper
1 head Boston lettuce, separated
into leaves
1 large tomato, sliced
6 seeded hamburger buns

1. Prepare a charcoal grill with hot coals, setting rack 6 inches from coals; or heat a gas grill to high; or heat broiler.

2. Combine ground chicken, cream cheese, cheddar, bread crumbs, onion, parsley, rosemary, salt and pepper in a large bowl. Form mixture into 6 equal patties.

3. Grill or broil burgers 4 minutes per side or until internal temperature registers 165° on an instant-read thermometer. Assemble with lettuce and tomato on buns.

PER SERVING
385 calories, 19 g fat (8 g saturated), 25 g protein, 29 g carbohydrate, 2 g fiber, 817 mg sodium, 129 mg cholesterol.

Chicken Caesar Burgers

MAKES 4 servings **PREP** 7 minutes
GRILL OR BROIL 6 minutes

1 egg
1 pound ground chicken
1 cup fresh bread crumbs (2 slices)
¼ cup grated Parmesan cheese
2 teaspoons anchovy paste
1 teaspoon Worcestershire sauce
1 teaspoon fresh lemon juice
1 clove garlic, finely chopped
¼ teaspoon black pepper
½ cup sour cream
½ cup Caesar salad dressing
4 pita breads (6-inch)
Shredded romaine lettuce

1. Prepare a charcoal grill with hot coals, setting rack 6 inches from coals; or heat a gas grill to high; or heat broiler.

2. Beat egg in a large bowl. Mix in chicken, bread crumbs, Parmesan, anchovy paste, Worcestershire sauce, lemon juice, garlic and pepper.

3. Coat 2 sheets of waxed paper with nonstick cooking spray. Divide chicken mixture into quarters; flatten into 5-inch patties between paper. Grill or broil 6 minutes or until internal temperature registers 165° on an instant-read thermometer, turning once.

4. Mix sour cream and dressing in a small bowl. Split each pita partway around its edge. Spoon 3 tablespoons sour cream mixture into each; add a burger and some lettuce. Drizzle with extra sour cream mixture.

PER SERVING
538 calories, 28 g fat (7 g saturated), 34 g protein, 36 g carbohydrate, 2 g fiber, 1,328 mg sodium, 167 mg cholesterol.

Honey-Sesame Chicken Kabobs

MAKES 6 servings **PREP** 20 minutes
REFRIGERATE 2 hours or overnight
GRILL OR BROIL 8 to 12 minutes

⅓   cup rice wine or dry sherry
⅓   cup reduced-sodium soy sauce
3   tablespoons apricot preserves
1   tablespoon dark Asian sesame oil
1   tablespoon minced fresh ginger
1   tablespoon sesame seeds, toasted
    (see page 232)
2   teaspoons liquid hot-pepper sauce
2   cloves garlic, chopped
2   scallions, finely chopped, including
    part of the green
½   teaspoon Chinese five-spice
    powder (optional)
1½   pounds boneless, skinless chicken
    breast halves, cut into 1-inch cubes
1   sweet red pepper, cored, seeded
    and cut into 1-inch pieces
1   sweet yellow or green pepper,
    cored, seeded and cut into 1-inch
    pieces
    Fruited Couscous (page 46) for
    serving (optional)

1. In a medium-size bowl, whisk wine, soy sauce, preserves, oil, ginger, ½ tablespoon sesame seeds, hot-pepper sauce, garlic, scallions and, if desired, five-spice powder.

2. Add chicken and red and yellow peppers to wine mixture. Cover; refrigerate 2 hours or overnight.

3. Meanwhile, prepare a charcoal grill with hot coals, setting rack 6 inches from coals; or heat a gas grill to high; or heat broiler.

4. Thread chicken onto 6 metal skewers, alternating with peppers.

5. Grill or broil kabobs 8 to 12 minutes or until cooked through, turning once. Arrange kabobs on plates with Fruited Couscous if desired. Sprinkle top with remaining ½ tablespoon sesame seeds.

PER SERVING
150 calories, 4 g fat (1 g saturated), 24 g protein, 5 g carbohydrate, 1 g fiber, 192 mg sodium, 63 mg cholesterol.

Mustardy Chicken Kabobs

MAKES 8 servings **PREP** 15 minutes
GRILL OR BROIL 10 to 12 minutes

⅓   cup spicy brown mustard
3   tablespoons dark-brown sugar
3   tablespoons olive oil
1   teaspoon garlic powder
2   pounds boneless, skinless chicken
    thighs, cut into 2-inch chunks
2   small zucchini, cut into ¾-inch-
    thick slices
2   small summer squash, cut into
    ¾-inch-thick slices
    Cooked rice for serving (optional)

1. Prepare a charcoal grill with hot coals, setting rack 6 inches from coals; or heat a gas grill to high; or heat broiler.

2. Whisk together mustard, brown sugar, oil and garlic powder in a cup.

3. Thread chicken onto 8 metal skewers, alternating with zucchini and squash. Brush mustard mixture over skewers.

4. Grill or broil skewers 10 to 12 minutes or until chicken is cooked, turning once. Serve over rice if desired.

PER SERVING
192 calories, 9 g fat (2 g saturated), 18 g protein, 9 g carbohydrate, 2 g fiber, 206 mg sodium, 71 mg cholesterol.

Buffalo Chicken Salad

MAKES 6 servings **PREP** 15 minutes
REFRIGERATE 30 minutes
BROIL about 14 minutes

Dressing

½   cup mayonnaise
¼   cup bottled barbecue sauce
½   cup crumbled blue cheese (about 3 ounces)
1   teaspoon liquid hot-pepper sauce
2   tablespoons milk

Salad

½   teaspoon liquid hot-pepper sauce
1¼ pounds boneless, skinless chicken breast halves
1   large carrot, shredded
½   head romaine lettuce, torn into bite-size pieces (3 cups)
1   small head iceberg lettuce, torn into bite-size pieces (4 cups)
4   ribs celery from the heart, cut into 1-inch-long matchstick strips
1   tablespoon crumbled blue cheese

1. Prepare dressing: Mix mayonnaise, barbecue sauce, blue cheese, hot-pepper sauce and milk in a small bowl.

2. Prepare salad: Mix ⅓ cup dressing and hot-pepper sauce in a glass pie plate. Add chicken; turn to coat. Cover; refrigerate 30 minutes.

3. Position broiler-pan rack 4 inches from heat. Heat broiler.

4. Transfer chicken to broiler-pan rack; discard marinade. Broil 8 minutes; turn and broil 6 minutes longer or until internal temperature registers 170° on an instant-read thermometer.

5. Meanwhile, mix carrot, romaine, iceberg lettuce and celery in a serving bowl. Add remaining dressing; toss.

6. Cut chicken into thin slices. Place on salad. Sprinkle with cheese.

PER SERVING
318 calories, 22 g fat (6 g saturated), 24 g protein, 6 g carbohydrate, 2 g fiber, 488 mg sodium, 76 mg cholesterol.

Maple-Nut Chicken Salad

MAKES 6 servings **PREP** 15 minutes

1½ cups shredded cooked chicken (about half a chicken)
1   bag (1 pound) broccoli coleslaw or cabbage coleslaw
1   can (about 15 ounces) black-eyed peas, drained and rinsed
⅓   cup maple syrup
⅓   cup cider vinegar
⅓   cup olive oil
½   teaspoon coarse-grained mustard
½   teaspoon salt
¼   teaspoon black pepper
½   cup smoked almonds

1. Toss together shredded chicken, broccoli coleslaw and black-eyed peas in a serving bowl.

2. Whisk together maple syrup, vinegar, oil, mustard, salt and pepper in a small bowl. Pour over salad; toss to combine. Add almonds just before serving.

PER SERVING
386 calories, 25 g fat (3 g saturated), 18 g protein, 27 g carbohydrate, 6 g fiber, 454 mg sodium, 31 mg cholesterol.

Warm Chicken Salad

MAKES 4 servings **PREP** 10 minutes
COOK about 10 minutes

¼   cup olive oil
¼   cup lemon juice
1   clove garlic, finely chopped
½   teaspoon grated lemon rind
¼   teaspoon salt
⅛   teaspoon black pepper
1   pound boneless, skinless chicken breasts, cut into strips
1   pound thin asparagus, tough ends trimmed
2   tablespoons snipped fresh dill
½   cup cherry tomatoes, halved
1   bag (8 ounces) salad greens
2   hard-cooked eggs, shelled and quartered

1. To make dressing, whisk together oil, lemon juice, garlic, lemon rind, salt and pepper in a small bowl until well blended.

2. Heat 2 tablespoons lemon dressing in a large nonstick skillet over medium heat. Add chicken and asparagus; stir-fry 8 to 10 minutes or until cooked through.

3. Meanwhile, stir chopped fresh dill into remaining lemon dressing.

4. Add cherry tomatoes and dressing to skillet; cook until heated through, about 1 minute.

5. Line a serving platter with salad greens. Spoon warm chicken and sauce onto greens. Top with eggs.

PER SERVING
315 calories, 19 g fat (3 g saturated), 29 g protein, 8 g carbohydrate, 3 g fiber, 243 mg sodium, 169 mg cholesterol.

Grilled Turkey-Tortellini Salad

MAKES 6 servings **PREP** 10 minutes
MARINATE 15 minutes
COOK tortellini about 12 minutes
(while marinating turkey)
GRILL OR BROIL turkey about 10 minutes

½   cup vegetable oil
¼   cup fresh lemon juice (2 small lemons)
1   large shallot, finely chopped (about 2 tablespoons)
2   teaspoons sugar
1   teaspoon Dijon mustard
¾   teaspoon salt
½   teaspoon black pepper
1½   pounds turkey cutlets
2   packages (9 ounces each) refrigerated cheese tortellini
2   cups packed spinach leaves, stemmed and torn
1   cup cherry tomatoes, halved
½   cup chopped walnuts, toasted (see page 232)

1. Whisk oil, lemon juice, shallot, sugar, mustard, ½ teaspoon salt and ¼ teaspoon pepper in a small bowl.

2. Transfer ¼ cup lemon juice mixture to a glass pie plate. Add cutlets; turn to coat. Marinate 15 minutes. Reserve remaining lemon juice mixture for dressing.

3. Prepare a charcoal grill with medium-hot coals; or heat a gas grill to medium-hot; or heat broiler. Position grill rack or broiler-pan rack 6 inches from heat.

4. Meanwhile, cook tortellini in a large pot of lightly salted boiling water until al dente, firm but tender. Drain.

5. Remove cutlets from marinade; discard marinade. Grill or broil cutlets 5 minutes per side or until internal temperature registers 170° on an instant-read thermometer. Cut into bite-size pieces.

6. Combine spinach and tomatoes in a large serving bowl. Add pasta, turkey, reserved dressing and walnuts. Sprinkle with remaining ¼ teaspoon salt and remaining ¼ teaspoon pepper. Toss to mix. Serve while slightly warm or refrigerate and serve chilled.

PER SERVING
614 calories, 30 g fat (2 g saturated), 39 g protein, 46 g carbohydrate, 1 g fiber, 662 mg sodium, 99 mg cholesterol.

Turkey Bolognese

MAKES 12 servings **PREP** 20 minutes
COOK 35 minutes
BAKE at 400° for 30 minutes

¾ **pound bow-tie pasta (farfalle)**
2 **tablespoons olive oil**
1 **small onion, finely chopped**
1 **small carrot, chopped (½ cup)**
1 **small rib celery, chopped (½ cup)**
2 **cloves garlic, finely chopped**
1½ **pounds ground turkey**
1 **can (28 ounces) crushed tomatoes**
1½ **teaspoons salt**
1 **teaspoon dried oregano**
½ **teaspoon red-pepper flakes**
¼ **cup heavy cream**
1 **package (10 ounces) frozen peas, thawed**
3 **cups shredded mozzarella cheese (12 ounces)**

1. Heat oven to 400°. Grease a 13 x 9 x 2-inch baking dish.

2. Cook bow-ties in a large pot of lightly salted boiling water until al dente, firm but tender. Drain well.

3. Meanwhile, heat oil in a medium-size skillet over medium heat. Add onion, carrot, celery and garlic; cook 12 minutes or until vegetables are softened.

4. Stir ground turkey into vegetable mixture; cook, breaking up clumps with a wooden spoon, 7 to 8 minutes or until turkey is cooked through and no longer pink.

5. Add tomatoes, salt, oregano and red-pepper flakes. Bring to boiling over high heat. Lower heat to medium; simmer, stirring occasionally, 15 minutes.

6. Remove from heat. Stir in cream. Stir in peas and bow-ties. Transfer to prepared baking dish. Top with mozzarella. Bake in heated 400° oven 30 minutes or until heated through.

PER SERVING
312 calories, 14 g fat (7 g saturated), 17 g protein, 29 g carbohydrate, 4 g fiber, 553 mg sodium, 57 mg cholesterol.

PANTRY PLUS: LIME JUICE

A touch of the tropics adds personality to everything poultry—and seafood as well.

• To make a zesty marinade for chicken or shrimp, combine 1 minced garlic clove, 2 tablespoons lime juice, 2 tablespoons olive oil, ¼ teaspoon ground cumin, a pinch of ground red pepper and salt to taste.

• Try this citrusy spread on turkey sandwiches: Mash 1 peeled, pitted avocado with 2 tablespoons lime juice, ½ cup mayonnaise and ½ teaspoon salt.

Apple Cider
Turkey Breast

MAKES 10 servings **PREP** 20 minutes
COOK about 2¼ hours

2   tablespoons vegetable oil
1   whole turkey breast, bone-in,
    with skin (5 to 7 pounds)
¼   cup dry white wine
1   large onion, sliced
1   large carrot, sliced
1   large rib celery, sliced
2   large cloves garlic, sliced
1   tablespoon dried sage
8   whole cloves
3   cups apple cider
1   can (14½ ounces) chicken broth
½   cup plus 1 tablespoon apple brandy
1   teaspoon salt

½   cup heavy cream
2   tablespoons cornstarch
2   tablespoons water

1. Heat oil in a large pot over medium-high heat. Add turkey; brown on all sides, about 10 minutes. Remove from pot. Add wine, scraping up browned bits from bottom of pot. Remove pot from heat.

2. Add onion, carrot, celery, garlic, sage and cloves to pot. Place turkey, meaty side down, on vegetables. Add cider, broth, ½ cup brandy and salt. Cover. Bring to boiling. Reduce heat to medium-low; simmer 1½ hours or until internal temperature of turkey registers 165° on an instant-read thermometer. Transfer turkey to a platter, cover loosely with aluminum foil and let stand until meat is cool enough to handle.

3. Meanwhile, strain liquid remaining in cooking pot through a sieve into a bowl; discard solids. Wipe inside of pot lightly with paper toweling. Return liquid to pot. Bring to boiling and boil until reduced to about 2 cups, about 30 minutes. Add cream and remaining 1 tablespoon brandy. Bring to simmering.

4. Stir together cornstarch and water in a small bowl. Stir into pot; cook over medium heat, whisking gently, until thickened slightly, about 1 minute. Taste and adjust seasonings as needed.

5. Remove skin from turkey. With a long thin knife, cut downward along each side of breast bone; remove meat in 2 large pieces. Slice across grain. Serve with sauce.

PER SERVING
300 calories, 7 g fat (3 g saturated), 41 g protein, 16 g carbohydrate, 0 g fiber, 466 mg sodium, 131 mg cholesterol.

Turkey Scaloppine

For a super quick meal, you can easily cook noodles and steam a vegetable at the same time you prepare the scaloppine.

MAKES 4 servings **PREP** 10 minutes
COOK 10 minutes

½	cup all-purpose flour
2	eggs
¾	cup dry plain bread crumbs
4	turkey cutlets (1½ pounds total), pounded thin
1	teaspoon salt
¼	cup (½ stick) butter or margarine
2	tablespoons vegetable oil
1	cup beef broth
½	cup water
1½	teaspoons Worcestershire sauce
1	teaspoon Dijon mustard
⅛	teaspoon black pepper

1. Place flour in a resealable plastic food-storage bag. Lightly beat eggs in a shallow bowl. Place bread crumbs in a pie plate.

2. Season turkey cutlets with salt; place in bag with flour. Shake to coat cutlets; remove and shake off excess flour. Reserve bag with flour. Dip cutlets in beaten egg; coat both sides with bread crumbs. Let stand a few minutes to dry.

3. Melt 1 tablespoon butter and 1 tablespoon oil in a large skillet over medium-high heat. Working in batches, add cutlets; cook 2 minutes on each side, adding 1 tablespoon oil and 1 tablespoon butter if needed. Transfer cutlets to a serving platter; keep warm.

4. Reduce heat to medium. In same skillet, melt remaining 2 tablespoons butter. Whisk in 2 tablespoons of reserved coating flour; cook, whisking, until smooth, about 1 minute. Stir in broth, water, Worcestershire sauce, mustard and pepper. Bring to boiling over high heat; boil 3 minutes. Serve with cutlets.

PER SERVING
452 calories, 23 g fat (9 g saturated), 47 g protein, 13 g carbohydrate, 1 g fiber, 944 mg sodium, 253 mg cholesterol.

Savory Sausage Sauce with Ziti

MAKES 6 servings **PREP** 5 minutes
COOK 25 minutes

1   teaspoon olive oil
½   small onion, chopped
1   clove garlic, finely chopped
4   links Italian-style turkey sausage
     (8 ounces total), casings removed
1   pound ziti
1   can (14½ ounces) diced tomatoes
1   cup fat-free half-and-half
¼   teaspoon salt
⅛   teaspoon black pepper
1   teaspoon cornstarch
1   tablespoon cold water
1   cup frozen peas, thawed

1. Heat oil in a large skillet over medium heat. Add onion and garlic; sauté until fragrant, about 1 minute. Crumble sausage into skillet; sauté, breaking up clumps with a wooden spoon, until lightly browned, about 7 minutes.

2. Cook ziti in a large pot of lightly salted boiling water until al dente, firm but tender. Drain well and keep warm.

3. Meanwhile, stir tomatoes, half-and-half, salt and pepper into skillet with sausage; simmer, uncovered, stirring occasionally, 15 minutes or until slightly thickened.

4. Dissolve cornstarch in water in a small bowl. Gently stir into sausage mixture. Add peas; cook until mixture is heated through.

5. Transfer ziti to a large serving bowl; top with sausage sauce.

PER SERVING
403 calories, 9 g fat (0 g saturated), 20 g protein, 80 g carbohydrate, 3 g fiber, 830 mg sodium, 47 mg cholesterol.

Summer Sausage Sauce over Grilled Polenta

MAKES 4 servings **PREP** 10 minutes
COOK about 20 minutes
GRILL OR BROIL 6 to 8 minutes

1   pound Italian-style turkey sausage
     links, cut into ½-inch-thick slices
1   small onion, chopped
6   medium tomatoes (about
     1½ pounds), peeled and chopped
1   tablespoon ketchup
½   teaspoon garlic salt
¼   teaspoon black pepper
2   tablespoons chopped fresh basil
     or 2 teaspoons dried basil
1   log (1 pound) prepared polenta,
     cut into twelve ½-inch-thick slices

1. Prepare a charcoal grill with hot coals, setting rack 6 inches from coals; or heat a gas grill to high; or heat broiler.

2. Coat a large nonstick skillet with olive oil cooking spray; heat over medium heat. Add sausage; sauté 3 minutes or until it starts to brown slightly. Add onion; sauté until softened, 3 minutes. Stir in tomatoes, ketchup, garlic salt and pepper; simmer 15 minutes or until slightly thickened but still chunky. Stir in basil.

3. Meanwhile, grill or broil polenta 3 to 4 minutes per side or until golden brown and heated through.

4. Arrange 3 slices polenta on each plate. Spoon sausage mixture on top, dividing equally.

PER SERVING
278 calories, 10 g fat (3 g saturated), 19 g protein, 29 g carbohydrate, 4 g fiber, 1,157 mg sodium, 71 mg cholesterol.

Spinach and Sausage Casserole

MAKES 4 servings **PREP** 5 minutes
COOK 35 minutes

1   teaspoon olive oil
1   medium onion, chopped
1   clove garlic, finely chopped
3   or 4 links hot Italian-style turkey sausage (8 ounces total), casings removed
1   can (13½ ounces) reduced-sodium chicken broth
2   tablespoons water
¾   cup quick-cooking barley
1   cup packaged shredded carrots
1   bag (10 ounces) fresh spinach, tough stems removed and leaves coarsely chopped

1. Heat oil in a large nonstick skillet over medium-high heat. Add onion and garlic; sauté until lightly colored, about 5 minutes. Crumble sausage into skillet; sauté, breaking up large clumps with a wooden spoon, until lightly browned, about 7 minutes.

2. Add broth, water, barley and carrots to sausage mixture; cover. Cook over low heat 10 minutes.

3. Add chopped spinach; simmer, covered, 8 to 10 minutes or until barley is tender.

PER SERVING
232 calories, 7 g fat (0 g saturated), 14 g protein, 44 g carbohydrate, 5 g fiber, 583 mg sodium, 35 mg cholesterol.

Turkey Amandine Casserole

MAKES 8 servings **PREP** 20 minutes
BAKE casserole at 350° for 1 hour

1   medium onion, chopped
4   ribs celery, thinly sliced (about 2 cups)
1   package (5½ ounces) croutons (about 3 cups)
2   cups shredded Swiss cheese (8 ounces)
1   pound turkey cutlets, cut into bite-size pieces
1   jar (17 ounces) Alfredo sauce
½   cup slivered almonds, toasted (see page 232)

1. Heat oven to 350°. Grease a 3-quart casserole.

2. Toss together onion, celery, croutons and cheese in a large bowl; stir in turkey. Stir in Alfredo sauce and spoon mixture into prepared casserole. Cover with foil.

3. Bake in heated 350° oven 45 minutes. Remove foil from casserole; sprinkle toasted almonds on top. Bake, uncovered, 15 minutes longer. Let casserole stand 5 minutes before serving.

PER SERVING
397 calories, 20 g fat (11 g saturated), 31 g protein, 22 g carbohydrate, 3 g fiber, 674 mg sodium, 91 mg cholesterol.

Turkey Fajitas with Peppers and Onions

MAKES 10 servings **PREP** 45 minutes
REFRIGERATE 1½ hours
GRILL OR BROIL about 15 minutes

Rub

1	tablespoon chili powder
1	teaspoon garlic powder
1	teaspoon onion powder
1	teaspoon black pepper
1	teaspoon salt
½	teaspoon ground cumin
¼	teaspoon ground red pepper (cayenne)

Fajitas

2	pounds turkey breast cutlets
1	tablespoon plus 2 teaspoons olive oil
¼	cup lime juice
1	poblano chile or green chile, cored, seeded and sliced into 1-inch-wide strips
1	sweet red pepper, cored, seeded and sliced into 1-inch-wide strips
1	sweet yellow pepper, cored, seeded and sliced into 1-inch-wide strips
1	large onion, cut crosswise into ½-inch-thick slices
1	bunch scallions, trimmed
10	flour tortillas (8-inch)

Garnishes (optional)

1	jar (16 ounces) salsa
1	large tomato, seeded and chopped
1	red onion, chopped
1	cup chopped fresh cilantro
1	cup reduced-fat sour cream

1. Prepare rub: Combine chili powder, garlic powder, onion powder, black pepper, salt, cumin and red pepper in a small bowl.

2. Prepare fajitas: Arrange cutlets in a single layer in a large shallow baking dish; coat with 2 teaspoons oil. Sprinkle all sides with rub, patting into meat. Marinate cutlets in refrigerator 1 hour. Add lime juice; turn cutlets to coat and marinate another 30 minutes in refrigerator.

3. Meanwhile, prepare a charcoal grill with hot coals, setting rack 6 inches from coals; or heat a gas grill to high; or heat broiler.

4. Combine poblano, sweet red and yellow peppers, onion, scallions and remaining 1 tablespoon oil in a medium-size bowl.

5. Grill or broil vegetables about 3 minutes per side or until nicely charred and cooked through. Arrange on a large platter. Grill turkey cutlets until cooked through, 4 to 5 minutes per side. Thinly slice turkey across grain on a diagonal. Arrange on platter with grilled vegetables.

6. Warm tortillas on grill or under broiler, following package directions, until soft and warm. Place in a cloth-lined basket and cover to keep warm.

7. To serve, have each diner roll up turkey and vegetables with desired garnishes in tortillas.

PER SERVING
322 calories, 9 g fat (3 g saturated), 27 g protein, 33 g carbohydrate, 4 g fiber, 920 mg sodium, 73 mg cholesterol.

Italian Turkey Burgers

MAKES 4 servings **PREP** 7 minutes
GRILL OR BROIL 10 minutes

1	egg
1	pound ground turkey
½	cup dry plain bread crumbs
¾	cup shredded mozzarella cheese (3 ounces)
¼	cup plus 3 tablespoons light creamy-style Italian salad dressing
4	teaspoons grated onion
1	teaspoon dried oregano
1	clove garlic, finely chopped
¼	teaspoon salt
¼	teaspoon black pepper
2	tablespoons light mayonnaise
4	sandwich-size English muffins, toasted
4	arugula sprigs
4	pieces bottled roasted red pepper

1. Prepare a charcoal grill with hot coals, setting rack 6 inches from coals; or heat a gas grill to high; or heat broiler.

2. Beat egg in a medium-size bowl. Mix in turkey, bread crumbs, ½ cup mozzarella, 3 tablespoons dressing, onion, oregano, garlic, salt and pepper. Shape mixture into four 4½-inch patties, dividing equally.

3. Grill or broil burgers 5 minutes. Turn; cook 3 minutes. Top with remaining ¼ cup mozzarella, dividing equally. Cook 2 minutes longer or until internal temperature registers 165° on an instant-read thermometer.

4. Mix mayonnaise and remaining ¼ cup dressing. Spread on muffins. Top with burgers, arugula and red peppers.

PER SERVING
653 calories, 25 g fat (8 g saturated), 39 g protein, 63 g carbohydrate, 1 g fiber, 1,252 mg sodium, 155 mg cholesterol.

Peanutty Crunch Burgers

Lettuce, tomato and pickles are the perfect garnishes for these burgers.

MAKES 6 servings **PREP** 20 minutes
COOK about 20 minutes

2	tablespoons olive oil
2	large onions, chopped (3 cups)
6	tablespoons water, as needed
¾	pound ground beef
¾	pound ground turkey
2	tablespoons soy sauce
1½	teaspoons dark Asian sesame oil
¾	cup finely chopped unsalted peanuts
6	Kaiser rolls, split and toasted

1. Heat 1 tablespoon oil in a large nonstick skillet over medium-high heat. Add onions; sauté until golden brown, 10 minutes, adding 2 tablespoons water each time skillet seems dry. Scrape into a large bowl.

2. Add beef, turkey, soy sauce and sesame oil to onions. Shape into 6 patties, each 4 inches in diameter. Spread peanuts on waxed paper; press one side of each patty into peanuts.

3. In same skillet, heat remaining 1 tablespoon oil over medium heat. Working in batches if necessary, add burgers, peanut side down, to skillet. Cook 5 minutes; turn; cook 5 to 7 minutes or internal temperature registers 165° on an instant-read thermometer.

4. Serve burgers on toasted rolls.

PER SERVING
545 calories, 29 g fat (7 g saturated), 33 g protein, 38 g carbohydrate, 4 g fiber, 689 mg sodium, 79 mg cholesterol.

Cheese-Stuffed Flank Steak

MAKES 6 servings **PREP** 20 minutes
REFRIGERATE 2 hours or overnight
ROAST at 425° for 25 minutes
BROIL 15 minutes

2   cloves garlic, chopped
2   tablespoons grated Parmesan cheese
1   tablespoon chopped fresh parsley
1   tablespoon olive oil
½   teaspoon dried Italian seasoning
½   teaspoon salt
¼   teaspoon black pepper
¼   teaspoon red-pepper flakes
1   flank steak (1½ pounds)
½   pound sliced provolone cheese
    (10 to 12 slices)
1   jar (7 ounces) roasted red
    peppers, drained
6   red onions, quartered

1. Mix garlic, Parmesan, parsley, oil, Italian seasoning, salt, black pepper and red-pepper flakes in a small bowl, forming a paste.

2. Place steak on a work surface. With a sharp knife, slice horizontally along length of steak, cutting almost all the way through; open like a book.

3. Rub steak all over on both sides with seasoning paste; place open side up again. Arrange slices of provolone on steak, leaving a 1-inch border all around. Top with roasted peppers. Starting at short end, roll up steak to enclose filling. Tie roll at 1-inch intervals with kitchen twine. Wrap in plastic wrap. Refrigerate 2 hours or overnight.

4. Heat oven to 425°. Meanwhile, remove plastic wrap from steak. Place steak on rack in a broiler pan. Let stand at room temperature while oven is heating (but not longer than 30 minutes). Arrange onion quarters around steak on rack.

5. Roast steak and onions in heated 425° oven 25 minutes. Turn on oven broiler. Broil steak and onions 4 inches from heat 15 minutes, turning once, or until internal temperature of meat registers 150° on an instant-read thermometer. Remove pan from oven. Let steak stand 15 minutes. To serve, remove twine and slice steak.

PER SERVING
402 calories, 23 g fat (11 g saturated), 35 g protein, 12 g carbohydrate, 2 g fiber, 522 mg sodium, 93 mg cholesterol.

Texas BBQ Pot Roast

MAKES 12 servings **PREP** 15 minutes
COOK 18 minutes
BAKE at 300° for 3 to 4 hours

1   teaspoon vegetable oil
1   pot roast (about 4 pounds), such
     as bottom round or chuck
1   cup bottled barbecue sauce
½   cup cider vinegar
½   cup chicken or beef broth
¼   cup packed light-brown sugar
1   tablespoon mustard
1   tablespoon Worcestershire sauce
1   tablespoon chili powder
1   large onion, chopped
2   large cloves garlic, crushed
1½   teaspoons dried thyme
12   rolls

1. Heat oven to 300°.

2. Heat oil in a large Dutch oven over medium-high heat. Add meat; brown well on all sides, about 15 minutes.

3. Add barbecue sauce, vinegar, broth, brown sugar, mustard, Worcestershire sauce, chili powder, onion, garlic and thyme to pot. Bring to boiling.

4. Cover pot and bake in heated 300° oven 3 to 4 hours, turning meat every hour, until fork-tender. Let stand at least 30 minutes in pan. Remove meat from pot. Skim fat from sauce in pan. Slice beef. Serve with sauce on rolls.

PER SERVING
406 calories, 12 g fat (4 g saturated), 36 g protein, 35 g carbohydrate, 2 g fiber, 571 mg sodium, 93 mg cholesterol.

Fiesta Roast Beef with Tropical Fruit Relish

MAKES 8 servings **PREP** 10 minutes
MICROWAVE 7 to 10 minutes

1 **can (15¼ ounces) tropical fruit salad**
1 **navel orange**
3 **teaspoons spicy brown mustard**
½ **teaspoon liquid hot-pepper sauce**
¼ **teaspoon salt**
1 **package (2 pounds) fully cooked beef tri-tip roast**
1 **small sweet green pepper, cored, seeded and diced**

1. Drain fruit salad, reserving 3 tablespoons juice. Dice fruit.

2. Grate 1 teaspoon rind from orange. Cut orange in half. Peel one half; cut flesh into small pieces and add to fruit salad. Juice other half.

3. Combine reserved fruit juice, orange juice, mustard, hot-pepper sauce and salt in a small bowl.

4. Drain liquid from tri-tip roast package into a small saucepan. Place beef in a microwave-safe dish; cover dish with plastic wrap. Microwave at 100% power 7 to 10 minutes or until heated through. Let stand, covered, 5 minutes.

5. Add ¼ cup fruit juice mixture to beef liquid in saucepan.

6. To make a relish, add reserved fruit and green pepper to remainder of fruit juice mixture in bowl. Cover and refrigerate until ready to use.

7. Carve roast across grain into thin slices. Bring mixture in saucepan to boiling. Remove saucepan from heat.

8. Arrange sliced beef and fruit relish on a serving platter. Spoon hot sauce over beef.

PER SERVING
298 calories, 15 g fat (5 g saturated), 27 g protein, 15 g carbohydrate, 1 g fiber, 344 mg sodium, 80 mg cholesterol.

Polynesian Beef

MAKES 6 servings **PREP** 10 minutes
REFRIGERATE 1 hour **COOK** 1½ to 2 hours

1   cup pineapple juice
¼   cup soy sauce
1½   teaspoons ground ginger
1   teaspoon salt
1   boneless beef chuck roast
     (3 pounds)
1   tablespoon vegetable oil
1   large onion, sliced ¼ inch thick
     and separated into rings
4   ribs celery, sliced (about 2 cups)
4   carrots, sliced lengthwise into
     ribbons
4   mushrooms, sliced
1   bag (10 ounces) fresh spinach,
     stemmed and washed
2   tablespoons cornstarch
2   tablespoons water

1. Combine pineapple juice, soy sauce, ginger and salt in a small bowl.

2. Place meat in a resealable plastic food-storage bag. Pour pineapple mixture over meat. Refrigerate 1 hour, turning several times.

3. Heat oil in a Dutch oven or heavy pot over medium heat. Add onion; cook 3 to 5 minutes or until softened.

4. Add meat and marinade. Cover; bring to simmering. Adjust heat to low and simmer 1 to 1½ hours or until tender.

5. Add celery; cook, covered, 5 minutes. Add carrots and mushrooms; cook, covered, 10 minutes or until softened. Add spinach; cook, covered, just until wilted, 3 to 4 minutes.

6. Transfer meat and vegetables to a serving platter; keep warm.

7. Stir cornstarch and water in a cup to make smooth paste; stir paste into pot. Bring to boiling over high heat. Boil, stirring, until sauce is thickened, 3 minutes. Serve with meat and vegetables.

PER SERVING
442 calories, 16 g fat (5 g saturated), 54 g protein, 20 g carbohydrate, 3 g fiber, 1,232 mg sodium, 156 mg cholesterol.

Orange Beef 'n' Rice

MAKES 4 servings **PREP** 10 minutes
COOK about 40 minutes

1   tablespoon vegetable oil
1   pound beef top round, cut into
     ½-inch cubes
1   cup diced onion
1   teaspoon bottled chopped garlic
½   pound packaged sliced mushrooms
1   cup packaged shredded carrots
¼   teaspoon dried Italian seasoning
¼   teaspoon black pepper
1   package (6 ounces) wild-and-
     white-rice pilaf mix
1   cup orange juice
1   cup beef broth
1   teaspoon grated orange rind

1. Heat oil in a Dutch oven over high heat. Add meat, onion and garlic; sauté 5 minutes.

2. Add mushrooms, carrots, Italian seasoning and black pepper; cook 4 minutes. Add pilaf mix, juice, broth and rind; simmer, covered, 30 minutes or until liquid has been absorbed.

PER SERVING
412 calories, 11 g fat (3 g saturated), 32 g protein, 46 g carbohydrate, 3 g fiber, 784 mg sodium, 72 mg cholesterol.

Tamale Pie

MAKES 6 servings **PREP** 15 minutes
COOK about 20 minutes
BAKE at 350° for 25 minutes

2 slices bacon, halved crosswise
1 medium onion, chopped
1 clove garlic, chopped
1 pound ground beef
1 can (10¾ ounces) condensed
   tomato soup
2 teaspoons chili powder
1½ teaspoons salt
¼ teaspoon paprika
1 large sweet green pepper, cut
   into 5 rings
8 large pimiento-stuffed olives,
   halved if desired
1 can (15¼ ounces) corn kernels,
   drained
1 cup all-purpose flour
1 cup yellow cornmeal
1 tablespoon sugar
1 tablespoon baking powder
1 egg, slightly beaten
1 cup milk
2 tablespoons butter, melted
1 can (8 ounces) tomato sauce
4 pimiento-stuffed olives, sliced

1. Heat oven to 350°.

2. Cook bacon in an ovenproof
   medium-size nonstick skillet over
   medium heat until crisp, 8 to
   10 minutes. Remove bacon from
   skillet with a slotted spoon and drain
   on paper toweling.

3. Add onion and garlic to bacon
   drippings in skillet; cook until slightly
   softened, 3 to 5 minutes. Add beef;
   cook, breaking up clumps with a
   wooden spoon, until meat is no

longer pink, about 5 minutes. Stir
in condensed soup, chili powder,
½ teaspoon salt and paprika. Transfer
to a large bowl.

4. Remove skillet from heat. Arrange
   pepper rings, reserved bacon and
   whole or halved olives in skillet
   bottom. Top with a layer of corn,
   then a layer of meat mixture.

5. Sift flour, cornmeal, sugar, baking
   powder and remaining 1 teaspoon
   salt into a medium-size bowl.

6. Mix egg, milk and butter in a small
   bowl. Pour into flour mixture; mix
   with a fork until combined. Spread
   batter evenly over meat mixture.

7. Bake in heated 350° oven about
   25 minutes or until top is golden
   and set. Remove from oven. Cover
   tightly; let stand 10 minutes.

8. Meanwhile, heat tomato sauce and
   sliced olives in a small saucepan until
   heated through, 5 to 7 minutes.

9. Invert tamale pie onto a serving
   platter. Cut into wedges. Serve with
   tomato-olive sauce.

PER SERVING
523 calories, 20 g fat (8 g saturated), 27 g protein,
60 g carbohydrate, 5 g fiber, 1,804 mg sodium,
111 mg cholesterol.

Oven-Braised Chili and Beans

MAKES 12 servings **PREP** 30 minutes
COOK about 35 minutes
BAKE at 300° for 3 hours

5	tablespoons vegetable oil
2	pounds trimmed lean beef chuck or bottom round, cut into 1-inch cubes
2	pounds trimmed boneless pork loin or leg, cut into 1-inch cubes
4¼	cups chopped onion (3 large onions)
5	large cloves garlic, crushed through a press
1½	tablespoons ground cumin
1½	tablespoons dried oregano
½	cup chili powder

1	tablespoon unsweetened cocoa powder
1	tablespoon sugar
2	teaspoons salt
1	bottle (12 ounces) beer
1	can (1 pound) diced tomatoes
3	tablespoons tomato paste
3	cans (1 pound each) small pink beans or kidney beans, drained and rinsed
	Sour cream for serving (optional)
	Shredded cheddar cheese for serving (optional)

1. Heat 1 tablespoon oil in a 6-quart Dutch oven over high heat. Add one-third of chuck and pork; cook without stirring until browned on one side, 4 to 5 minutes. Turn; cook 1 minute. With a slotted spoon, transfer meat to a platter. Repeat with 2 more batches of chuck and pork.

2. Heat oven to 300°.

3. Heat remaining 2 tablespoons oil in same pot over medium-high heat. Add onion; sauté 10 minutes. Stir in garlic, cumin and oregano; cook 1 minute. Stir in chili powder, cocoa powder, sugar and salt; cook 1 minute. Pour in beer, scraping any browned bits from bottom of pot with a wooden spoon. Stir in tomatoes and tomato paste. Return meat with any accumulated juices to pot.

4. Bake, covered, in heated 300° oven about 2 hours, stirring once, or until meat is tender. Add beans. Bake, covered, 1 hour longer. If desired, serve topped with sour cream and shredded cheddar cheese.

PER SERVING
428 calories, 18 g fat (4 g saturated), 43 g protein, 31 g carbohydrate, 9 g fiber, 787 mg sodium, 98 mg cholesterol.

Best Meatballs

MAKES 8 servings PREP 20 minutes
BAKE at 450° for 1 hour 25 minutes
COOK 1 minute

½ cup dry plain bread crumbs
⅓ cup milk
2 eggs
2 pounds lean ground sirloin
¼ cup tomato sauce
2 teaspoons salt
½ teaspoon dried oregano
½ teaspoon dried basil
¼ teaspoon ground nutmeg
¼ teaspoon black pepper
1½ tablespoons olive oil
1 can (14½ ounces) beef broth
1 can (14½ ounces) crushed
    tomatoes
2 tablespoons tomato paste
1½ tablespoons cornstarch
3 tablespoons water
    Mashed Potatoes (page 129) for
    serving (optional)

1. Position oven rack in top third of
    oven. Heat oven to 450°. Lightly oil
    a 13 x 9 x 2-inch casserole.

2. Mix bread crumbs and milk in a large
    bowl. Let soften 2 minutes. Add eggs,
    meat, tomato sauce, salt, oregano,
    basil, nutmeg and pepper. Shape into
    meatballs, using ¼ cup mixture for
    each. Place in casserole; brush with oil.

3. Bake in heated 450° oven about
    25 minutes or until browned. Remove
    casserole from oven; leave oven on.
    Pour off any excess fat from casserole.
    Mix broth, tomatoes and tomato
    paste in a medium-size bowl. Add
    to casserole.

4. Cover casserole. Bake 1 hour.
    Transfer meatballs to a deep platter
    and keep warm. Pour liquid from
    casserole into a saucepan.

5. Stir together cornstarch and water
    in a small bowl. Whisk into liquid
    in saucepan. Bring to boiling over
    medium heat, whisking, until
    thickened, 1 minute. Pour over
    meatballs. Serve with Mashed
    Potatoes if desired.

PER SERVING
276 calories, 12 g fat (4 g saturated), 31 g protein,
11 g carbohydrate, 1 g fiber, 1,111 mg sodium,
131 mg cholesterol.

BBQ Mini Meat Loaves

MAKES 6 servings PREP 5 minutes
BAKE at 350° for 30 minutes

1   egg
¾   pound ground beef
¾   pound ground pork
1⅓   cups hickory-smoked barbecue sauce
½   cup dry plain bread crumbs (see note)
⅓   cup chopped fresh parsley
2   tablespoons grated onion
1   clove garlic, finely chopped
½   teaspoon salt

1. Heat oven to 350°.

2. Beat egg in a medium-size bowl. Mix in beef, pork, ⅔ cup barbecue sauce, bread crumbs, parsley, onion, garlic and salt. Shape mixture into six 4 x 2 x 1-inch loaves. Place on a jelly-roll pan. Top each loaf with about 2 tablespoons of remaining barbecue sauce.

3. Bake in heated 350° oven 30 minutes or until internal temperature of loaves registers 160° on an instant-read thermometer. Remove from oven and let stand on pan 10 minutes.

4. Serve immediately; or cool completely, refrigerate and serve cold.

   Note: For softer-textured meat loaves, use 1½ cups fresh bread crumbs (about 3 slices white bread).

PER SERVING
346 calories, 16 g fat (6 g saturated), 24 g protein, 25 g carbohydrate, 0 g fiber, 1,118 mg sodium, 114 mg cholesterol.

Meatball Ratatouille

MAKES 4 servings PREP 12 minutes
COOK about 30 minutes

1   pound ground beef
¼   cup milk
½   teaspoon dried Italian seasoning
1   teaspoon onion powder
1   teaspoon salt
½   teaspoon black pepper
⅛   teaspoon garlic powder
1   tablespoon olive oil
1   small eggplant, cut into ½-inch cubes
1   zucchini, cut into ½-inch cubes
1   sweet red pepper, cored, seeded and cut into ½-inch pieces
1   cup frozen baby onions, thawed
1   can (14½ ounces) Italian-style stewed tomatoes
       Fresh oregano sprigs for garnish (optional)

1. Mix beef, milk, Italian seasoning, onion powder, ½ teaspoon salt, ¼ teaspoon black pepper and garlic powder in a medium-size bowl. Shape mixture into about twenty 1¼-inch meatballs.

2. Heat oil in a large deep skillet over medium-high heat. Working in 2 batches, brown meatballs 4 minutes. Transfer to a plate lined with paper toweling to drain.

3. Add eggplant, zucchini, red pepper, onions, remaining ½ teaspoon salt and remaining ¼ teaspoon black pepper to skillet; cook 3 minutes.

4. Add meatballs and tomatoes to skillet. Cover; simmer 18 minutes or until vegetables are tender. Garnish with oregano if desired.

PER SERVING
331 calories, 16 g fat (6 g saturated), 26 g protein, 19 g carbohydrate, 4 g fiber, 857 mg sodium, 83 mg cholesterol.

Spiced Beef

MAKES 6 servings **PREP** 5 minutes
COOK 15 minutes

1   pound ground beef
1   envelope (1¼ ounces) taco
     seasoning mix
1   can (19 ounces) kidney beans,
     undrained
1   can (19 ounces) stewed tomatoes
1   pound egg noodles (1 bag)

1. Cook ground beef in a large nonstick
    skillet over medium heat 5 minutes,
    breaking up clumps with a wooden
    spoon. Add taco seasoning mix;
    cook 5 minutes or until meat is no
    longer pink.

2. Drain beans, reserving ¼ cup of
    liquid. Rinse beans and add to skillet
    along with reserved liquid and
    tomatoes; cook 5 minutes.

3. Meanwhile, cook noodles in a large
    pot of lightly salted boiling water
    until al dente, firm but tender.
    Drain well. Serve Spiced Beef over
    drained noodles.

PER SERVING
505 calories, 15 g fat (5 g saturated), 26 g protein,
66 g carbohydrate, 9 g fiber, 1,017 mg sodium,
108 mg cholesterol.

Meat and Veggie Stir-Fry

MAKES 4 servings **PREP** 5 minutes
COOK 11 minutes

½   pound ground beef
½   pound ground pork
1   cup snow peas, trimmed, or
     1 package (6 ounces) frozen
     snow peas, thawed and drained
1½   cups shredded carrots
½   cup stir-fry sauce
2   tablespoons water
2   teaspoons reduced-sodium
     soy sauce
     Cooked rice for serving (optional)

1. Heat a wok or 10-inch nonstick skillet
    over medium-high heat. Add beef
    and pork; stir-fry about 5 minutes or
    until no longer pink; do not break
    up clumps of meat. Transfer to a
    plate; keep warm.

2. Add snow peas and carrots to wok;
    stir-fry 5 minutes or until crisp-
    tender. Mix in stir-fry sauce, water
    and soy sauce. Return meat to wok;
    stir-fry about 1 minute or until
    heated through.

3. Serve over rice if desired.

PER SERVING
299 calories, 16 g fat (6 g saturated), 25 g protein,
13 g carbohydrate, 2 g fiber, 1,226 mg sodium,
75 mg cholesterol.

Pesto Steak with Croutons and Coleslaw

You'll cook once but get two different meals from this recipe, which yields enough steak and potatoes to be used the next day for Pesto Steak Salad (opposite). If you wish to serve 12 with this recipe, prepare twice the amount of croutons and coleslaw.

MAKES 6 servings **PREP** potatoes and steak about 5 minutes; croutons 5 minutes; coleslaw 5 minutes
COOK potatoes 5 to 7 minutes
GRILL OR BROIL potatoes 3 to 5 minutes; steak 14 minutes; croutons 3 to 4 minutes

1 **pound small red new potatoes, halved**
2 **top round steaks (3 pounds total)**
½ **cup pesto (see note)**
   Pesto Croutons (opposite)
   Pesto Coleslaw (left)

1. Prepare a charcoal grill with hot coals, setting rack 6 inches from coals; or heat a gas grill to high; or heat broiler.

2. Cook potatoes in boiling salted water 5 to 7 minutes or until partially cooked; drain.

3. With a knife, score both sides of each steak. Spread 2 tablespoons pesto on each side of both steaks.

4. Grill or broil potatoes until golden, 3 to 5 minutes. Grill or broil steaks to desired doneness, 7 minutes per side for medium-rare or until internal

Pesto Coleslaw

Whisk together 1 cup sour cream, 1 tablespoon white-wine vinegar, ¼ cup pesto, 1 teaspoon salt and ½ teaspoon black pepper in a large bowl. Add 1-pound package coleslaw mix; toss to combine.

MAKES 6 servings

PER SERVING
157 calories, 13 g fat (6 g saturated), 4 g protein, 8 g carbohydrate, 2 g fiber, 496 mg sodium, 20 mg cholesterol.

temperature registers 145° on an instant-read thermometer. Slice 1 steak. Serve with croutons and coleslaw. Refrigerate remaining steak and potatoes, wrapped separately, for another use.

Note: To make all three components of this recipe, you'll need 14 ounces, or about 1¾ cups, pesto.

PER SERVING (with croutons and coleslaw)
669 calories, 32 g fat (13 g saturated), 41 g protein, 55 g carbohydrate, 4 g fiber, 1,156 mg sodium, 106 mg cholesterol.

Pesto Croutons

Combine 2 tablespoons softened butter and 2 tablespoons pesto in a small bowl. Cut 1 loaf white bread (1 pound 2 ounces) into 12 slices. If broiling, broil to toast 1 side. Spread an untoasted side of each slice with butter mixture. Grill or broil, butter side up, until golden, 3 to 4 minutes. To serve, cut each slice in half diagonally.

MAKES 6 servings

Note: French, sourdough, whole wheat or rye bread would all make excellent pesto croutons.

PER CROUTON
89 calories, 6 g fat (1 g saturated), 1 g protein, 7 g carbohydrate, 0 g fiber, 135 mg sodium, 0 mg cholesterol.

Pesto Steak Salad

Here's a delicious way to use leftover steak and potatoes from Pesto Steak with Croutons and Coleslaw.

MAKES 6 servings **PREP** about 7 minutes

¾ **cup buttermilk**
⅔ **cup pesto**
¼ **cup mayonnaise**
12 **cups mixed salad greens**
1½ **pounds Pesto Steak (opposite)**
½ **pound small red new potatoes, halved and grilled (see Pesto Steak, opposite)**
2 **plum tomatoes, cored and quartered**

1. For dressing, stir together buttermilk, pesto and mayonnaise in a small bowl. Toss together greens with ½ cup dressing in a large bowl.

2. Thinly slice steak across grain. Arrange on a large serving platter with dressed greens, potatoes and tomatoes. Serve salad with extra dressing on the side.

PER SERVING
492 calories, 30 g fat (7 g saturated), 38 g protein, 18 g carbohydrate, 4 g fiber, 427 mg sodium, 88 mg cholesterol.

Sesame and Soy Grilled Steak Salad

MAKES 6 servings **PREP** 20 minutes
MARINATE 1 hour
GRILL OR BROIL 16 minutes

1¾ **pounds top sirloin steak (about 1½ inches thick)**
½ **cup reduced-sodium soy sauce**
⅓ **cup sugar**
3 **tablespoons sake, rice wine or dry sherry**
1 **teaspoon dark Asian sesame oil**
6 **cloves garlic, finely chopped**
4 **scallions, chopped, including part of the green**
1 **tablespoon sesame seeds, toasted (see page 232)**
½ **teaspoon hot paprika**
½ **teaspoon black pepper**
12 **cups mixed greens, including romaine**
   Pear Dressing (right)

1. Place steak in a baking dish.
2. Mix soy sauce, sugar, sake, oil, garlic, scallions, sesame seeds, paprika and pepper in a small bowl. Pour over steak. Marinate 1 hour in refrigerator, turning after 30 minutes.
3. Meanwhile, prepare a charcoal grill with hot coals, setting rack 6 inches from coals; or heat a gas grill to high; or heat broiler.
4. Grill or broil steak 8 minutes per side or until temperature registers at least 145° for medium-rare. Thinly slice steak across grain.
5. Toss greens with half of Pear Dressing; top with steak. Serve remaining dressing on the side.

PER SERVING
256 calories, 8 g fat (3 g saturated), 32 g protein, 11 g carbohydrate, 2 g fiber, 455 mg sodium, 87 mg cholesterol.

Pear Dressing

In a small bowl, mash 1 finely chopped garlic clove and 2 teaspoons sugar to a smooth paste with back of a spoon. Add ½ cup reduced-sodium soy sauce; ½ cup sake, rice wine or dry sherry; and 3 tablespoons plus 1 teaspoon sugar. Whisk to dissolve sugar. Peel, core and chop 1 Asian pear. Finely chop 4 scallions, including part of the green. Stir pear, scallions and 1 tablespoon toasted sesame seeds into soy sauce mixture.

MAKES 2 cups

PER 1 TABLESPOON
14 calories, 0 g fat (0 g saturated), 0 g protein, 2 g carbohydrate, 0 g fiber, 98 mg sodium, 0 mg cholesterol.

Beef "Taco" Salad

MAKES 6 servings **PREP** 30 minutes
BAKE tortillas at 425° for 8 minutes
COOK about 8 minutes

¼	cup fresh lime juice (about 3 limes)
3	tablespoons olive oil
1	small red onion, diced
1	small jalapeño chile, seeded and diced
½	teaspoon ground cumin
½	teaspoon chili powder
½	teaspoon salt
½	teaspoon black pepper
¼	teaspoon liquid hot-pepper sauce
¼	cup sour cream
1	teaspoon sugar
1	package (12 ounces) corn tortillas (ten 6-inch tortillas)
1	pound ground beef
1	can (10 ounces) corn kernels, drained
1	ripe avocado
1	large head romaine lettuce, torn into pieces (about 12 cups)
½	cup shredded cheddar cheese (2 ounces)
2	plum tomatoes, diced

1. Heat oven to 425°.
2. Whisk lime juice, oil, onion, jalapeño, cumin, ¼ teaspoon chili powder, ¼ teaspoon salt, ¼ teaspoon pepper, and hot-pepper sauce in a small bowl. Pour half of mixture into a large skillet. Whisk sour cream and sugar into remaining mixture in bowl. Set aside bowl and skillet.
3. Cut 4 tortillas in half and then into ¼-inch-wide strips. Place on a baking sheet; coat with nonstick cooking spray. Sprinkle evenly with remaining ¼ teaspoon chili powder, remaining ¼ teaspoon salt and remaining ¼ teaspoon pepper. Bake in heated 425° oven 8 minutes or until crisp.
4. Meanwhile, bring lime juice mixture in skillet to simmering over medium-high heat. Add beef; cook 6 minutes or until no longer pink, breaking up clumps with a wooden spoon. Add corn; heat through.
5. Cut avocado in half; remove seed. Scoop flesh from one half into sour cream mixture; mash into a smooth dressing. Scoop out flesh from other half; chop.
6. Meanwhile, warm remaining 6 tortillas according to package directions.
7. Mix lettuce, cheese and tomatoes in a serving bowl. Add tortilla crisps and chopped avocado. Top with beef-corn mixture. Add dressing; toss. Serve with warmed tortillas.

PER SERVING
479 calories, 29 g fat (9 g saturated), 23 g protein, 41 g carbohydrate, 6 g fiber, 500 mg sodium, 65 mg cholesterol.

PANTRY PLUS: PITTING AVOCADOS

Removing the pit from an avocado is a snap when you know the right moves.

- First slice avocado in half lengthwise around pit. Gently twist top half to separate it from bottom half.
- Hold half with pit in one hand. Hold a sturdy knife in your other hand; firmly strike pit with midpoint of knife blade. Pull up blade—the pit will pop right out.

BBQ Beef and Veggie Fajitas

Shown on page 23.

MAKES 4 servings **PREP** 10 minutes
COOK 15 minutes

2   tablespoons vegetable oil
1   medium onion, sliced
1   pound beef strips for stir-fry
2   zucchini, cut into matchstick strips
1   cup frozen sweet pepper strips
½   teaspoon chili powder
½   teaspoon salt
¼   teaspoon black pepper
⅓   cup barbecue sauce
8   flour tortillas (6-inch)
½   cup shredded cheddar cheese
    (2 ounces)
¼   cup sour cream

1. Heat oil in a large skillet over medium-high heat. Add onion; cook 5 minutes. Add beef and zucchini; cook 3 to 4 minutes.

2. Add pepper strips, chili powder, salt and black pepper; cook 2 minutes or until meat is cooked through. Add barbecue sauce. Heat through.

3. Warm tortillas according to package directions. Divide beef filling among tortillas. Top each with cheese and sour cream, dividing equally; roll up.

PER SERVING
558 calories, 30 g fat (9 g saturated), 36 g protein, 37 g carbohydrate, 3 g fiber, 1,083 mg sodium, 80 mg cholesterol.

Sliced Steak Sandwich

MAKES 6 servings **PREP** 10 minutes
MARINATE 15 minutes
GRILL OR BROIL 8 to 10 minutes

1½   pounds flank steak
¼   cup teriyaki sauce
1   tablespoon vegetable oil
2   scallions, chopped, including part of the green
1   envelope (0.9 ounces) Béarnaise sauce mix
6   slices black bread

1. Prepare a charcoal grill with hot coals, setting rack 6 inches from coals; or heat a gas grill to high; or heat broiler.

2. Place steak, teriyaki sauce, oil and scallions in a plastic food-storage bag. Marinate 15 minutes.

3. Meanwhile, prepare Béarnaise sauce, according to package directions.

4. Remove steak from bag. Discard remaining marinade. Grill or broil steak to desired doneness, 4 to 5 minutes per side for medium-rare or until internal temperature registers 145° on an instant-read thermometer. Thinly slice steak across grain.

5. Place a bread slice on each dinner plate. Arrange steak on bread. Ladle sauce over top.

PER SERVING
476 calories, 20 g fat (10 g saturated), 29 g protein, 20 g carbohydrate, 2 g fiber, 567 mg sodium, 85 mg cholesterol.

Roast Stuffed Loin of Pork

MAKES 12 servings **PREP** 20 minutes
ROAST at 450° for 10 minutes; then at 350° for 55 to 60 minutes

1   box (6 ounces) stuffing mix
1   boneless center-cut pork loin roast (about 3 pounds), excess fat trimmed
3   tablespoons olive oil
¼   cup all-purpose flour
1   teaspoon salt
½   teaspoon black pepper
3   pounds sweet potatoes (about 9), unpeeled, cut into 1½-inch chunks

1. Heat oven to 450°.

2. Prepare stuffing mix in a large bowl according to package directions.

3. Place pork loin, fat side up, on a work surface. With a sharp knife, slice horizontally along length of loin, cutting almost all the way through; open like a book.

4. Spoon stuffing down center of loin. Fold meat over stuffing. Wrap loin with kitchen twine and tie closed; space ties about 1½ inches apart. Rub loin with 1 tablespoon oil.

5. Stir together flour, salt and pepper in a small bowl. Rub mixture evenly over loin.

6. Toss together sweet potato chunks and remaining 2 tablespoons oil in a roasting pan; spread evenly over bottom of pan. Place loin, fat side up, on top of potatoes.

7. Roast in heated 450° oven about 10 minutes. Lower oven temperature to 350°. Roast 55 to 60 minutes or until internal temperature of meat registers 150° to 155° on an instant-read thermometer and potatoes are fork-tender.

8. Remove loin from oven; keep potatoes warm. Let loin stand 10 minutes; internal temperature should rise to 160°. Remove twine; slice pork and serve with potatoes.

PER SERVING
364 calories, 15 g fat (4 g saturated), 27 g protein, 30 g carbohydrate, 2 g fiber, 503 mg sodium, 67 mg cholesterol.

Pork Loin Preparation

Slice horizontally along length of loin, cutting almost all the way through.

Open loin like a book. Spoon stuffing down center of loin and shape evenly with your fingers.

Sausage, Veal, Spinach and Polenta Casserole

MAKES 12 servings **PREP** 30 minutes
COOK about 50 minutes
BAKE at 400° for 30 minutes

¼   cup vegetable oil
½   pound sweet Italian sausage,
     casings removed (see note)
1½   pounds boneless veal, cut into
     1-inch cubes (see note)
1   medium onion, thinly sliced
2   cloves garlic, finely chopped
½   pound mushrooms, sliced
1   sweet green pepper, cored, seeded
     and cut into ½-inch-wide strips

1   sweet red pepper, cored, seeded
     and cut into ½-inch-wide strips
2   tablespoons all-purpose flour
1   can (14½ ounces) beef broth
¼   teaspoon salt
⅛   teaspoon black pepper
     Polenta with Cheese (opposite)
2   packages (10 ounces each) frozen
     chopped spinach, thawed and
     squeezed dry
1½   cups shredded Fontina cheese
     (6 ounces)

1. Heat oven to 400°. Grease a 13 x 9 x
    2-inch baking dish.

2. Heat 2 tablespoons oil in a large skillet
    over medium-high heat. Working in
    batches to avoid crowding skillet, add
    sausage and veal; cook, breaking up
    sausage with a wooden spoon, until
    lightly colored, 4 to 5 minutes.
    Transfer to a plate or bowl.

3. Heat remaining 2 tablespoons oil in
    same skillet. Add onion; cook until
    softened, about 3 minutes. Add garlic,
    mushrooms and green and red peppers;
    cook, stirring occasionally, 5 minutes
    or until softened.

4. Sprinkle flour over vegetables; cook,
    stirring constantly, 1 minute. Gradually
    add broth, stirring and scraping up
    any browned bits from bottom of
    skillet; cook 1 to 2 minutes or until
    mixture is thickened slightly. Stir in
    salt and black pepper.

5. Return sausage and veal to skillet;
    cook, covered, over medium-high
    heat 15 minutes. Uncover; cook
    15 minutes more or until meat is
    cooked through.

6. Spread half of polenta in bottom of prepared baking dish. Spread spinach on top; sprinkle evenly with Fontina. Top with remaining polenta. Spoon sausage and veal mixture evenly on top. Bake in heated 400° oven 30 minutes or until heated through.

Note: Veal cut from a blade roast, arm roast or boneless shoulder arm roast all will work in this recipe. Or you can use all sausage or all veal, for a total of 2 pounds.

PER SERVING (with polenta)
415 calories, 20 g fat (8 g saturated), 26 g protein, 31 g carbohydrate, 3 g fiber, 823 mg sodium, 91 mg cholesterol.

Polenta with Cheese

Bring 4 cups milk and 2 cups water to boiling in a large saucepan over high heat. Add 1½ teaspoons salt, ½ teaspoon garlic powder, ½ teaspoon onion powder and ¼ teaspoon black pepper. Gradually stir in 2 cups instant polenta; cook, stirring, 3 to 5 minutes or until mixture thickens and pulls away from sides of pan. Stir in ¼ cup grated Parmesan cheese and 3 tablespoons butter. Remove from heat.

MAKES 7¼ cups (12 servings)

PER SERVING
184 calories, 6 g fat (4 g saturated), 15 g protein, 25 g carbohydrate, 1 g fiber, 370 mg sodium, 21 mg cholesterol.

Pork Saltimbocca

We substituted pork cutlets for veal in this take on a typical Italian recipe—with terrific results.

MAKES 4 servings **PREP** 5 minutes
COOK 8 to 12 minutes

4 pork cutlets (¾ pound total)
1 teaspoon salt
½ teaspoon dried sage
½ teaspoon black pepper
4 slices prosciutto (2 ounces total)
2 tablespoons butter
½ cup Marsala wine
½ cup beef broth
1 cup shredded Fontina cheese (4 ounces)

1. Place cutlets between sheets of plastic wrap and pound lightly. Sprinkle each with salt, sage and pepper, dividing equally. Lay 1 slice prosciutto on each cutlet.

2. Heat butter in a large skillet over medium-high heat. Working in batches if necessary, cook cutlets, starting with prosciutto side down, 2 minutes per side. Remove cutlets to a plate. Add Marsala and broth to skillet; cook 2 minutes.

3. Return cutlets to skillet, prosciutto side up; top each with ¼ cup Fontina. Cover and cook 2 minutes or until cheese melts. Remove cutlets to a platter and keep warm.

4. Reduce sauce over medium-high heat to a syrupy consistency, 4 minutes. Spoon over cutlets.

PER SERVING
332 calories, 23 g fat (11 g saturated), 29 g protein, 1 g carbohydrate, 0 g fiber, 1,460 mg sodium, 112 mg cholesterol.

Glazed Pork and Vegetables

MAKES 6 servings **PREP** 20 minutes
COOK about 1¼ hours

2   tablespoons vegetable oil
2   pounds trimmed boneless pork
    for stew, cut into 1-inch cubes
¼   cup sugar
¾   cup plus 1 tablespoon water
3   tablespoons Asian fish sauce
1   tablespoon lemon juice
¼   teaspoon black pepper
3   carrots, peeled and sliced
1   large sweet red pepper, cored,
    seeded and cut into 2 x 1½-inch
    strips
4   scallions, chopped, including
    part of the green
    Cooked rice for serving (optional)

1. Heat 1 tablespoon oil in a large skillet
    or Dutch oven. Add half of pork;
    cook without stirring until browned
    on one side, about 3 minutes. Turn;
    cook 3 minutes. Transfer to a platter.
    Repeat with remaining oil and pork.

2. Combine sugar and 1 tablespoon
    water in a small heavy nonstick
    saucepan; cook over medium-high
    heat, shaking pan until sugar melts
    and turns deep caramel brown, about
    8 minutes. Carefully add ¼ cup water
    and fish sauce. Remove from heat.

3. Stir lemon juice, remaining ½ cup
    water and black pepper into fish sauce
    mixture. Heat through over low heat,
    stirring if caramel hardens. Add fish
    sauce mixture to skillet over low heat,
    scraping up browned bits from
    bottom with a wooden spoon. Add
    meat to skillet. Bring to simmering;
    cover. Cook over low heat 1 hour.

4. Add carrots and red pepper strips to
    skillet. Bring to simmering; cover.
    Cook 20 minutes.

5. Add scallions to skillet; cook
    10 minutes or until vegetables are
    tender. Serve with rice if desired.

PER SERVING
343 calories, 20 g fat (6 g saturated), 26 g protein,
14 g carbohydrate, 1 g fiber, 747 mg sodium,
88 mg cholesterol.

Asian Pork Kabobs

MAKES 8 servings **PREP** 17 minutes
BROIL kabobs 8 to 10 minutes
COOK pasta while broiling kabobs

Peanut Dressing
1   cup creamy peanut butter
⅔   cup water
½   cup teriyaki sauce
1   tablespoon dark Asian sesame oil
2   teaspoons chopped garlic
2   teaspoons grated fresh ginger
¾   teaspoon ground red pepper
    (cayenne)

Kabobs
2   pounds pork tenderloin, cut into
    2-inch chunks
2   small sweet green peppers, cored,
    seeded and cut into 1-inch pieces
2   small sweet red peppers, cored,
    seeded and cut into 1-inch pieces
1   large red onion, cut into 1-inch
    wedges
1   pound angel hair pasta

1. Heat broiler.

2. Prepare peanut dressing: Whisk
    together peanut butter, water, teriyaki
    sauce, oil, garlic, ginger and ground
    red pepper in a small bowl. Pour
    ¾ cup dressing into a measuring cup;
    reserve remainder.

3. Prepare kabobs: Thread pork onto 8 metal skewers, alternating with sweet peppers and onion and using about 5 pieces pork per skewer. Brush skewers with dressing from cup.

4. Broil 8 to 10 minutes, turning halfway through cooking.

5. Meanwhile, cook pasta in a large pot of lightly salted boiling water until al dente, firm but tender. Drain well. Transfer to a large serving bowl; toss with reserved dressing. Serve pasta topped with kabobs.

PER SERVING
604 calories, 23 g fat (5 g saturated), 41 g protein, 59 g carbohydrate, 6 g fiber, 890 mg sodium, 67 mg cholesterol.

Mediterranean Pork Skewers

MAKES 6 servings **PREP** 10 minutes
BROIL 10 minutes

4   ounces (½ package) flavored feta cheese, crumbled
½   cup sour cream
1   small onion, diced
¼   teaspoon black pepper
1   seasoned pork tenderloin (about 1½ pounds), cut into 1-inch cubes
1   zucchini (about 1 pound), halved lengthwise and cut into ½-inch-thick slices
12 cherry tomatoes
2   boxes (5.6 ounces each) flavored couscous
1   tablespoon chopped fresh parsley

1. To make a sauce, whirl feta, sour cream, onion and pepper in a food processor until smooth. Refrigerate until ready to serve.

2. Heat broiler. Spray broiler-pan rack with nonstick cooking spray.

3. Thread pork cubes alternately with zucchini and cherry tomatoes onto six 14-inch metal skewers.

4. Broil skewers 5 inches from heat 10 minutes, turning once halfway through cooking.

5. Meanwhile, prepare couscous according to package directions.

6. Spoon couscous onto a serving platter. Top with skewers; sprinkle with parsley. Serve with sauce on the side.

PER SERVING
382 calories, 11 g fat (6 g saturated), 26 g protein, 47 g carbohydrate, 1 g fiber, 901 mg sodium, 59 mg cholesterol.

BBQ Ribs with Two Sauces

MAKES 6 servings **PREP** 10 minutes
BAKE at 450° for 1¼ hours
REFRIGERATE overnight **GRILL** 15 minutes

1 **rack (about 2½ pounds) pork loin back ribs, cut in half crosswise Easy BBQ Sauce or Soy-Ginger Sauce (right)**

1. Heat oven to 450°.

2. Brush ribs with ⅓ cup Easy BBQ Sauce or ¼ cup Soy-Ginger Sauce; refrigerate remaining sauce. Place ribs in a large extra-heavy-duty aluminum foil baking bag. Double-fold open end of bag. Place in a 1-inch-deep baking pan. Bake in 450° oven 1¼ hours.

3. Remove pan from oven. Carefully open bag; let ribs cool. Remove ribs from bag. Refrigerate ribs, covered, overnight.

4. Prepare a charcoal grill with hot coals, setting rack 6 inches from coals; or heat a gas grill to high. Coat ribs with ⅓ cup of your choice of sauce; reserve remaining sauce. Grill ribs, turning once, 15 minutes or until hot. Boil reserved sauce 3 minutes and serve alongside ribs.

PER SERVING (with Easy BBQ Sauce)
356 calories, 26 g fat (10 g saturated), 22 g protein, 9 g carbohydrate, 0 g fiber, 612 mg sodium, 102 mg cholesterol.

PER SERVING (with Soy-Ginger Sauce)
369 calories, 30 g fat (10 g saturated), 22 g protein, 2 g carbohydrate, 0 g fiber, 617 mg sodium, 102 mg cholesterol.

Easy BBQ Sauce

In a small bowl, whisk together 1 bottle (12 ounces) chili sauce, 2 tablespoons brown sugar, 2 tablespoons cider vinegar, 1 tablespoon Worcestershire sauce, 1 teaspoon chili powder, 1 teaspoon salt and 1 teaspoon garlic powder. Cover sauce and refrigerate.

MAKES 1½ cups

PER TABLESPOON
20 calories, 0 g fat (0 g saturated), 0 g protein, 5 g carbohydrate, 0 g fiber, 294 mg sodium, 0 mg cholesterol.

Soy-Ginger Sauce

In a small bowl, whisk together ⅓ cup soy sauce, 2 tablespoons peanut oil, 2 tablespoons rice-wine vinegar, 2 tablespoons Asian chili paste, 4 teaspoons dark Asian sesame oil, 2 teaspoons brown sugar and 4 chopped scallions. Cover sauce and refrigerate.

MAKES 1 cup

PER TABLESPOON
31 calories, 3 g fat (0 g saturated), 0 g protein, 1 g carbohydrate, 0 g fiber, 340 mg sodium, 0 mg cholesterol.

Orange-Glazed Ham

MAKES about 24 servings
PREP 10 minutes **BAKE** according to
ham package directions

1	fully cooked boneless ham (6 to 6 ½ pounds)
½	cup water
¼	cup Dijon mustard
	Grated rind of 1 large orange
¼	cup fresh orange juice
¼	cup ketchup
¼	cup packed dark-brown sugar
2	tablespoons vegetable oil
2	teaspoons garlic salt
5	thin orange slices
10	whole cloves

1. Heat oven according to ham package directions. Place ham in a roasting pan; add water to pan. Cover loosely with aluminum foil.

2. Bake ham in heated oven according to package directions.

3. Meanwhile, to make a glaze, whisk together mustard, orange rind, orange juice, ketchup, brown sugar, oil and garlic salt in a small bowl. Cover with plastic wrap and set aside.

4. Half an hour before ham is done, remove foil. Spoon ½ cup glaze over ham; reserve remaining glaze. Place orange slices over ham in a decorative fashion, using 2 cloves to attach each slice. Bake 30 minutes longer or until internal temperature registers 140° on an instant-read thermometer.

5. Slice ham; serve with reserved glaze.

PER SERVING
183 calories, 7 g fat (2 g saturated), 25 g protein, 3 g carbohydrate, 0 g fiber, 1,574 mg sodium, 55 mg cholesterol.

Ham and Whipped Potato Casserole

MAKES 12 servings **PREP** 20 minutes
COOK ham filling 4 to 5 minutes
BAKE at 400° for 30 minutes

2	tablespoons butter
2	tablespoons all-purpose flour
2	cups milk
¼	teaspoon salt
¼	teaspoon ground red pepper (cayenne)
⅛	teaspoon ground nutmeg
1¼	pounds cooked ham, cut into ½-inch cubes
2	scallions, thinly sliced
2	cans (15¼ ounces each) corn kernels, drained
½	cup grated Parmesan cheese
	Rich Whipped Potatoes (page 129)

1. Heat oven to 400°. Grease a 13 x 9 x 2-inch baking dish.

2. Melt butter in a large skillet over medium heat. Stir in flour; cook, stirring, 1 minute or until golden. Gradually stir in milk. Bring to simmering over medium-high heat; cook, stirring constantly, 2 to 3 minutes or until thickened. Stir in salt, red pepper, nutmeg, ham and scallions. Remove from heat.

3. Spread ham mixture in prepared baking dish. Spread corn on top. Sprinkle evenly with Parmesan. Spread potatoes over all.

4. Bake in heated 400° oven 30 minutes or until heated through.

PER SERVING (with potatoes)
365 calories, 20 g fat (11 g saturated), 15 g protein, 33 g carbohydrate, 3 g fiber, 1,000 mg sodium, 76 mg cholesterol.

Sausage and Potato Salad

Shown on page 23.

MAKES 6 servings **PREP** 15 minutes
COOK about 20 minutes

1½ pounds red new potatoes
½   cup chicken broth
¼   cup red-wine vinegar
2   teaspoons sugar
½   teaspoon dry mustard
½   teaspoon salt
¼   teaspoon black pepper
¼   teaspoon fennel seeds, crushed
1   pound hot Italian sausage, cut into bite-size pieces
1   sweet red pepper, cored, seeded and cut into thin strips
1   sweet yellow pepper, cored, seeded and cut into thin strips
1   medium onion, halved lengthwise and sliced crosswise
3   cups packed escarole, cut into bite-size pieces

1. Place potatoes in a medium-size saucepan; add enough water to cover. Bring to boiling; boil gently 20 minutes or until knife-tender.

2. Meanwhile, mix broth, vinegar, sugar, dry mustard, salt, black pepper and fennel seeds in small saucepan. Heat to simmering; keep warm.

3. Cook sausage in a large skillet over medium-high heat 7 minutes or until beginning to brown. Add sweet peppers and onion; reduce heat to medium-low and cook 9 minutes or until vegetables are tender and sausage is cooked through.

4. Drain potatoes; cut into halves or quarters. Place in a large bowl.

Add warm dressing and sausage mixture; toss to coat. Divide escarole among individual plates; top with warm potato salad.

PER SERVING
229 calories, 11 g fat (4 g saturated), 12 g protein, 22 g carbohydrate, 4 g fiber, 627 mg sodium, 31 mg cholesterol.

Asian Pork and Noodle Salad

MAKES 6 servings **PREP** 20 minutes
COOK 10 minutes
ROAST at 400° for 15 to 20 minutes

Sauce
1   cup orange juice
2   tablespoons soy sauce
1   tablespoon rice-wine vinegar
2   teaspoons dark Asian sesame oil
1   tablespoon cornstarch
4   scallions, chopped, including part of the green
1   clove garlic, chopped
1   teaspoon finely chopped fresh ginger
1   teaspoon grated orange rind
¼   teaspoon salt
¼   teaspoon red-pepper flakes
¼   teaspoon black pepper

Salad
½   teaspoon salt
¼   teaspoon red-pepper flakes
¼   teaspoon black pepper
1   teaspoon dark Asian sesame oil
1   pork tenderloin (¾ pound)
½   pound thin spaghetti
2   oranges, peeled and sectioned
1   bunch watercress, stemmed

1. Prepare sauce: Whisk orange juice, soy sauce, vinegar, and oil in a small bowl. Whisk in cornstarch, then add scallions, garlic, ginger, orange rind, salt, red-pepper flakes and black pepper. Set aside.

2. Heat oven to 400°.

3. Prepare salad: Combine salt, red-pepper flakes, black pepper and oil in a cup. Rub onto pork.

4. Heat a medium-size cast-iron skillet over medium-high heat. Add pork; sear on all sides, 5 minutes total. Transfer skillet to heated 400° oven. Roast 15 to 20 minutes or until internal temperature of pork registers 145° on an instant-read thermometer. Remove skillet from oven; let stand 10 minutes.

5. Meanwhile, cook spaghetti in a large pot of lightly salted boiling water until al dente, firm but tender. Drain well; transfer to a serving bowl.

6. Transfer pork to a cutting board. Whisk sauce and add to skillet; cook over medium heat 3 to 5 minutes or until bubbly and thickened.

7. Add orange sections and watercress to spaghetti in bowl. Thinly slice pork; halve any large pieces. Add to bowl along with sauce. Toss to coat.

PER SERVING
294 calories, 5 g fat (1 g saturated), 19 g protein, 43 g carbohydrate, 3 g fiber, 649 mg sodium, 34 mg cholesterol.

Quick Ham and Macaroni Salad

MAKES 6 servings **PREP** 15 minutes

2 pounds deli macaroni salad
¾ pound deli ham, cut into 1½ x ¼-inch strips
½ pound sugar snap peas, strings removed
1 bag (8 ounces) cheddar and mozzarella cheese cubes
½ cup crumbled cooked bacon (8 slices)

Toss together macaroni salad and ham in a large bowl. Slice any large sugar snap peas in half. Add to bowl, along with cheese and bacon. Toss to combine. Chill until ready to serve.

PER SERVING
395 calories, 18 g fat (8 g saturated), 29 g protein, 39 g carbohydrate, 2 g fiber, 1,848 mg sodium, 82 mg cholesterol.

MARBLED PUMPERNICKEL RYE (PAGE 109)

TOMATO-HERB CHEESE POTATOES AU GRATIN (PAGE 130)

CARROT SALAD (PAGE 124)

Side
Dishes

Split-Top Butter Loaf

MAKES 2 loaves (12 slices each)
PREP 25 minutes **RISE** about 2¼ hours
BAKE at 350° for 35 minutes

1   teaspoon sugar
¾   cup warm water (105° to 115°)
1   envelope active dry yeast
1½ cups buttermilk
¼   cup honey
1   egg
1   tablespoon salt
3   tablespoons butter, cut into pieces
6   cups bread flour
2   tablespoons butter, melted, for brushing

1. Mix sugar and warm water in a small bowl. Sprinkle yeast over top. Let stand until foamy, 5 to 10 minutes.

2. Meanwhile, whisk together buttermilk, honey, egg and salt in a small saucepan until well blended. Add butter pieces. Heat over low heat, stirring, until butter is melted. Let cool until mixture registers 110° to 120° on an instant-read thermometer. Pour into a large bowl.

3. Beat 2 cups flour into buttermilk mixture with a wooden spoon until mixture is smooth. Stir in yeast mixture. Stir in enough of remaining flour, ½ cup at a time, to make dough come together and pull away from sides of bowl.

4. Turn out dough onto a lightly floured surface. Knead until smooth and elastic, 8 to 10 minutes, adding more flour as needed to prevent sticking. Place in a greased large bowl, turning to coat. Cover with a clean kitchen towel or plastic wrap. Let rise in a warm place until doubled in volume, about 1 hour.

5. Punch down dough. Let rest 5 minutes. Meanwhile, grease two 9¼ x 5¼ x 2¾-inch loaf pans.

6. Turn out dough; divide in half; lightly coat halves with flour. Gently pat each half into a 7 x 5-inch rectangle. Transfer to prepared pans. Cover with a clean kitchen towel. Let rise in a warm place until doubled in volume, about 1¼ hours.

7. Heat oven to 350°. Using a razor blade or very sharp knife, slash top of each loaf in half lengthwise.

8. Bake in heated 350° oven 15 minutes. Brush loaves with some of melted butter. Bake 15 minutes longer. Brush again with butter. Bake 5 minutes or until loaves sound hollow when tapped. Remove loaves from pans; cool on wire racks.

PER SLICE
143 calories, 3 g fat (2 g saturated), 5 g protein, 26 g carbohydrate, 1 g fiber, 286 mg sodium, 16 mg cholesterol.

Tangy Herb Yogurt Cheese

This savory spread offers a nice change of pace from butter.

Line a strainer with paper toweling; place over a small bowl. Spoon in 8 ounces plain yogurt; refrigerate 2 hours. Discard liquid in bowl; transfer yogurt to bowl and stir in 1 tablespoon pesto and pinch of salt.

MAKES about ¾ cup

PER TABLESPOON
18 calories, 1 g fat (0 g saturated), 1 g protein, 1 g carbohydrate, 0 g fiber, 35 mg sodium, 2 mg cholesterol.

Egg Knot

MAKES 2 loaves (16 slices each)
PREP 30 minutes **RISE** 2½ to 3 hours
BAKE at 375° for 30 to 35 minutes

2   cups bread flour
3   cups all-purpose flour
1   envelope active dry yeast
3   tablespoons sugar
2½ teaspoons salt
1   cup water
¼   cup (½ stick) butter, cut up
4   eggs

1. Combine 1 cup bread flour, 1 cup all-purpose flour, yeast, sugar and salt in a large bowl.

2. Heat water and butter in a small saucepan until butter melts. Let cool to 120° to 130°. Add to flour mixture; beat with a wooden spoon until combined. Beat in 3 eggs. Stir in enough of remaining 1 cup bread flour and 2 cups all-purpose flour, 1 cup at a time, to make dough come together and pull away from sides of bowl.

3. Turn out dough onto a lightly floured surface. Knead until smooth and elastic, 8 to 10 minutes, adding more flour as needed to prevent sticking. Place in a greased large bowl, turning to coat. Cover with a clean kitchen towel or plastic wrap. Let rise in a warm place until doubled in volume, about 1½ hours.

4. Punch down dough. Let rest 5 minutes. Meanwhile, grease two 8½ x 4½ x 2⅝-inch loaf pans.

5. Turn out dough; divide into 4 equal pieces. Shape 2 pieces into 7 x 3-inch rectangles; place 1 rectangle in bottom of each loaf pan.

6. Roll each of the remaining 2 pieces of dough into a 12-inch rope. Cut each rope into 12 equal pieces. With floured hands, shape pieces into balls. Arrange 12 balls, with their sides touching, on top of dough in each pan. Cover pans with a clean kitchen towel. Let dough rise in a warm place until doubled in volume, 1 to 1½ hours.

7. Heat oven to 375°.

8. Lightly beat remaining egg in a small bowl just to blend together. Brush evenly over tops of risen loaves, being careful not to deflate dough.

9. Bake in heated 375° oven 30 to 35 minutes or until loaves are golden and sound hollow when lightly tapped on top. Remove loaves from pans; run a knife around sides to separate if they stick to pans. Cool on wire racks.

PER SLICE
95 calories, 2 g fat (1 g saturated), 3 g protein, 16 g carbohydrate, 1 g fiber, 175 mg sodium, 30 mg cholesterol.

Egg Knot Know-How

Shape each piece into a ball. Place 12 balls, sides touching, in each pan.

Wisconsin Cheddar-Beer Bread

MAKES 2 loaves (16 slices each)
PREP 20 minutes **RISE** 1½ hours
BAKE at 350° for 30 to 35 minutes

4   to 4¼ cups bread flour
1   envelope fast-acting yeast
1   sweet Italian sausage (about 4 ounces), casing removed
1   bottle (12 ounces) amber or regular beer
2   tablespoons sugar
2   teaspoons salt
1   cup shredded cheddar cheese (4 ounces)
½   cup chopped scallions, including part of the green
2   tablespoons butter, melted, for brushing

1. Mix together 2 cups flour and yeast in a large bowl.

2. Cook sausage in a small skillet over medium heat, breaking up clumps with a wooden spoon, until cooked through, about 5 minutes. Drain if needed. Set aside.

3. Heat beer, sugar and salt in a saucepan over medium heat until temperature registers 120° to 130° on an instant-read thermometer. Pour into flour mixture in bowl. Beat with a wooden spoon, about 100 strokes.

4. Beat in remaining 2 cups flour, ½ cup at a time. Add sausage, ½ cup cheese and scallions; knead into dough with your hands.

5. Turn out dough onto a lightly floured surface. Knead until smooth and elastic, about 8 minutes, adding more flour as needed to prevent sticking. Place in a greased large bowl, turning to coat. Cover with a clean kitchen towel or plastic wrap. Let rise in a warm place until doubled in volume, about 1 hour.

6. Punch down dough. Turn out onto a work surface and divide in half. Let rest 5 minutes. Meanwhile, grease a baking sheet.

7. Shape each piece of dough into an oblong loaf about 10 x 3 inches. Transfer to prepared baking sheet. Cover with a clean kitchen towel. Let rise in a warm place until doubled in volume, 30 minutes.

8. Heat oven to 350°. Using a razor blade or very sharp knife, slash top of each loaf lengthwise. Sprinkle ¼ cup cheese over each slash.

9. Bake in heated 350° oven 15 minutes. Brush each loaf with 1 tablespoon melted butter. Bake 15 to 20 minutes longer or until loaves are golden and sound hollow when tapped on bottom. Remove from baking sheet; cool on a wire rack. Serve slightly warm if desired.

PER SLICE
81 calories, 2 g fat (1 g saturated), 3 g protein, 12 g carbohydrate, 1 g fiber, 172 mg sodium, 7 mg cholesterol.

Cottage Cheese and Rosemary Bread

This bread makes a great gift. Wrap the cooled loaf in plastic wrap and then gift wrap as desired.

MAKES 1 loaf (15 slices) **PREP** 30 minutes
RISE 1½ hours **BAKE** at 400° for 30 minutes

1   **cup warm water (105° to 115°)**
2   **tablespoons packed light-brown sugar**
1   **package active dry yeast**
4   **cups bread flour**
1   **tablespoon coarse kosher salt**
1   **tablespoon dried rosemary**
½   **teaspoon black pepper**
1   **cup cottage cheese or ricotta cheese**

1. Combine ¼ cup warm water, brown sugar and yeast in a small glass measuring cup; stir to dissolve yeast. Let stand 10 minutes.

2. Combine flour, salt, rosemary, pepper, remaining ¾ cup warm water and cottage cheese in a large bowl. Pour in yeast mixture; stir with a wooden spoon until dough is well combined.

3. Using an electric mixer fitted with a dough hook, knead dough 8 minutes. Turn out dough onto a lightly floured surface; knead by hand about 2 minutes. (To knead dough without a mixer, knead on lightly floured surface 8 to 10 minutes.) Place dough in a greased large bowl, turning to coat. Cover with lightly oiled waxed paper or a kitchen towel. Let rise in a warm place until doubled in volume, about 1 hour.

4. Punch down dough. Turn out onto a lightly floured surface. Shape dough into a 15 x 9-inch rectangle. If dough pulls back, let rest 10 minutes.

5. Lifting from a short end, fold dough into thirds and place in an 11½ x 5½ x 3-inch loaf pan (see note). Cover with lightly oiled waxed paper or a clean kitchen towel. Let rise in a warm place until doubled in volume, about 30 minutes.

6. Heat oven to 400°. If a crisp crust is desired, pour 2 to 3 cups water into a heavy pan and place on floor of oven.

7. Bake bread in heated 400° oven 30 minutes or until loaf sounds hollow when tapped and is golden brown. (Check after 20 minutes; if loaf is getting too brown, loosely cover with aluminum foil.)

8. Cool loaf in pan on a wire rack 10 minutes. Remove loaf from pan to rack and cool completely.

Note: To make 2 loaves, divide rectangle of dough in half and then fold into thirds. Place in two 8½ x 4½ x 2⅝-inch loaf pans. Complete recipe as directed.

PER SLICE
131 calories, 1 g fat (0 g saturated), 6 g protein, 26 g carbohydrate, 1 g fiber, 438 mg sodium, 2 mg cholesterol.

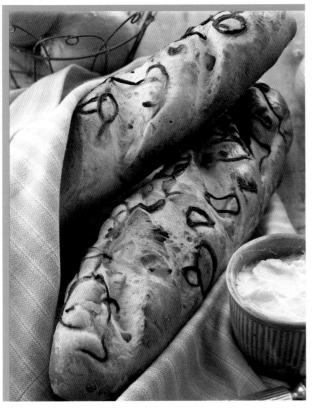

Onion Baguettes

MAKES 2 baguettes (16 slices each)
PREP 25 minutes **COOK** 8 minutes
RISE 1½ hours
BAKE at 400° for 35 to 40 minutes

2	**cups bread flour**
1	**cup all-purpose flour**
1	**envelope active dry yeast**
2	**teaspoons sugar**
¼	**teaspoon onion powder**
2	**teaspoons salt**
1	**cup very warm water (120° to 130°)**
2	**tablespoons olive oil**
	Cornmeal for dusting baking sheet

Topping

1	**small yellow onion, sliced and separated into rings**
¼	**teaspoon salt**
1	**egg yolk**
1	**tablespoon milk**

1. Combine bread flour, all-purpose flour, yeast, sugar, onion powder and salt in a large bowl. Stir in very warm water and oil.

2. Turn out dough onto a lightly floured surface. Knead until well blended and stiff, about 10 minutes, adding more flour as needed to prevent sticking. Place in a greased large bowl, turning to coat. Cover with a clean kitchen towel or plastic wrap. Let rise in a warm place until almost tripled in volume, about 1½ hours.

3. Meanwhile, prepare topping: Bring a small saucepan of water to boiling. Add sliced onion; cook until softened, about 8 minutes. Drain. Sprinkle with salt. Set aside.

4. Punch down dough. Let rest, covered, 10 minutes. Meanwhile, dust a baking sheet with cornmeal.

5. Turn out dough. Divide in half and shape into two 12 x 2-inch baguettes. Transfer to prepared baking sheet. Using a razor blade or very sharp knife, make 4 diagonal slashes across top of each loaf.

6. Whisk together egg yolk and milk in a small bowl. Brush over loaves. Top with prepared onion rings.

7. Place baking sheet with baguettes in cold oven. Turn oven on to 400°. Bake 35 to 40 minutes or until loaves are puffed, golden and sound hollow when tapped on bottom. Transfer to a wire rack to cool; serve warm if desired.

PER SLICE
52 calories, 1 g fat (0 g saturated), 2 g protein, 9 g carbohydrate, 0 g fiber, 151 mg sodium, 7 mg cholesterol.

Marbled Pumpernickel Rye

Shown on page 102.

MAKES 1 loaf (12 slices) **PREP** 45 minutes
RISE 3 hours
BAKE at 350° for 30 to 35 minutes

Pumpernickel Dough

⅔ cup warm water (105° to 115°)
½ teaspoon sugar
1 envelope active dry yeast
1 cup plus 2 tablespoons bread flour
¾ cup rye flour
1½ teaspoons salt
1 teaspoon caraway seeds
2 tablespoons unsweetened cocoa powder
2 teaspoons espresso powder
2 tablespoons unsulfured molasses
1 tablespoon cider vinegar

Rye Dough

⅔ cup warm water (105° to 115°)
½ teaspoon sugar
1 envelope active dry yeast
1 cup plus 2 tablespoons bread flour
¾ cup rye flour
1½ teaspoons salt
1 teaspoon caraway seeds
2 tablespoons unsulfured molasses
1 tablespoon cider vinegar

Topping

1 egg white, lightly beaten
½ teaspoon caraway seeds

1. Prepare pumpernickel dough: Mix ⅓ cup warm water and sugar in a small bowl. Sprinkle yeast over top. Let stand until foamy, 5 to 10 minutes.

2. Mix bread flour, rye flour, salt and caraway seeds in a large bowl. Whisk in cocoa powder and espresso powder. Mix molasses, vinegar and remaining ⅓ cup warm water in a small bowl. Stir vinegar mixture and yeast mixture into flour mixture. Add more bread flour if dough is too sticky to handle.

3. Turn out dough onto a floured work surface. With floured hands, knead until smooth and elastic, about 10 minutes; dough will be slightly stiff.

4. Place dough in a greased large bowl, turning to coat. Cover with a clean kitchen towel or plastic wrap. Let rise in a warm place until doubled in volume, about 1½ hours.

5. Meanwhile, prepare rye dough: Follow steps 1 through 3 above, omitting espresso and cocoa powders. Place dough in a second greased large bowl, turning to coat. Cover and let rise in a warm place until doubled in volume, about 1¼ hours.

6. Punch down doughs; transfer each to a floured work surface. Let rest 5 minutes. Meanwhile, grease an 8½ x 4½ x 2⅝-inch loaf pan.

7. Roll each dough into an 11 x 8-inch rectangle. Place pumpernickel dough on top of rye, overlapping so a 1-inch border of rye dough extends at one end. Fold up border over pumpernickel edge; firmly roll up doughs together. Pinch edges together along spiral ends; turn ends under. Transfer to prepared pan. Cover and let rise until doubled in volume, about 1½ hours.

8. Heat oven to 350°. Lightly brush top of risen loaf with beaten egg white. Sprinkle with caraway seeds.

9. Bake loaf in heated 350° oven 30 to 35 minutes or until it is puffed, golden and sounds hollow when tapped. Remove from pan; cool on a wire rack.

PER SLICE
149 calories, 0 g fat (0 g saturated), 5 g protein,
33 g carbohydrate, 3 g fiber, 541 mg sodium,
0 mg cholesterol.

Multigrain Bread

Shown on page 3.

MAKES 1 round loaf (12 slices)
PREP 30 minutes **RISE** about 1¼ hours
BAKE at 375° for 30 to 35 minutes

¼ cup plus 2 teaspoons honey
½ cup warm water (105° to 115°)
2 envelopes active dry yeast
¾ cup milk
1 egg
2 teaspoons salt
3 tablespoons unsalted butter, cut into small pieces
2 cups whole-wheat flour
2 cups bread flour
⅓ cup wheat-and-barley cereal bits
½ cup old-fashioned rolled oats
½ cup sunflower seeds

Topping

1 teaspoon sunflower seeds
1 teaspoon old-fashioned rolled oats
1 egg white, lightly beaten

1. Stir 2 teaspoons honey and warm water in a small bowl until well blended. Sprinkle yeast over top. Let stand until mixture is foamy, 5 to 10 minutes.

2. Meanwhile, whisk together remaining ¼ cup honey, milk, egg and salt in a small saucepan until well blended. Add butter. Heat over low heat, stirring, until butter is melted. Remove saucepan from heat and let mixture cool until it registers 115° to 120° on an instant-read thermometer. Pour into a large bowl.

3. Beat 1 cup whole-wheat flour and 1 cup bread flour into butter mixture with a wooden spoon until mixture is smooth. Add yeast mixture, wheat-and-barley cereal, oats and sunflower seeds; stir to combine.

4. Stir in enough of remaining 1 cup whole-wheat flour and 1 cup bread flour, ½ cup at a time, to make dough come together and pull away from sides of bowl.

5. Turn out dough onto a lightly floured surface. Knead until smooth and elastic, 8 to 10 minutes, adding more flour as needed to prevent sticking. Place in a greased large bowl, turning to coat. Cover with a clean kitchen towel or plastic wrap. Let rise in a warm place until doubled in volume, about 1 hour.

6. Punch down dough. Let rest 5 minutes. Meanwhile, grease a baking sheet.

7. Turn out dough. Shape into a round loaf, 6 inches in diameter. Transfer to prepared baking sheet. Cover and let rise in a warm place until doubled in volume, 30 to 45 minutes.

8. Heat oven to 375°.

9. Prepare topping: Mix sunflower seeds and oats in a small bowl. Brush top of risen loaf with egg white. Sprinkle evenly with seed mixture.

10. Bake in heated 375° oven 30 to 35 minutes or until loaf sounds hollow when lightly tapped on bottom. Transfer to a wire rack to cool.

PER SLICE
262 calories, 8 g fat (3 g saturated), 9 g protein, 43 g carbohydrate, 4 g fiber, 396 mg sodium, 28 mg cholesterol.

Sesame Breadsticks

MAKES about 16 breadsticks
PREP 25 minutes **RISE** about 2 hours
BAKE at 425° for 12 to 15 minutes

1   teaspoon honey
1   cup warm water (105° to 115°)
1   envelope active dry yeast
1½   cups bread flour
1½   cups all-purpose flour
1   teaspoon sugar
1   teaspoon salt
¼   cup plus 1 tablespoon sesame seeds, toasted (see page 232)
2   tablespoons dark Asian sesame oil
     Cornmeal for dusting baking sheet
1   egg white, lightly beaten
1   teaspoon coarse salt

1. Mix honey and ¼ cup warm water in a small bowl. Sprinkle yeast over top. Let stand until foamy, 5 to 10 minutes.

2. Combine bread flour, all-purpose flour, sugar, salt and ¼ cup toasted sesame seeds in a large bowl. Stir in yeast mixture, remaining ¾ cup warm water and sesame oil. Stir until dough pulls away from sides of bowl.

3. Turn out dough onto a lightly floured surface. Knead until smooth and elastic, 8 to 10 minutes, adding more flour as needed to prevent sticking. Place in a greased large bowl, turning to coat. Cover with a clean kitchen towel or plastic wrap. Let rise in a warm place until doubled in volume, 45 minutes to 1 hour.

4. Punch down dough. Let rest 5 minutes. Meanwhile, dust 2 baking sheets with cornmeal.

5. Turn out dough onto a lightly floured surface. Roll into a 16 x 9-inch rectangle. Using a pizza cutter or sharp knife, cut dough crosswise into sixteen 1-inch-wide strips. Transfer dough strips to prepared baking sheets, placing about 1 inch apart.

6. Brush dough strips with egg white. Sprinkle with salt and remaining tablespoon of sesame seeds. Cover with a clean dish towel. Let rise in a warm place until doubled in volume, 45 minutes to 1 hour.

7. Heat oven to 425°. Bake breadsticks 12 to 15 minutes or until surface is golden and hard. Serve warm.

PER BREADSTICK
116 calories, 3 g fat (0 g saturated), 4 g protein, 19 g carbohydrate, 1 g fiber, 255 mg sodium, 0 mg cholesterol.

Old-Fashioned Crumb Buns

MAKES 16 servings **PREP** 30 minutes
RISE 2½ to 3 hours
BAKE at 375° for 30 minutes

¼   cup milk
⅓   cup solid vegetable shortening
¼   cup granulated sugar
½   teaspoon salt
¼   cup warm water (105° to 115°)
1   envelope active dry yeast
2   eggs, lightly beaten
2½ cups all-purpose flour

Topping

2   cups all-purpose flour
1   cup packed light-brown sugar
1   teaspoon ground cinnamon
¼   teaspoon ground nutmeg
¼   teaspoon salt
1   cup (2 sticks) butter, melted
¼   cup confectioners' sugar for dusting

1. Heat milk, shortening, granulated sugar and salt in a small saucepan over medium heat just until shortening is melted. Let mixture cool until lukewarm.

2. Meanwhile, pour warm water into a large bowl. Sprinkle yeast over top. Let stand until foamy, about 5 minutes. Stir to dissolve yeast. Add cooled milk mixture, eggs and ½ cup flour. Beat with a wooden spoon until smooth. Stir in remaining flour until dough comes together. Turn out onto a floured surface. Knead 5 minutes or until smooth and silky.

3. Place dough in a greased large bowl, turning to coat. Cover; let rise in a warm place until doubled in volume, 1½ to 2 hours.

4. Coat a 13 x 9 x 2-inch baking pan with nonstick cooking spray. Punch down dough. Press into pan; cover. Let rise 1 hour or until almost doubled in volume.

5. Heat oven to 375°.

6. Prepare topping: Whisk flour, brown sugar, cinnamon, nutmeg and salt in a medium-size bowl. Stir in melted butter until mixture is crumbly. Crumble topping evenly over dough in pan.

7. Bake in heated 375° oven 30 minutes or until a knife inserted in center comes out clean and crumbs are lightly brown and crisp. Cool in pan on rack 30 minutes. Sprinkle with confectioners' sugar. Cut into 16 squares. Serve warm or at room temperature.

PER SERVING
350 calories, 17 g fat (9 g saturated), 5 g protein, 45 g carbohydrate, 1 g fiber, 127 mg sodium, 58 mg cholesterol.

**PANTRY PLUS:
THE LOWDOWN ON YEAST**

This so-called magic ingredient comes in several varieties. Here is a helpful primer:

- Active dry yeast is generally dissolved in warm water (105° to 115°, comfortably warm to the touch) and then added to other ingredients. It can also be used in the same way as fast-acting yeast.

- Fast-acting yeast is generally mixed dry with other dry ingredients. The liquid added to these must be very warm (120° to 130°) but not hot enough to burn your skin.

- Bread-machine yeast should not be dissolved before use. Follow instructions on the label.

Cheese-Filled Crowns

MAKES 16 crowns **PREP** 25 minutes
RISE 1¼ hours **REFRIGERATE** 45 minutes
BAKE at 350° for 15 to 20 minutes

Dough

½ cup warm water (105° to 115°)
¼ cup plus 2 teaspoons maple syrup
2 envelopes active dry yeast
6 tablespoons butter, melted
1 whole egg
¼ cup sweetened dried cranberries, chopped
3 to 3¼ cups bread flour
1½ teaspoons salt

Filling

4 ounces berry-flavored cream cheese (½ cup)
1 tablespoon berry preserves
3 tablespoons all-purpose flour
1 egg yolk
1 teaspoon vanilla
   Pinch ground nutmeg
¼ cup chopped pecans

Topping

1 teaspoon sugar
¼ teaspoon ground cinnamon

1. Prepare dough: Mix warm water and 2 teaspoons maple syrup in a small bowl. Sprinkle yeast over top. Let stand until foamy, 5 to 10 minutes.

2. Combine remaining ¼ cup maple syrup, butter, whole egg, cranberries, 2 cups flour and salt in a large bowl. Add yeast mixture. Beat with mixer on medium speed 3 minutes or until well combined. Stir in enough of remaining flour to make a soft dough.

3. Turn out dough onto a lightly floured surface. Knead until smooth and elastic, 5 to 8 minutes, adding more flour as needed to prevent sticking. Place in a greased large bowl, turning to coat. Cover with a clean kitchen towel or plastic wrap. Let rise in a warm place until doubled in volume, about 1¼ hours.

4. Punch down dough. Let rest 5 minutes.

5. Meanwhile, prepare filling: Beat cream cheese, preserves, flour, egg yolk, vanilla and nutmeg in a small bowl until smooth.

6. Turn out dough onto a floured surface. Flour a rolling pin and roll out dough into a 16 x 11-inch rectangle. Spread filling over dough, leaving a 1-inch border. Sprinkle with pecans. Roll up from a long side. Cover with greased plastic wrap. Refrigerate 15 minutes to firm slightly.

7. Meanwhile, grease 16 cups in 2 standard 12-muffin pans.

8. Cut chilled roll into 16 equal slices. Place each slice, cut side up, in a greased muffin cup. Using kitchen shears held point down, cut each slice into quarters; spread dough pieces apart with your fingertips. Cover pans. Let rise until doubled in volume, 25 to 30 minutes.

9. Heat oven to 350°.

10. Prepare topping: Mix sugar and cinnamon. Sprinkle over crowns.

11. Bake in heated 350° oven 15 to 20 minutes or until golden brown. Transfer pan to a wire rack to cool slightly, about 10 minutes. Remove crowns from pan and serve warm.

PER CROWN
192 calories, 8 g fat (4 g saturated), 4 g protein, 26 g carbohydrate, 1 g fiber, 228 mg sodium, 44 mg cholesterol.

Chocolate and Peanut Butter Bread

MAKES 1 round loaf (24 slices)
PREP 25 minutes **RISE** 1¼ hours
BAKE at 375° for 30 to 35 minutes

¾ **cup warm water (105° to 115°)**
⅓ **cup plus 2 teaspoons sugar**
2 **envelopes active dry yeast**
¼ **cup creamy peanut butter**
2 **tablespoons butter, at room temperature**
1 **egg**
3 **to 3¼ cups bread flour**
1 **teaspoon salt**
26 **mini chocolate–peanut butter cups**
1 **tablespoon milk**

1. Mix together warm water and 2 teaspoons sugar in a small bowl. Sprinkle yeast over top. Let stand until foamy, 5 to 10 minutes.

2. Mix together peanut butter, butter, egg, 2 cups flour, salt and remaining ⅓ cup sugar in a large bowl. Add yeast mixture. Beat with a mixer on medium speed 3 minutes or until well combined. Stir in 1 cup flour or more as needed for dough to come together.

3. Turn out dough onto a lightly floured surface. Knead until smooth and elastic, about 8 minutes, adding more flour as needed to prevent sticking. Place in a greased bowl, turning to coat. Cover with a clean kitchen towel or plastic wrap. Let rise in a warm place until doubled in volume, about 1¼ hours.

4. Punch down dough. Let rest 5 minutes. Turn out onto a floured surface. Gently roll or pat into a 9-inch square. With a sharp knife or pizza cutter, cut into 36 equal squares (6 across by 6 down).

5. Unwrap 18 mini peanut butter cups. Cut each in half. Grease a 6-cup bundt pan or 9-inch round layer-cake pan.

6. Enclose each peanut butter cup half in a dough square, pinching dough edges together to seal and form a ball. Place balls, smooth side down, in bottom of prepared pan; add balls in layers until all are used.

7. Place pan in cold oven. Turn oven on to 375°. Bake 30 to 35 minutes or until top of bread is golden and puffed. Immediately remove bread from pan; cool on a wire rack.

8. Meanwhile, unwrap remaining 8 mini peanut butter cups. Melt in a small saucepan over very low heat. Stir in milk until smooth. Drizzle over bread.

9. To serve, cut bread into slices or pull pieces apart.

PER SLICE
137 calories, 5 g fat (2 g saturated), 4 g protein, 20 g carbohydrate, 1 g fiber, 130 mg sodium, 12 mg cholesterol.

Cherry-Nut Mini Loaves

MAKES 3 mini loaves (8 slices each)
PREP 15 minutes
BAKE at 350° for 30 to 40 minutes

1 **package (3 ounces) dried tart cherries (¾ cup)**
½ **cup brandy**
2¼ **cups all-purpose flour**
1 **teaspoon baking soda**
1 **teaspoon baking powder**
½ **teaspoon salt**
½ **teaspoon ground allspice**
2 **eggs**
¾ **cup granulated sugar**

¼ **cup packed light-brown sugar**
½ **cup buttermilk**
¼ **cup vegetable oil**
¾ **cup walnuts, coarsely chopped**
Confectioners' sugar for dusting
(optional)

1. Heat cherries and brandy in a small saucepan over low heat just until mixture starts to simmer. Remove from heat; let stand 5 minutes to allow cherries to soften.

2. Heat oven to 350°. Coat 3 miniature loaf pans, 6 x 3 x 2 inches each, with nonstick cooking spray. (See note.)

3. Mix together flour, baking soda, baking powder, salt and allspice in a large bowl.

4. Beat eggs, granulated sugar and brown sugar in a medium-size bowl on high speed until well blended. On low speed, beat in buttermilk and oil.

5. Stir egg mixture into flour mixture until moistened and batter just comes together. Do not overmix. Fold in walnuts and cherries with soaking liquid. Divide batter equally among prepared pans.

6. Bake in heated 350° oven 30 to 40 minutes or until a wooden pick inserted in centers comes out clean. Let loaves cool in pans on a wire rack 10 minutes. Turn out onto rack to cool completely.

7. Dust loaves with confectioners' sugar if desired.

Note: If you prefer, make one 9 x 5 x 3-inch loaf; bake in heated 350° oven about 1 hour.

PER SLICE
137 calories, 5 g fat (1 g saturated), 3 g protein, 21 g carbohydrate, 1 g fiber, 129 mg sodium, 18 mg cholesterol.

Banana-Coconut Loaf

MAKES 1 loaf (12 slices) **PREP** 15 minutes
BAKE at 350° for 1 hour 10 minutes

2 **cups all-purpose flour**
1 **teaspoon baking powder**
1 **teaspoon ground cinnamon**
½ **teaspoon baking soda**
½ **teaspoon salt**
2 **eggs**
¾ **cup sugar**
½ **cup vegetable oil**
¼ **cup buttermilk**
1 **cup mashed ripe banana**
1 **teaspoon vanilla**
⅔ **cup shredded sweetened flake coconut**
½ **cup pecan halves**
½ **cup semisweet chocolate chips**

1. Heat oven to 350°. Coat a 9 x 5 x 3-inch loaf pan with nonstick cooking spray.

2. Mix flour, baking powder, cinnamon, baking soda and salt in a large bowl.

3. Beat eggs and sugar in a medium-size bowl on high speed until blended. On low speed, beat in oil, buttermilk, banana and vanilla.

4. Stir egg mixture into flour mixture until moistened and batter just comes together. Do not overmix. Fold in ⅓ cup coconut, nuts and chocolate chips. Pour into prepared pan. Sprinkle with remaining ⅓ cup coconut.

5. Bake in heated 350° oven 1 hour 10 minutes or until a wooden pick inserted in center comes out almost clean. Let loaf cool in pan on a wire rack 10 minutes. Turn out onto rack to cool completely.

PER SLICE
321 calories, 17 g fat (4 g saturated), 4 g protein, 41 g carbohydrate, 2 g fiber, 201 mg sodium, 36 mg cholesterol.

Red-Pepper Corn Muffins

Cactus molds are an apt choice for this recipe, but the muffins taste just as good baked in standard pans.

MAKES 18 muffins **PREP** 15 minutes
COOK 1 to 2 minutes
BAKE at 400° for 18 minutes

¼	cup plus 1 tablespoon vegetable oil
1	sweet red pepper, cored, seeded and diced
2	teaspoons chopped fresh rosemary
1½	cups coarse yellow cornmeal
1½	cups all-purpose flour
1	tablespoon sugar
2	teaspoons salt
1	teaspoon baking soda
1	teaspoon baking powder
¼	teaspoon black pepper
2	eggs
2	cups buttermilk
1	cup shredded Jarlsberg cheese (4 ounces)

1. Heat oven to 400°. Coat 18 cups in standard 12-muffin pans or cast-iron cactus muffin pans with nonstick cooking spray.

2. Heat 1 tablespoon oil in a skillet over medium-high heat. Add sweet pepper and cook 1 minute or until softened. Add rosemary. Remove from heat.

3. Mix cornmeal, flour, sugar, salt, baking soda, baking powder and black pepper in a large bowl. Beat eggs, buttermilk and remaining ¼ cup oil in a small bowl.

4. Stir egg mixture into flour mixture until moistened and batter just comes together. Do not overmix. Fold in sweet pepper and cheese. Spoon a slightly rounded ¼ cup batter into each prepared muffin cup.

5. Bake in heated 400° oven 18 minutes (16 minutes if using cactus muffin pans) or until slightly crusty around edges. Let muffins cool in pans on wire racks 5 minutes. Serve warm.

PER MUFFIN
159 calories, 7 g fat (2 g saturated), 5 g protein, 20 g carbohydrate, 1 g fiber, 380 mg sodium, 30 mg cholesterol.

Jumbo Pumpkin-Pecan Muffins

MAKES 6 jumbo muffins **PREP** 15 minutes
BAKE at 375° for 28 to 30 minutes

2½ cups all-purpose flour
2 teaspoons pumpkin pie spice
1 teaspoon baking powder
1 teaspoon baking soda
½ teaspoon salt
2 eggs
½ cup granulated sugar
¼ cup packed light-brown sugar
1 cup canned pumpkin puree
(not pie filling)
½ cup buttermilk
¼ cup vegetable oil
1 teaspoon vanilla
½ cup pecans, coarsely chopped

Topping
¼ cup (½ stick) butter, at room
temperature
⅓ cup packed light-brown sugar
⅓ cup pecans, finely chopped
¼ cup all-purpose flour

1. Heat oven to 375°. Coat a jumbo 6-muffin pan with nonstick cooking spray.

2. Mix flour, pumpkin pie spice, baking powder, baking soda and salt in a large bowl.

3. Beat eggs, granulated sugar and brown sugar in a separate large bowl on high speed. On medium speed, beat in pumpkin, then buttermilk, oil and vanilla until smooth.

4. Stir egg mixture into flour mixture until moistened and batter just comes together. Do not overmix. Fold in

pecans. Spoon batter into muffin cups, dividing equally.

5. Prepare topping: Using a fork, mix butter, brown sugar, pecans and flour in a small bowl until crumbly. Sprinkle topping over batter in muffin cups, dividing equally.

6. Bake in heated 375° oven 28 to 30 minutes or until a wooden pick inserted in centers comes out clean. Let muffins cool in pan on a wire rack 5 minutes. Turn out onto rack to cool completely.

PER MUFFIN
635 calories, 31 g fat (7 g saturated), 11 g protein, 82 g carbohydrate, 4 g fiber, 503 mg sodium, 92 mg cholesterol.

speed until blended. On low speed, beat in milk and oil.

3. Stir egg mixture into flour mixture until moistened and batter just comes together. Do not overmix. Fold in apple and nuts. Spoon a rounded ¼ cup batter into each muffin cup.

4. Bake in heated 375° oven 20 minutes or until a wooden pick inserted in centers comes out clean. Let muffins cool in pan on a wire rack 5 minutes. Turn out onto rack to cool completely.

PER MUFFIN
220 calories, 9 g fat (1 g saturated), 5 g protein, 31 g carbohydrate, 1 g fiber, 199 mg sodium, 37 mg cholesterol.

Apple-Walnut Muffins

MAKES 12 muffins **PREP** 10 minutes
BAKE at 375° for 20 minutes

2 cups all-purpose flour
1 tablespoon baking powder
1 teaspoon ground cinnamon
½ teaspoon salt
2 eggs
¾ cup sugar
¼ cup plus 2 tablespoons milk
¼ cup vegetable oil
1 cup diced peeled apple
½ cup walnuts, coarsely chopped

1. Heat oven to 375°. Coat a standard 12-muffin pan with nonstick cooking spray.

2. Mix flour, baking powder, cinnamon and salt in a large bowl. Beat eggs and sugar in a medium-size bowl on high

Savory Cheddar Muffins

MAKES 12 muffins **PREP** 15 minutes
COOK 5 to 6 minutes
BAKE at 375° for 20 to 22 minutes

6 slices bacon, cut crosswise into ¼-inch-wide slices
4 scallions, chopped, including part of the green
2½ cups all-purpose flour
1 tablespoon plus 1 teaspoon sugar
1 tablespoon plus 1 teaspoon baking powder
1 teaspoon salt
¼ teaspoon ground red pepper (cayenne)
1 cup milk
1 egg
3 tablespoons vegetable oil
1 cup shredded sharp cheddar cheese (4 ounces)

1. Heat oven to 375°. Coat a standard 12-muffin pan with nonstick cooking spray.

2. Cook bacon in a large skillet over medium-high heat 3 to 4 minutes or

until almost crispy. Add scallions; cook 2 minutes or until softened.

3. Mix flour, sugar, baking powder, salt and red pepper in a large bowl. Beat milk and egg in a small bowl until well combined.

4. Make a well in center of flour mixture. Add bacon and scallion mixture with any bacon fat from skillet, then milk mixture, oil and cheese. Stir until flour mixture is moistened and batter just comes together. Spoon batter into muffin cups, dividing equally.

5. Bake in heated 375° oven 20 to 22 minutes or until golden brown. Let muffins cool in pan on a wire rack 2 minutes. Turn out onto rack; serve warm or allow to cool completely.

PER MUFFIN
243 calories, 13 g fat (4 g saturated), 9 g protein, 23 g carbohydrate, 1 g fiber, 532 mg sodium, 39 mg cholesterol.

Carrot Muffins

MAKES 12 muffins **PREP** 20 minutes
BAKE at 375° for 20 minutes

1½	cups all-purpose flour
½	cup whole-wheat flour
1	teaspoon baking soda
1	teaspoon ground cinnamon
½	teaspoon salt
⅛	teaspoon ground cloves
½	cup chopped walnuts
1	egg
½	cup sugar
¼	cup vegetable oil
½	teaspoon vanilla
1	cup unsweetened applesauce
1	cup grated carrots (8 ounces)
¼	cup golden raisins, chopped Cream Cheese Spread (right) for serving (optional)

1. Heat oven to 375°. Coat a standard 12-muffin pan with nonstick cooking spray.

2. Mix flours, baking soda, cinnamon, salt, cloves and nuts in a large bowl.

3. Beat egg and sugar in a medium-size bowl on high speed until blended. On low speed, beat in oil, then vanilla and applesauce.

4. Stir egg mixture into flour mixture until moistened and batter just comes together. Do not overmix. Fold in carrots and raisins. Spoon ⅓ cup batter into each muffin cup.

5. Bake in heated 375° oven 20 minutes or until a wooden pick inserted in centers comes out clean. Let muffins cool in pan on a wire rack 2 minutes. Turn out onto rack; serve warm or allow to cool completely. Serve with Cream Cheese Spread.

PER MUFFIN (with 2 tablespoons spread)
325 calories, 19 g fat (7 g saturated), 5 g protein, 36 g carbohydrate, 2 g fiber, 261 mg sodium, 49 mg cholesterol.

Cream Cheese Spread

Allow 1 package (8 ounces) cream cheese and ¼ cup (½ stick) butter to reach room temperature. Beat them together in a small bowl until smooth. Beat in ½ teaspoon vanilla. Gradually beat in ½ cup confectioners' sugar until fluffy.

MAKES about 1½ cups

PER 2 TABLESPOONS
117 calories, 10 g fat (7 g saturated), 2 g protein, 5 g carbohydrate, 0 g fiber, 56 mg sodium, 31 mg cholesterol.

Chocolate Chip Muffins

MAKES 12 muffins **PREP** 10 minutes
BAKE at 400° for 17 minutes

2	**cups all-purpose flour**
⅓	**cup packed light-brown sugar**
1	**tablespoon baking powder**
½	**teaspoon salt**
1	**cup skim milk**
¼	**cup jarred prune puree**
1	**egg**
½	**teaspoon vanilla**
2	**tablespoons butter, melted**
⅓	**cup mini semisweet chocolate chips**

1. Heat oven to 400°. Coat a standard 12-muffin pan with nonstick cooking spray.

2. Mix flour, sugar, baking powder and salt in a large bowl. Beat milk, prune puree, egg and vanilla in a medium-size bowl until blended.

3. Stir milk mixture into flour mixture until moistened and batter just comes together. Stir in butter and chocolate chips. Do not overmix. Spoon batter into muffin cups, dividing equally.

4. Bake in heated 400° oven 17 minutes. Transfer pan to a wire rack; cool muffins in pan 5 minutes. Serve warm.

PER MUFFIN
165 calories, 4 g fat (2 g saturated), 3 g protein, 29 g carbohydrate, 1 g fiber, 212 mg sodium, 23 mg cholesterol.

Chocolate-Zucchini Mini Muffins

MAKES 3 dozen mini muffins
PREP 15 minutes
BAKE at 375° for 20 minutes

1¾	**cups all-purpose flour**
½	**cup granulated sugar**
¼	**cup packed light-brown sugar**
3	**tablespoons unsweetened cocoa powder**
¾	**teaspoon baking powder**
½	**teaspoon baking soda**
½	**teaspoon salt**
2	**eggs**
¾	**cup vegetable oil**
1	**teaspoon vanilla**
1¼	**cups grated zucchini (about 8 ounces)**
½	**cup semisweet mini chocolate chips**
½	**cup unsalted dry-roasted peanuts, chopped**

Garnish (optional)

⅓	**cup semisweet mini chocolate chips**
¼	**teaspoon vegetable oil**
2	**tablespoons chopped unsalted dry-roasted peanuts**

1. Heat oven to 375°. Coat three 12-mini-muffin pans with nonstick cooking spray.

2. Sift flour, granulated sugar, brown sugar, cocoa powder, baking powder, baking soda and salt into a large bowl.

3. Beat eggs, oil and vanilla in a medium-size bowl until well combined. Stir in zucchini.

4. Stir egg mixture into flour mixture until moistened and a stiff batter just comes together. Do not overmix. Fold in chocolate chips and peanuts. Spoon 1 heaping tablespoon batter into each muffin cup.

5. Bake in heated 375° oven 20 minutes or until muffins are set. Let muffins cool in pans on a wire rack 5 minutes. Turn out onto rack to cool completely.

6. Prepare garnish if desired: Melt chocolate chips and oil in top of a double boiler over barely simmering, not boiling, water until smooth. Drizzle on muffin tops. Sprinkle with nuts.

PER MUFFIN
106 calories, 7 g fat (1 g saturated), 2 g protein, 11 g carbohydrate, 1 g fiber, 60 mg sodium, 12 mg cholesterol.

Banana-Pecan Waffles

MAKES 8 waffles (4-inch squares)
PREP 20 minutes
COOK 3 to 4 minutes per waffle

1¾ cups all-purpose flour
1 tablespoon sugar
½ teaspoon baking powder
½ teaspoon baking soda
½ teaspoon ground cinnamon
¼ teaspoon salt
¾ cup mashed banana
2 eggs
3 tablespoons butter or margarine, melted
1 cup buttermilk
1 teaspoon vanilla
½ cup finely chopped pecans

Toppings (optional)
   Butter
   Maple syrup
   Sliced bananas
   Chopped pecans

1. Heat a nonstick Belgian or standard waffle iron.

2. Combine flour, sugar, baking powder, baking soda, cinnamon and salt in a large bowl.

3. Beat together banana and eggs in a medium-size bowl. Beat in butter, buttermilk, vanilla and pecans.

4. Make a well in center of flour mixture. Add banana mixture to well, stirring quickly, just until blended.

5. Coat waffle iron with nonstick cooking spray. For each 4-inch waffle, spoon slightly rounded ⅓ cup batter onto hot iron, quickly spreading to cover entire surface. Cook according to manufacturer's instructions.

6. Serve waffles hot with an assortment of desired toppings.

PER WAFFLE
245 calories, 11 g fat (4 g saturated), 6 g protein, 31 g carbohydrate, 2 g fiber, 218 mg sodium, 66 mg cholesterol.

Green Salad with Walnut Vinaigrette

MAKES 6 servings **PREP** 15 minutes

Walnut Vinaigrette
¼   **cup balsamic vinegar**
¼   **cup raspberries**
2   **rounded tablespoons walnut pieces**
2   **teaspoons minced fresh parsley**
1   **teaspoon sugar**
½   **teaspoon black pepper**
½   **teaspoon salt**
½   **cup canola oil**
½   **cup walnut oil**

Salad
8   **cups assorted baby salad greens**
½   **cup cherry tomatoes**
½   **cup raspberries**
½   **cup walnuts, toasted (see page 232)**

1. Prepare vinaigrette: Place vinegar, raspberries, walnuts, parsley, sugar, pepper and salt in a food processor; whirl to combine. With machine running, slowly add oils until combined.

2. Prepare salad: Place greens on 6 plates; top with tomatoes and raspberries. Drizzle each serving with 2 tablespoons dressing. Sprinkle with toasted walnuts.

PER SERVING
421 calories, 43 g fat (4 g saturated), 3 g protein, 9 g carbohydrate, 3 g fiber, 199 mg sodium, 0 mg cholesterol.

Spinach-Tabbouleh-Stuffed Tomatoes

MAKES 6 servings **PREP** 15 minutes
COOK 2 minutes **STAND** 15 minutes

1   **cup water**
¾   **cup bulgur**
6   **ripe medium tomatoes**
½   **cup low-fat mayonnaise**
1   **tablespoon lemon juice**
¼   **teaspoon liquid hot-pepper sauce**
1   **bag (5 ounces) fresh baby spinach, washed and coarsely chopped**
2   **tablespoons chopped fresh mint**
½   **teaspoon salt**
2   **tablespoons pine nuts, toasted (see page 232)**
     Fresh mint sprigs for garnish (optional)

1. Bring water to boiling in a small saucepan. Add bulgur; stir. Remove from heat. Cover; let stand 15 minutes.

2. Slice ¼ inch from stem end of each tomato. Scoop out insides. Invert tomatoes on paper toweling to drain.

3. Meanwhile, whisk together mayonnaise, lemon juice and hot-

pepper sauce in a small bowl. Mix bulgur, spinach, mint and salt in a large bowl. Stir in mayonnaise mixture.

4. Fill each tomato with ½ cup bulgur mixture. Sprinkle with nuts. Garnish with mint sprigs if desired.

PER SERVING
148 calories, 4 g fat (0 g saturated), 5 g protein, 26 g carbohydrate, 5 g fiber, 413 mg sodium, 0 mg cholesterol.

Double Nutty Salad

MAKES 8 servings **PREP** 30 minutes
STAND 1 hour **REFRIGERATE** 1 hour

1½ cups bulgur
    Warm water
¼   cup lemon juice
1   large apple, cored and coarsely chopped (2 cups)
1   large cucumber, peeled, halved lengthwise, seeded and coarsely chopped (1⅓ cups)
1   small sweet green pepper, cored, seeded and chopped (1 cup)
1   cup coarsely chopped walnuts, toasted (see page 232)
½   cup coarsely chopped cashews
1   medium tomato, chopped
½   cup chopped scallions, including part of the green
½   cup chopped fresh parsley
½   cup chopped fresh mint
¼   cup olive oil
1½ teaspoons salt
¼   teaspoon ground black pepper
    Romaine lettuce leaves

Garnishes (optional)
    Fresh mint sprigs
    Walnuts

1. Mix bulgur with enough warm water to cover in a medium-size bowl; stir.

Drain bulgur in a fine-mesh sieve. Repeat rinsing and draining. Return bulgur to bowl. Cover with warm water. Let stand 1 hour.

2. In another large bowl, drizzle lemon juice over apple; gently toss to coat apple. Add cucumber, green pepper, walnuts, cashews, tomato, scallions, parsley, mint, oil, salt and pepper; gently stir to mix well.

3. Drain bulgur, gently squeezing out excess water. Add to apple mixture in bowl; stir to combine well. Cover bowl and refrigerate at least 1 hour or until thoroughly chilled.

4. Arrange lettuce on a platter or individual plates. Top with bulgur salad. Garnish with mint sprigs and walnuts if desired.

PER SERVING
326 calories, 21 g fat (3 g saturated), 8 g protein, 33 g carbohydrate, 7 g fiber, 466 mg sodium, 0 mg cholesterol.

Italian Tomato Salad

MAKES 8 servings **PREP** 8 minutes
REFRIGERATE 1 hour or overnight

- 2 **pounds tomatoes, diced**
- 1 **Italian sweet frying pepper, seeded and thinly sliced**
- 3 **cloves garlic, sliced**
- ¼ **cup extra-virgin olive oil**
- ¾ **teaspoon salt**
- ¼ **teaspoon black pepper**
- ¼ **teaspoon crushed red-pepper flakes**

Mix together tomatoes, frying pepper, garlic, oil, salt, black pepper and red-pepper flakes in a large bowl. Cover and refrigerate 1 hour or overnight.

PER SERVING
88 calories, 7 g fat (1 g saturated), 1 g protein, 6 g carbohydrate, 2 g fiber, 230 mg sodium, 0 mg cholesterol.

Carrot Salad

Shown on pages 3 and 103.

MAKES 6 servings **PREP** 5 minutes
REFRIGERATE 2 hours or overnight

- ¼ **cup olive oil**
- 2 **tablespoons lemon juice**
- 1 **tablespoon chopped fresh parsley**
- 1 **teaspoon Dijon mustard**
- 1 **teaspoon salt**
- ½ **teaspoon sugar**
- 1 **bag (10 ounces) shredded carrots**
- ½ **cup dried cranberries**
- 1 **small red onion, chopped**
- ½ **cup slivered almonds, toasted (see page 232)**

1. To make dressing, whisk together oil, lemon juice, parsley, mustard, salt and sugar in a small bowl until well blended.

2. Combine carrots, cranberries, onion and almonds in a large bowl. Add dressing. Cover and refrigerate 2 hours or overnight.

PER SERVING
208 calories, 15 g fat (2 g saturated), 3 g protein, 18 g carbohydrate, 3 g fiber, 395 mg sodium, 0 mg cholesterol.

Tangy Coleslaw

MAKES 12 servings **PREP** 15 minutes
REFRIGERATE 1 hour or overnight

- 1 **cup plain yogurt**
- 1 **cup mayonnaise**
- 1 **tablespoon cider vinegar**
- 2 **tablespoons sugar**
- 1 **teaspoon salt**
- ½ **teaspoon black pepper**
- ⅛ **teaspoon ground red pepper (cayenne)**
- 8 **cups shredded green cabbage**
- 2 **cups shredded red cabbage**
- 2 **large carrots, shredded**

Whisk yogurt, mayonnaise, vinegar, sugar, salt, black pepper and red pepper in a large bowl. Add green cabbage, red cabbage and carrots; stir until completely coated. Cover with plastic wrap. Refrigerate at least 1 hour or preferably overnight.

PER SERVING
175 calories, 15 g fat (2 g saturated), 2 g protein, 9 g carbohydrate, 2 g fiber, 311 mg sodium, 12 mg cholesterol.

Garlicky Spinach and Carrots

MAKES 8 servings **PREP** 15 minutes
COOK 20 minutes

2   tablespoons butter
1   tablespoon olive oil
4   large cloves garlic, finely chopped
5   carrots, shredded (about 2 cups)
2   teaspoons chicken-flavor bouillon
    granules
4   bags (6 ounces each) fresh baby
    spinach
¼   teaspoon salt
¼   teaspoon black pepper

1. Heat 1 tablespoon butter and oil in a large nonstick pot over medium-low heat. Add garlic; sauté 8 minutes, adjusting heat so as not to burn garlic.

2. Adjust heat to medium-high. Add carrots and bouillon granules; cook 4 minutes or until carrots are almost tender. Add spinach, salt and pepper; cook, stirring, 6 to 8 minutes or until spinach is tender but not overcooked. Stir in remaining 1 tablespoon butter.

PER SERVING
72 calories, 5 g fat (2 g saturated), 2 g protein,
6 g carbohydrate, 2 g fiber, 348 mg sodium,
8 mg cholesterol.

Green Bean, Potato and Tomato Medley

MAKES 8 servings **PREP** 15 minutes
COOK 25 minutes

1   pound small red new potatoes,
    scrubbed and halved
1   pound green beans, trimmed
1   tablespoon olive oil
1   medium onion, chopped
2   tomatoes, seeded and chopped
1   tablespoon tomato paste
1   teaspoon salt
¼   teaspoon black pepper

1. Cook potatoes in a medium-size pot of lightly salted boiling water 10 minutes or until almost tender. Add green beans; cook 6 to 7 minutes or until potatoes and beans are tender. Drain. Transfer to a serving bowl.

2. Meanwhile, heat oil in a small skillet over medium-high heat. Add onion; cook 3 minutes or until softened. Add tomatoes; cook 3 minutes. Stir in tomato paste; cook 1 minute. Add salt and pepper.

3. Add onion mixture to potatoes and beans; stir together.

PER SERVING
81 calories, 2 g fat (0 g saturated), 3 g protein,
14 g carbohydrate, 3 g fiber, 880 mg sodium,
0 mg cholesterol.

Harvest Stir-Fry

MAKES 4 servings **PREP** 30 minutes
COOK about 14 minutes

Sauce

⅓   cup reduced-sodium soy sauce
2   tablespoons honey
2   tablespoons rice-wine vinegar
1   clove garlic, chopped
1   teaspoon dark Asian sesame oil
     (optional)
¼   teaspoon ground ginger
2   tablespoons canola oil

Stir-Fry

1   tablespoon canola oil
1   small onion, chopped
2   cups broccoli flowerets

4   small summer squash (about
     1 pound 10 ounces), trimmed,
     halved lengthwise and cut
     crosswise into ¼-inch-thick slices
1   sweet red pepper, cored, seeded
     and sliced
⅓   pound green beans, trimmed and
     cut into 1-inch pieces (1 cup)
1   cup chopped arugula leaves
     (about ¼ pound)
1   cup thickly sliced bok choy
     (about ¼ pound) or thickly sliced
     celery ribs
½   pound angel hair pasta
2   tablespoons sesame seeds, toasted
     (see page 232)

1. Prepare sauce: Stir together soy
    sauce, honey, vinegar, garlic, sesame
    oil, if using, and ginger in a small
    bowl. Whisk in canola oil.

2. Prepare stir-fry: Heat oil in a large
    nonstick skillet over medium-high
    heat. Add onion; sauté 2 minutes. Add
    broccoli, squash, red pepper, green
    beans and ½ cup sauce; cook 3 to
    5 minutes. Add arugula and bok choy;
    stir until wilted. Add remaining sauce.
    Bring to boiling; cover and cook until
    beans and broccoli are tender, about
    7 minutes.

3. Meanwhile, cook pasta in a large pot
    of lightly salted boiling water until
    al dente, firm but tender. Drain well.
    Return to pot. Add vegetables and
    toss to combine. Sprinkle sesame
    seeds over each serving.

PER SERVING
459 calories, 14 g fat (1 g saturated), 14 g protein,
73 g carbohydrate, 11 g fiber, 734 mg sodium,
0 mg cholesterol.

Vegetable Mixed Grill with Romesco Sauce

The mixed grill includes 4 tomatoes to be used in the Romesco sauce.

MAKES 8 servings **PREP** 15 minutes
GRILL OR BROIL 10 to 12 minutes

Vegetable Mixed Grill

¼   cup extra-virgin olive oil
1   teaspoon salt
1   teaspoon black pepper
8   plum tomatoes (about 1½ pounds), halved
4   zucchini (about 1½ pounds), halved
2   sweet red peppers, cored, seeded and quartered
2   sweet yellow peppers, cored, seeded and quartered
4   Belgian endives, cored and halved lengthwise
1   pound asparagus, tough ends trimmed and stems peeled
1   pound large mushrooms, stemmed
2   tablespoons balsamic vinegar

Romesco Sauce

¼   cup whole blanched almonds, toasted (see page 232)
1   slice white bread, toasted and torn into pieces
1   large clove garlic, peeled
8   grilled tomato halves (from Vegetable Mixed Grill, above)
1   tablespoon sherry vinegar
2   tablespoons extra-virgin olive oil
½   teaspoon salt
¼   teaspoon black pepper

1. Prepare a charcoal grill with hot coals, setting rack 6 inches from coals; or heat a gas grill to high; or heat broiler.

2. Prepare mixed grill: Mix oil, salt and pepper in a large bowl. Add vegetables; toss to coat well.

3. Grill or broil vegetables, working in batches if necessary, 5 to 6 minutes per side or until cooked through. Transfer vegetables to a serving platter, reserving 8 tomato halves for Romesco sauce. Sprinkle balsamic vinegar over vegetables while still hot.

4. Prepare sauce: Place almonds, bread and garlic in a food processor. Whirl until almonds are ground. Add reserved grilled tomatoes, sherry vinegar, oil, salt and pepper. Whirl until you have a thick paste.

5. Serve vegetables with sauce on the side.

Note: Sauce can be covered and stored in refrigerator up to 1 day. Let come to room temperature before serving.

PER SERVING
163 calories, 8 g fat (1 g saturated), 6 g protein, 20 g carbohydrate, 6 g fiber, 252 mg sodium, 0 mg cholesterol.

Grilled Corn with Chili Butter

MAKES 8 servings **PREP** 10 minutes
BAKE at 450° for 45 minutes
OR GRILL for 15 to 20 minutes

4 tablespoons butter, softened
Juice of 1 lime
1¼ teaspoons chili powder
¾ teaspoon salt
¼ teaspoon ground red pepper (cayenne)
8 ears fresh corn, shucked

1. Heat oven to 450°; or prepare a charcoal grill with medium-hot coals, setting rack 6 inches from coals; or heat a gas grill to medium-high.

2. Stir together butter, lime juice, chili powder, salt and red pepper in a small bowl until smooth and thoroughly combined. Generously coat each ear of corn with chili butter. Securely wrap each in foil.

3. Roast in heated 450° oven 45 minutes or until tender. Or grill 15 to 20 minutes, turning occasionally.

PER SERVING
172 calories, 7 g fat (4 g saturated), 4 g protein, 29 g carbohydrate, 4 g fiber, 227 mg sodium, 16 mg cholesterol.

Scalloped Corn

MAKES 12 servings **PREP** 10 minutes
BAKE at 350° for 90 minutes

2 cups fresh or frozen corn kernels
1 can (14¾ ounces) cream-style corn
1 container (8 ounces) French onion sour cream dip
1 egg, lightly beaten
1 box (8½ ounces) corn muffin mix
¼ cup (½ stick) butter or margarine, melted
1 jar (4 ounces) sliced sweet red pimientos, drained and chopped
¼ teaspoon ground red pepper (cayenne)
¾ teaspoon salt
¼ teaspoon black pepper

1. Heat oven to 350°. Coat a deep 8-cup casserole with nonstick cooking spray.

2. Mix together corn kernels, cream-style corn, sour cream dip, egg, muffin mix and butter in a large bowl. Fold in pimientos, red pepper, salt and black pepper. Scrape into prepared casserole.

3. Bake in heated 350° oven 90 minutes or until set and lightly golden. Serve immediately.

PER SERVING
206 calories, 10 g fat (5 g saturated), 4 g protein, 26 g carbohydrate, 2 g fiber, 579 mg sodium, 58 mg cholesterol.

Rich Whipped Potatoes

MAKES 12 servings **PREP** 10 minutes
COOK 25 to 30 minutes

2½ **pounds Yukon Gold potatoes, peeled and cut into eighths**
1   **cup heavy cream**
3   **tablespoons butter**
½   **teaspoon salt**
¼   **black pepper**
¼   **cup chopped fresh parsley**

1. Place potatoes in a large pot; cover with salted cold water. Bring to boiling over high heat. Reduce heat to medium; cook 25 to 30 minutes or until fork-tender. Drain.

2. Return potatoes to pot; cook over low heat 1 minute to dry out. Remove from heat.

3. Heat cream and butter in a small saucepan over medium heat until butter melts. Add salt and pepper. Add cream mixture to potatoes. Beat on low speed until fluffy, about 2 minutes. Stir in parsley.

PER SERVING
166 calories, 10 g fat (6 g saturated), 2 g protein, 17 g carbohydrate, 2 g fiber, 110 mg sodium, 35 mg cholesterol.

Mashed Potatoes

Shown on page 85.

MAKES 8 servings **PREP** 10 minutes
COOK 15 to 20 minutes

3   **pounds russet potatoes**
¾   **cup milk**
¼   **cup (½ stick) butter**
1½   **teaspoons salt**
¼   **teaspoon black pepper**
¼   **teaspoon ground nutmeg**
¼   **cup fresh parsley, chopped**

1. Peel potatoes; cut into 1-inch chunks. Place in a large pot with enough salted water to cover. Bring to boiling. Reduce heat; simmer 15 to 20 minutes or until knife-tender. Drain; place in a large bowl.

2. Add milk, butter, salt, pepper and nutmeg. Beat with a handheld mixer on low speed or use a potato masher. Stir in parsley.

PER SERVING
214 calories, 7 g fat (4 g saturated), 4 g protein, 36 g carbohydrate, 3 g fiber, 420 mg sodium, 19 mg cholesterol.

PANTRY PLUS: PERFECT POTATOES

For fluffy, flavorful mashed potatoes, choose russets—large and oblong, with coarse, dark skin, or Yukon gold potatoes—with buttery yellow to golden flesh and skin.

- Choose potatoes that are heavy for their size, with firm, clean, smooth skins. Avoid those that are sprouting, bruised, mushy in spots or dappled with green.

- Store potatoes in a well-ventilated, dark, cool spot for up to 2 months. Avoid moist warm areas such as under the sink.

Tomato–Herb Cheese Potatoes au Gratin

Shown on page 103.

MAKES 8 servings **PREP** 25 minutes
COOK 20 to 23 minutes
BAKE at 375° for 1 hour 10 minutes

1 tablespoon butter
2 small onions, thinly sliced
2½ pounds all-purpose potatoes, peeled and thinly sliced
1½ teaspoons salt
3 plum tomatoes, thinly sliced
2 cups shredded Gruyère or Swiss cheese (8 ounces)
2 cups half-and-half
3 tablespoons all-purpose flour
1 package (4.4 ounces) spreadable creamy herb cheese
¼ cup grated Parmesan cheese
½ teaspoon black pepper

1. Heat oven to 375°. Coat a 2½-quart baking dish with nonstick cooking spray.

2. Melt butter in a medium-size skillet over medium heat. Add onions; cook, stirring occasionally, until softened and lightly browned, 12 to 15 minutes.

3. Spread one-third of potato slices in a single layer, slightly overlapping, in bottom of prepared dish. Sprinkle with ¼ teaspoon salt. Layer with half of sliced tomatoes. Top with half of onions, then half of Gruyère. Continue layering with another third of potatoes, sprinkling with ¼ teaspoon salt, remaining tomato slices, onions and Gruyère. Layer remaining third of potatoes on top.

4. Whisk together half-and-half and flour in medium-size saucepan. Cook over medium-high heat, stirring constantly, just until warmed through, about 8 minutes. Remove from heat. Whisk in remaining 1 teaspoon salt, herb cheese, 2 tablespoons Parmesan and pepper. Pour over layered potato mixture in dish. Cover with aluminum foil.

5. Bake in heated 375° oven 40 minutes, placing a baking sheet underneath to catch drips. Remove foil from dish. Sprinkle casserole with remaining 2 tablespoons Parmesan. Bake, uncovered, 30 minutes longer, until top is browned and potatoes are knife-tender. Remove from oven and let stand 15 minutes before serving.

PER SERVING
390 calories, 24 g fat (14 g saturated), 15 g protein, 31 g carbohydrate, 2 g fiber, 718 mg sodium, 81 mg cholesterol.

Cabbage Casserole

MAKES 6 servings **PREP** 10 minutes
COOK 20 minutes
BAKE at 325° for 30 minutes

½ cup (1 stick) butter
1 medium head green cabbage (about 2½ pounds), cored and thinly sliced
1 large onion, finely chopped
1½ cups milk
4 eggs, lightly beaten
15 saltines, finely crushed (about ¾ cup)
1 teaspoon salt
¼ teaspoon black pepper

1. Heat oven to 325°. Butter a shallow 10-cup casserole.

2. Melt butter in a large pot over medium heat. Add cabbage and onion; cook until softened, about 20 minutes.

3. Stir milk into cabbage mixture; bring to boiling. Lower heat to medium-low; simmer 5 minutes. Remove pot from heat. Let cool slightly.

4. Gently stir in eggs. Add ½ cup crushed crackers, salt and pepper. Pour into prepared casserole. Sprinkle remaining ¼ cup crackers evenly on top.

5. Bake in heated 325° oven 30 minutes or until heated through and top is golden brown.

PER SERVING
260 calories, 20 g fat (11 g saturated), 7 g protein, 15 g carbohydrate, 4 g fiber, 542 mg sodium, 183 mg cholesterol.

Old-Fashioned Baked Beans

MAKES 12 servings **PREP** 10 minutes
BAKE at 350° for 3½ hours
STAND about 45 minutes

6 **slices thick-cut smoked bacon, 3 slices cut crosswise into slivers**
6 **cans (15½ ounces each) pinto beans, drained and rinsed**
1½ **cups ketchup**
1 **cup water**
1 **large onion, chopped**
¼ **cup molasses**
¼ **cup packed dark-brown sugar**
2 **tablespoons spicy brown mustard**
3 **teaspoons salt**
1 **teaspoon dried thyme**
1 **teaspoon liquid hot-pepper sauce**
½ **teaspoon black pepper**

1. Heat oven to 350°. Coat a 13 x 9 x 2-inch baking dish or a 4-quart casserole with nonstick cooking spray.

2. Combine bacon slivers, beans, ketchup, water, onion, molasses, brown sugar, mustard, salt, thyme, hot-pepper sauce and black pepper in a large bowl. Spoon bean mixture into prepared baking dish, spreading evenly. Arrange remaining 3 bacon slices on top. Cover dish with foil.

3. Bake in heated 350° oven 3½ hours. Remove dish from oven; let stand before serving until thickened, about 45 minutes.

Note: Recipe can be prepared a day ahead through step 2. Refrigerate until ready to bake and then allow extra baking time.

PER SERVING
133 calories, 2 g fat (1 g saturated), 4 g protein, 25 g carbohydrate, 2 g fiber, 1,180 mg sodium, 5 mg cholesterol.

PANTRY PLUS: DRIED BEAN PREP

If you wish to cook dried beans to use in recipes calling for canned, follow these steps.

• Pick beans over, discarding shriveled ones and bits of dirt. Rinse well. Place in a bowl with enough cold water to cover by 2 inches. Soak 8 hours or overnight.

• Discard soaking water; rinse beans well.

• Place drained beans in a large pot; add enough water to cover by 1 inch. Add any seasonings. DO NOT ADD SALT; it will toughen beans. Add salt after cooked beans become tender.

• Bring beans slowly to boiling; remove any scum that rises to top. Simmer, covered, for time indicated on package; add more water as needed.

• Cooked beans should be tender to the bite, but still firm enough to hold their shape.

CRAN-APPLE PIE (PAGE 151)

Desserts

Banana Shortcakes

These fruit-laced biscuits layered with chocolate ice cream and banana coins are a scrumptious twist on the strawberry classic.

MAKES 8 shortcakes **PREP** 35 minutes
BAKE at 425° for 15 to 20 minutes
FREEZE at least 4 hours

Ice Cream

1   quart chocolate ice cream
2   firm bananas, peeled, quartered lengthwise and chopped
½   cup walnuts, chopped

Shortcake

2½   cups buttermilk baking mix
½   cup milk
¼   cup semisweet mini chocolate chips
¼   cup sugar
2   ripe bananas, mashed (about 1 cup)
¼   cup walnuts, chopped
3   tablespoons butter, melted

Garnishes (optional)

Whipped cream or nondairy whipped topping
Chopped walnuts

1. Prepare ice cream: Let ice cream soften in a medium-size bowl 15 minutes or until it can be stirred. Stir in chopped bananas and walnuts. Cover with plastic wrap and freeze at least 4 hours or until ready to serve.

2. Prepare shortcake: Heat oven to 425°.

3. Stir together baking mix, milk, chocolate chips, sugar, mashed bananas, walnuts and melted butter in a large bowl. Drop 8 heaping ¼ cupfuls onto an ungreased baking sheet; spread slightly.

4. Bake in heated 425° oven 15 to 20 minutes or until golden. Remove shortcakes to a wire rack to cool.

5. Split each shortcake in half horizontally. Sandwich each with about ½ cup ice cream. Dollop with whipped cream and sprinkle with chopped nuts if desired.

PER SHORTCAKE
519 calories, 27 g fat (11 g saturated), 8 g protein, 68 g carbohydrate, 3 g fiber, 532 mg sodium, 36 mg cholesterol.

Mint Chocolate Chip Cake

Transform a handful of supermarket basics into this rich, stunning masterpiece.

MAKES 16 servings **PREP** 20 minutes
ASSEMBLY 1 hour
FREEZE about 4 hours plus overnight

½   gallon mint chocolate chip ice cream
1   package (8½ ounces) fudge-covered creme-filled wafer cookies
1   jar (18 ounces) hot fudge topping
1   package (7 ounces) oval-shaped mint sandwich cookies
1   loaf marbled pound cake (12 ounces)

1. Place half of ice cream in a medium-size bowl; return remainder to freezer. Let ice cream in bowl soften slightly at room temperature, then stir until a spreadable consistency, similar to peanut butter. Line an 8 x 8 x 2-inch metal baking pan with plastic wrap. Spoon ice cream into pan, spreading evenly. Freeze 1 hour.

2. Crush 12 wafer cookies in a plastic bag. Transfer fudge topping to a microwave-safe bowl. Microwave at 100% power until heated through but not hot, about 30 seconds. Pour half of topping (about ¾ cup) into a small bowl; stir in crushed cookies.

3. Coat a 9 x 9 x 2-inch metal baking pan with nonstick cooking spray. Line bottom and sides with plastic wrap. Line bottom of pan with waxed paper; coat paper with spray. Line edges of pan with mint cookies and remaining wafer cookies, standing cookies on end and alternating them; 1 mint cookie will remain.

4. Pour fudge topping mixture into bottom of cookie-lined pan; spread evenly to touch standing cookies. Freeze 20 minutes or until topping is almost solid.

5. Place pound cake on its side on a cutting board, with top to your right. Using a long serrated knife, cut off top of cake to make a flat side; discard top or reserve for another purpose. Keep cake in same position and cut it lengthwise into 4 equal slices, each about ½ inch thick.

6. Remove both pans from freezer. Invert ice cream square into cookie-lined pan; remove plastic wrap; spread ice cream slightly toward edges. Freeze 45 minutes.

7. Arrange 2 cake slices, side by side, in pan on top of ice cream. Freeze 45 minutes.

8. Reheat remaining fudge topping in microwave oven at 100% power 15 to 20 seconds or until fluid but not hot. Spread over top of cake layer in pan. Freeze 45 minutes.

9. Remove remaining ice cream from freezer; transfer to a medium-size bowl and stir until spreadable. Spread over fudge topping layer in pan. Top with remaining cake. Cover with plastic wrap. Freeze overnight or until firm.

10. Remove plastic wrap from top of ice cream cake. Invert cake onto a platter. Remove pan, plastic wrap and waxed paper. Crumble last mint cookie; sprinkle on top of cake.

PER SERVING
545 calories, 25 g fat (14 g saturated), 7 g protein, 72 g carbohydrate, 2 g fiber, 370 mg sodium, 84 mg cholesterol.

Chocolate Chip Cake Hints

Remove plastic wrap after inverting frozen ice cream square into cookie-lined pan.

Arrange 2 cake slices, side by side, in pan on top of ice cream.

Golden Baked Alaska

For a homemade crust, prepare the dough for Chocolate Chip Sugar Cookies on page 202, adding ½ cup walnuts. Use half of the recipe, shaping into a disc and chilling 10 minutes. If making your own dough, skip step 4.

MAKES 8 servings **PREP** 20 minutes
FREEZE several hours or overnight
BAKE crust at 350° for 12 to 15 minutes; meringue at 475° for 2 to 4 minutes

Filling

1 **pint strawberry ice cream or frozen yogurt, softened**
1 **pint chocolate ice cream or frozen yogurt, softened**

Dough

9 **ounces (half of 18-ounce tube) refrigerated chocolate chip cookie dough**
¼ **cup finely chopped walnuts, toasted (see page 232)**

Meringue

⅓ **cup powdered egg whites (see page 232)**
⅔ **cup warm water**
½ **cup sugar**

1. Heat oven to 350°.
2. Prepare filling: Line a 1-quart round bowl with plastic wrap, leaving a generous overhang. Scoop strawberry ice cream into bowl; pack in and smooth top until level. Top with chocolate ice cream; pack and smooth. Fold overhanging plastic wrap over top of ice cream. Freeze several hours or overnight, until very firm.
3. Prepare dough: Line a baking sheet with aluminum foil; grease an area 8 inches in diameter in center.
4. Using a wooden spoon, work together dough and walnuts in a large bowl until blended. Shape dough into a disc. (If this makes dough too soft to work with, wrap it and return to refrigerator until firm, about 10 minutes.)
5. Place dough in center of greased foil. Pat with hands or roll with a floured rolling pin into 8-inch round. Bake in heated 350° oven 12 to 15 minutes or until cookie is lightly browned at edges. Transfer cookie, still on foil, to a wire rack to cool completely. Increase oven temperature to 475°.
6. Prepare meringue: Remove bowl with ice cream from freezer; let stand at room temperature while preparing

meringue. Stir dried egg whites into warm water in a small bowl to dissolve completely. Beat with a mixer on high speed until fluffy. Gradually add sugar, beating until meringue forms stiff peaks.

7. Loosen cookie from foil, then return to same piece of foil; transfer to an insulated baking sheet.

8. Lift ice cream from bowl with its plastic wrapping; it may be necessary to loosen sides by gently running a long, thin metal spatula between bowl and plastic wrap. Fold back plastic wrap from top of ice cream; invert ice cream onto center of cookie. Peel off plastic wrap. Completely cover ice cream with meringue, swirling to within ¼ inch of cookie edge.

9. Bake in heated 475° oven 2 to 4 minutes or until meringue is lightly browned. Using a wide spatula, gently slide Alaska from foil onto a serving platter. Serve immediately.

PER SERVING
356 calories, 15 g fat (7 g saturated), 5 g protein, 51 g carbohydrate, 1 g fiber, 116 mg sodium, 27 mg cholesterol.

Baked Alaska Technique

Fold back plastic wrap from flat side of molded ice cream. Then invert ice cream onto cookie. Peel off plastic wrap.

Peach Pie Ice Cream

Look for waffle bowls in the ice cream cone section of your supermarket.

MAKES 8 servings **PREP** 15 minutes
FREEZE 6 hours or overnight

1   **quart vanilla ice cream**
1¼   **cups frozen peach pieces, thawed**
⅓   **cup peach nectar**
     Pinch ground nutmeg
     Pinch ground cinnamon
¼   **cup pecans, coarsely chopped and toasted (see page 232)**
¾   **cup coarsely broken vanilla wafers (about 15 cookies)**
     Waffle bowls or ice cream cones for serving (optional)

1. Let ice cream soften slightly at room temperature. Place half of peach pieces in a blender. Pour peach nectar into a glass measure; stir in nutmeg and cinnamon. Add to blender, whirl to puree. Add ice cream. Pulse 6 to 8 times or until blended. Pour ice cream mixture into an 8 x 8 x 2-inch metal pan.

2. Finely dice remaining peach pieces. Stir diced peaches, pecans and cookie pieces into pan with ice cream mixture until well blended. Freeze until mixture is firm, about 6 hours or overnight. Serve in waffle bowls if desired.

PER SERVING
228 calories, 12 g fat (6 g saturated), 4 g protein, 25 g carbohydrate, 1 g fiber, 79 mg sodium, 25 mg cholesterol.

Chocolate-Cherry Sandwiches

MAKES 12 sandwiches **PREP** 25 minutes
BAKE at 350° for 10 minutes
FREEZE about 4 hours or overnight

- ½ **gallon cherry ice cream (in rectangular container)**
- 1 **box (about 18 ounces) chocolate cake mix**
- 2 **eggs**
- ½ **cup vegetable oil**
- 1 **jar (about 6 ounces) maraschino cherries, drained and chopped**
- ½ **teaspoon cherry extract**

1. Line a baking sheet with waxed paper.
2. Unwrap ice cream and place on a cutting board. Using a sharp knife, cut 6 lengthwise slices, each ½ inch thick. Place each slice on prepared baking sheet. Rewrap remaining ice cream and return to freezer. Cover baking sheet with plastic wrap and freeze 45 minutes or until firm.
3. Meanwhile, heat oven to 350°.
4. Stir together cake mix, eggs, oil, cherries and cherry extract in a large bowl until a stiff dough comes together. Divide into 24 pieces (about 1½ tablespoons each). Roll into balls. Place 3 inches apart on ungreased baking sheets, about 8 balls per sheet. Using bottom of a glass, flatten each ball into a 3-inch round; if dough is sticky, grease bottom of glass.
5. Bake cookies in heated 350° oven 10 minutes or until firm. Cool on baking sheet 2 minutes, then transfer to a wire rack to cool completely.
6. Remove ice cream slices from freezer; remove covering. Using a 3-inch round or scalloped cookie cutter, quickly cut 2 rounds out of each slice, for a total of 12 rounds. Place a cookie on a piece of plastic wrap. Using a spatula, transfer an ice cream round onto the cookie; top with another cookie. Enclose sandwich in plastic wrap. Repeat, making a total of 12 sandwiches. (If ice cream begins to melt, return baking sheet to freezer.) Freeze 3 hours or overnight.

PER SANDWICH
391 calories, 23 g fat (6 g saturated), 5 g protein, 46 g carbohydrate, 1 g fiber, 395 mg sodium, 59 mg cholesterol.

Neapolitan Pie

MAKES 12 servings **PREP** 20 minutes
BAKE at 375° for 15 to 18 minutes
FREEZE 4 hours or overnight

- 1 **tube (18 ounces) refrigerated chocolate chip cookie dough**
- ¼ **cup all-purpose flour**
- 1 **pint vanilla ice cream**
- 1 **pint chocolate ice cream**
- 1 **pint strawberry ice cream**
- ½ **cup strawberry jam**

1. Heat oven to 375°. Coat a 9-inch glass pie plate with nonstick cooking spray.
2. Set aside 1 cup cookie dough. Knead flour into remaining dough. Press dough over bottom and up sides of prepared pie plate. Prick all over with a fork. Line with foil; fill with dried beans or pie weights.

3. To prepare cookies, divide remaining 1 cup dough into 12 equal pieces (1 tablespoon each). Roll each into a ball. Place balls on an ungreased baking sheet.

4. Bake cookies and pie shell in heated 375° oven 10 minutes. Carefully remove aluminum foil and weights from pie shell. Bake cookies and pie shell another 5 to 8 minutes or until lightly browned. Remove to a wire rack, transferring cookies from baking sheet to rack; let cool completely.

5. Crush 4 cookies. Break remaining 8 cookies into halves or quarters. When pie shell has cooled, scoop half of each pint of ice cream into it, alternating colors and stacking as you go. Sprinkle crushed cookies on top. Continue scooping and stacking remaining ice cream. Tuck cookie pieces in between scoops. Cover loosely with plastic wrap. Freeze until firm, 4 hours or overnight.

6. Shortly before serving, gently heat jam in a small saucepan until spreadable (or heat in a small bowl in a microwave oven). Let cool to room temperature. Transfer to a small plastic food-storage bag. Snip off a corner; drizzle jam over pie. Or spoon jam over pie. Let pie stand at room temperature until easy to cut into serving pieces, about 10 minutes.

PER SERVING
368 calories, 16 g fat (8 g saturated), 5 g protein, 53 g carbohydrate, 1 g fiber, 130 mg sodium, 32 mg cholesterol.

Peanut Butter Chunk Ice Cream

MAKES 8 servings **PREP** 20 minutes
FREEZE 4 hours or overnight

¼ cup creamy or chunky peanut butter
2 tablespoons warm water
1 tablespoon corn syrup
1 quart vanilla ice cream
½ cup honey-roasted peanuts, coarsely chopped
6 chocolate chip cookies, crumbled
½ cup hot fudge topping
Chopped honey-roasted peanuts for garnish (optional)

1. Whisk together peanut butter, warm water and corn syrup in a small bowl.

2. Place ice cream in a large metal bowl. Let stand at room temperature 15 minutes to soften. Stir in peanut butter mixture, peanuts and cookie pieces. Freeze 1 hour or until consistency of very thick oatmeal.

3. Stir fudge sauce in a small bowl to loosen, or microwave at 100% power 15 seconds, until slightly thinned but not hot. Remove ice cream from freezer. Swirl in fudge. Freeze until firm, about 3 hours or overnight.

4. To serve, garnish with nuts if desired.

PER SERVING
351 calories, 18 g fat (8 g saturated), 8 g protein, 39 g carbohydrate, 2 g fiber, 216 mg sodium, 25 mg cholesterol.

constantly, until walnuts are fragrant and stick together in a thick, syrupy mixture. Immediately pour walnut mixture onto prepared baking sheet, spreading quickly with a metal spatula until as thin as possible. Cool at least 10 minutes.

3. Peel nuts away from foil. Divide walnut mixture in half. Coarsely chop one half of mixture; break other half into small pieces.

4. In 8 parfait glasses, arrange ingredients in layers as follows, dividing equally: half of pie filling, half of ice cream, chopped nuts, half of pie filling and half of ice cream. Sprinkle tops with remaining small pieces of nuts.

PER SERVING
322 calories, 18 g fat (7 g saturated), 4 g protein, 39 g carbohydrate, 2 g fiber, 134 mg sodium, 38 mg cholesterol.

Pumpkin Parfaits

MAKES 8 servings **PREP** 10 minutes
COOK about 5 minutes

2   tablespoons butter
¼   cup sugar
1   tablespoon dark corn syrup
1   cup walnut halves or pieces
1   can (15 ounces) pumpkin pie filling
1   quart vanilla ice cream

1. Line a small baking sheet with aluminum foil. Butter foil.

2. Heat together butter, sugar and corn syrup in a small saucepan over medium-low heat, stirring, until melted, smooth and bubbly. Stir in walnuts. Increase heat to medium-high; cook 3 to 5 minutes, stirring

Cool 'n' Creamy Coconut Sandwiches

MAKES 19 sandwiches **PREP** 10 minutes
FREEZE filling 1 hour; sandwiches 3 hours or overnight

1   pint vanilla frozen nonfat yogurt
¼   cup sweetened flake coconut
2   teaspoons coconut extract
38   chocolate wafer cookies
2   tablespoons sweetened flake coconut, toasted (see page 232)

1. Soften frozen yogurt in a medium-size freezer-proof bowl. Stir in ¼ cup coconut and coconut extract. Place in freezer until firm, about 1 hour.

2. Using a small melon-ball cutter or 1 rounded tablespoon, spoon frozen yogurt onto 19 chocolate wafers. Top each with another wafer. Roll edges in toasted coconut. Freeze 3 hours or overnight.

PER SANDWICH
80 calories, 2 g fat (1 g saturated), 2 g protein, 13 g carbohydrate, 0 g fiber, 99 mg sodium, 1 mg cholesterol.

Chocolate Almond Bars

MAKES 12 bars **PREP** 1 hour
FREEZE 5 hours

½ gallon premium coffee or vanilla ice cream (in rectangular container)

12 flat wooden sticks

1 cup whole almonds, toasted (see page 232)

2 pounds semisweet or bittersweet chocolate or a combination of both, chopped

3 tablespoons solid vegetable shortening

1. Line a baking sheet with waxed paper.

2. Unwrap ice cream and place on a cutting board. Cut block crosswise into thirds; rewrap two-thirds and return to freezer. Working quickly, cut ice cream on cutting board crosswise into 8 equal slices, each about ½ inch thick.

3. Using a spatula, transfer 4 ice cream slices to prepared baking sheet. Gently press a wooden stick lengthwise onto half of each piece,

extending one end for a handle. Top each piece with another ice cream piece to make a bar, lining up edges. Cover with waxed paper or plastic wrap. Place baking sheet in freezer. Repeat with each remaining third of ice cream and remaining 8 wooden sticks, transferring assembled bars to baking sheet in freezer. Freeze until firm but not solid, about 1 hour.

4. Finely chop almonds. Place in a pie plate. Using a spatula, remove bars, one at a time, from baking sheet and transfer to pie plate; press chopped nuts onto sides and edges. Return bars to baking sheet, placing under wrapping. Freeze until firm, about 2 hours.

5. Place chocolate and shortening in a microwave-safe shallow dish. Microwave at 100% power 2 minutes. Stir until mixture is blended and chocolate is completely melted. If chocolate is not completely melted, microwave 30 to 60 seconds more, then stir mixture again.

6. Remove wrapping from baking sheet in freezer. Remove bars from freezer, one at a time, and quickly dip into chocolate mixture; use a spoon or rubber spatula to coat any exposed nuts with chocolate. Return bars to baking sheet. Chocolate should harden almost immediately. Freeze 2 hours. Serve bars or store in plastic food-storage bags in freezer.

PER BAR
659 calories, 50 g fat (25 g saturated), 12 g protein, 58 g carbohydrate, 4 g fiber, 70 mg sodium, 33 mg cholesterol.

Chocolate Sauce

Melt 8 ounces semisweet chocolate, chopped, and 2 tablespoons butter in a small saucepan over medium heat, stirring until smooth. Slowly add 1 cup heavy cream, stirring until smooth and glossy. Remove from heat. Stir in ¾ teaspoon almond or vanilla extract.

MAKES 1¾ cups

PER TABLESPOON
76 calories, 7 g fat (4 g saturated), 1 g protein, 4 g carbohydrate, 0 g fiber, 4 mg sodium, 14 mg cholesterol.

Butterscotch Sauce

Combine ½ cup packed light-brown sugar, ½ cup corn syrup, 2 tablespoons butter, ⅛ teaspoon cinnamon and ⅛ teaspoon ginger in a small saucepan (not nonstick). Cook over medium heat, stirring occasionally, until sugar is dissolved, about 8 minutes. Increase heat to medium-high. Bring mixture just to boiling. Remove from heat. Stir in 2 tablespoons half-and-half. Serve warm or at room temperature.

MAKES 1¼ cups

PER TABLESPOON
56 calories, 1 g fat (1 g saturated), 0 g protein, 12 g carbohydrate, 0 g fiber, 13 mg sodium, 4 mg cholesterol.

Coconut Bonbons

MAKES 8 servings **PREP** 1 hour
COOK 1 minute **FREEZE** 2 hours

- **1   pint vanilla ice cream**
- **⅔   cup sweetened flake coconut, toasted (see page 232)**
- **⅔   cup cornflake crumbs**
- **¼   teaspoon ground cinnamon**
  Chocolate and Butterscotch Sauces (left)

1. Line 2 baking sheets with waxed paper. Scoop about 18 ice cream balls (about 1 heaping tablespoon each) onto 1 prepared baking sheet; cover with plastic wrap and place in freezer. Repeat with second baking sheet and remaining ice cream. Freeze 1 hour.

2. Mix coconut, cornflake crumbs and cinnamon in a plastic food-storage bag.

3. Remove 1 baking sheet from freezer. Transfer 9 ice cream balls to a shallow dish; place baking sheet with remaining balls in refrigerator. One at a time, place balls in bag with coconut mixture; shake to coat; press coating into sides, reshaping ball if necessary. As soon as each ball is coated, return it to baking sheet in refrigerator. Repeat with remaining 9 balls on baking sheet, then return baking sheet to freezer. Repeat with remaining 18 balls on second baking sheet. If balls begin to melt, return to freezer.

4. To serve, drizzle sauces on 8 dessert plates. Top each with 3 or 4 bonbons.

PER SERVING
131 calories, 6 g fat (4 g saturated), 2 g protein, 17 g carbohydrate, 0 g fiber, 121 mg sodium, 13 mg cholesterol.

Blackberry-Lime Sherbet

MAKES 6 cups **PREP** 30 minutes
FREEZE 4 to 6 hours

1½ cups sugar
1½ cups water
1   bag (12 ounces) frozen
     blackberries, thawed, or 2½ cups
     fresh blackberries
1   bag (12 ounces) frozen blueberries,
     thawed, or 2½ cups fresh
     blueberries
¼   cup fresh lime juice
     Red and blue liquid food colors
2   cups heavy cream or half-and-half
     Pinch salt
½   pint fresh blackberries for garnish

1. Combine sugar and water in a small
   saucepan; bring to boiling over high
   heat. Lower heat; simmer 6 minutes.
   Let syrup cool.

2. Puree blackberries and blueberries
   in a food processor (do not use a
   blender). Strain through a fine-mesh
   sieve into a medium-size bowl,
   forcing through with a rubber
   spatula; discard solids. Stir in lime
   juice and 5 drops each food color.

3. Add sugar syrup, cream and salt to
   berry puree, stirring until blended.
   Pour into a 13 x 9 x 2-inch baking
   pan. Freeze 2 hours.

4. Spoon mixture into a food processor.
   Pulse to break up; don't overprocess.
   Return mixture to pan. Freeze 2 hours.
   Repeat pulsing in processor; return to
   pan. Freeze until firm. To serve,
   garnish with fresh berries if desired.

PER ½ CUP
268 calories, 15 g fat (9 g saturated), 1 g protein,
35 g carbohydrate, 2 g fiber, 27 mg sodium,
54 mg cholesterol.

Mango-Mandarin Sherbet

Prepare step 1 of Blackberry-Lime
Sherbet. In step 2, substitute
2 drained 11-ounce cans Mandarin
orange segments for blackberries
and blueberries. Puree orange
segments in a food processor.
Pour into a large measuring cup;
add enough mango nectar to make
2½ cups. Stir in ¾ teaspoon grated
fresh ginger; omit lime juice and
food colors. Continue with step 3.

PER ½ CUP
273 calories, 15 g fat (9 g saturated), 1 g protein,
37 g carbohydrate, 1 g fiber, 30 mg sodium,
54 mg cholesterol.

Raspberry-Strawberry Sherbet

Prepare Blackberry-Lime Sherbet,
substituting raspberries and
strawberries for blackberries and
blueberries, omitting food colors
and replacing lime juice with
lemon juice.

PER ½ CUP
274 calories, 15 g fat (9 g saturated), 1 g protein,
37 g carbohydrate, 2 g fiber, 28 mg sodium,
54 mg cholesterol.

Rainbow Pops

Use any two flavors of gelatin to make these pretty frozen treats.

MAKES 12 pops **PREP** 15 minutes
FREEZE 4 to 6 hours

2	**cups water**
1	**box (3 ounces) lime-flavored gelatin**
1	**box (3 ounces) lemon-flavored gelatin**
1	**jar (about 7 ounces) marshmallow cream**
12	**flat wooden sticks**

1. Heat 1 cup water to boiling in a small saucepan. Stir in lime-flavored gelatin until dissolved. Transfer mixture to a blender; let cool about 15 minutes.

2. Add ¾ cup marshmallow cream (about half of jar) to gelatin mixture in blender. Whirl until mixture is smooth and creamy.

3. Grease a standard 12-muffin pan. Divide gelatin mixture equally among cups, placing about 2½ tablespoons mixture in each. Place muffin pan in freezer 1 hour.

4. Line a baking sheet with waxed paper; lightly coat paper with nonstick cooking spray. To remove gelatin discs from muffin cups, run a butter knife around edges of each, gently pry up one edge and slide fingers under; lift out disc and place, smaller side (bottom) down, on prepared baking sheet. Repeat with remaining discs.

5. Lay a wooden stick across top of each disc, aligning one end of stick with edge of disc and letting other end extend for a handle. Cover discs with another sheet of waxed paper. Freeze while continuing with step 6.

6. Repeat steps 1, 2 and 3, using remaining 1 cup water, lemon-flavored gelatin and remaining half of marshmallow cream to make another batch of gelatin discs.

7. Remove baking sheet and muffin pan from freezer. Uncover baking sheet. One at a time, remove discs from muffin cups and invert onto discs on baking sheet, aligning edges. Cover baking sheet and return to freezer. Freeze until firm, about 2 hours. To remove pops from baking sheet, lift with a spatula. Serve or store in plastic food-storage bags in freezer.

PER POP
107 calories, 0 g fat (0 g saturated), 1 g protein, 26 g carbohydrate, 0 g fiber, 44 mg sodium, 0 mg cholesterol.

Ginger-Orange Cheesecake Mousse

MAKES 10 servings **PREP** 15 minutes
REFRIGERATE 1 to 1½ hours

1   large orange
½   cup sweetened dried cranberries
1   package (8 ounces) regular or less-fat cream cheese
⅓   cup honey
1⅓ cups heavy cream, chilled
2   cups crumbled gingersnaps (about 40 cookies)

1. Grate rind from orange; set rind aside. Squeeze juice from orange; you should have at least ½ cup. Measure 5 tablespoons into a microwave-safe bowl or a saucepan; add cranberries. Reserve remainder of juice. Microwave cranberry mixture at 100% power or cook over medium heat until simmering. Remove from microwave or heat; let stand10 minutes or until berries are cooled and plump.

2. Using a mixer on medium speed, beat together cream cheese, honey, orange rind and 3 tablespoons reserved orange juice in a medium-size bowl until smooth. Add cream; beat until mixture is stiff. Drain juice (if any has not been absorbed) from cranberries into a small bowl. Add 3 tablespoons cranberries to bowl; set aside. Fold remaining cranberries into cheese mixture.

3. Sprinkle ⅔ cup cookie crumbs over bottom of a 1½-quart glass serving dish. Dollop with half of cranberry mousse; sprinkle with ⅔ cup crumbs; cover with remaining mousse. Sprinkle remaining ⅔ cup crumbs around edge.

Spoon reserved cranberries and any juice in center. Refrigerate 1 to 1½ hours or until firm.

PER SERVING
360 calories, 22 g fat (13 g saturated), 7 g protein, 37 g carbohydrate, 1 g fiber, 263 mg sodium, 85 mg cholesterol.

Strawberry Fluff

MAKES 6 servings **PREP** 10 minutes
REFRIGERATE 3 to 4 hours

1   box (3 ounces) strawberry-flavored gelatin
1   cup boiling water
1¼ cups ice cubes, or as needed
1   cup sour cream
1   cup sliced strawberries
    Whipped cream for garnish (optional)
    Sliced strawberries for garnish (optional)

1. Sprinkle gelatin over water in a 4-cup glass measuring cup; stir until gelatin is completely dissolved. Add ice cubes a few at a time, stirring until ice melts; continue until mixture equals 2 cups.

2. Place gelatin mixture, sour cream and strawberries in a food processor. Whirl until smooth, 1 to 2 minutes.

3. Pour mixture into 6 sherbet dishes, dividing equally. Cover with plastic wrap. Refrigerate until set, 3 to 4 hours. If desired, garnish each with a dollop of whipped cream and sliced strawberries.

PER SERVING
144 calories, 8 g fat (5 g saturated), 2 g protein, 16 g carbohydrate, 0 g fiber, 57 mg sodium, 17 mg cholesterol.

Cream Hearts

You'll create some scraps while making these—
happy snacking!

MAKES 6 hearts **PREP** 10 minutes
REFRIGERATE 24 hours

12	ounces cream cheese, at room temperature
1½	teaspoons coconut extract
1	cup heavy cream
½	cup confectioners' sugar
¼	cup light rum
1	tablespoon cornstarch
1	cup pineapple juice
2	tablespoons granulated sugar
⅓	cup unsweetened flake coconut, toasted (see page 232)

1. Line an 8 x 8 x 2-inch baking dish with plastic wrap, leaving an overhang on 2 opposite sides.

2. Beat together cream cheese and coconut extract in a medium-size bowl until light and fluffy, about 2 minutes.

3. Beat cream and confectioners' sugar in a second medium-size bowl until soft peaks form. Using a rubber spatula, gently fold one-quarter of whipped cream into cheese mixture. Fold in remaining whipped cream mixture. Spoon into prepared baking dish; smooth top with a spatula. Cover dish with plastic wrap. Refrigerate 24 hours.

4. To make pineapple sauce, whisk together rum and cornstarch in a small bowl until cornstarch is dissolved. Mix pineapple juice and granulated sugar in a small saucepan; bring to boiling. Whisk in cornstarch mixture; cook, whisking, until thickened, about 1 minute. Transfer to a small bowl; cover with plastic wrap. Refrigerate sauce until ready to use.

5. When ready to serve, lift plastic wrap out of baking dish to remove cream cheese mixture; place plastic with mixture on a work surface. Using a 2¾-inch heart-shaped cookie cutter, cut out 6 heart shapes.

6. Spoon pineapple sauce onto middle of 6 dessert plates, dividing equally. Using a spatula, place a cheese heart on each pool of sauce. Garnish top of each with a sprinkling of toasted coconut.

PER HEART
305 calories, 24 g fat (15 g saturated), 3 g protein, 19 g carbohydrate, 1 g fiber, 112 mg sodium, 70 mg cholesterol.

Tiramisu

For homemade cookie layers, use the dough for Mocha Sugar Cookies on page 203, omitting the espresso powder; shape into a disc and chill 10 minutes. If making your own dough, skip step 2.

MAKES 12 servings **PREP** 25 minutes
BAKE at 350° for 8 to 10 minutes
REFRIGERATE 8 to 24 hours

Dough

- 1 **tube (18 ounces) refrigerated sugar-cookie dough**
- ¼ **cup unsweetened cocoa powder**

- 2 **tablespoons granulated sugar**
- 2 **cups heavy cream**
- ¼ **cup confectioners' sugar**
- 1 **tablespoon vanilla**
- ⅔ **cup milk**
- 1 **to 2 tablespoons instant coffee powder**
- 1 **package (8 ounces) cream cheese, at room temperature**
- 1 **square (1 ounce) semisweet chocolate, grated (optional)**

1. Heat oven to 350°.
2. Prepare dough: Using a wooden spoon, work together dough and cocoa powder in a large bowl until well blended and smooth. (If this makes dough too soft to work with, cover and return to refrigerator until firm, about 10 minutes.)
3. Drop dough by slightly rounded teaspoonfuls, 2 inches apart, onto large ungreased baking sheets (you should have about 40 cookies). Measure granulated sugar onto a piece of waxed paper. For each cookie, dampen bottom of a small glass with water; dip into sugar; press down on cookie to flatten to about 2 inches in diameter.
4. Bake in heated 350° oven 8 to 10 minutes or until cookies are puffed and slightly crisp around edges. Transfer baking sheets to a wire rack and cool cookies 1 minute. Remove cookies from sheet to rack and cool completely.
5. With a mixer on high speed, beat together cream, confectioners' sugar and vanilla in a small bowl until stiff peaks form. Pour milk into a glass measure, add instant coffee and stir until dissolved. Place cream cheese in a second small bowl; gradually beat in milk mixture until smooth and well blended. Fold in half of whipped cream.
6. Coarsely break about one-third of cookies into bottom of an 11 x 7-inch baking dish. Spread half of cream cheese mixture evenly over top of cookies. Layer with another third of broken cookies and remaining cream cheese mixture. Top with remaining broken cookies and remaining whipped cream. Sprinkle with grated chocolate if desired.
7. Cover tightly. Refrigerate at least 8 hours or up to 24 hours to allow cookies to soften.

PER SERVING
441 calories, 32 g fat (16 g saturated), 5 g protein, 35 g carbohydrate, 1 g fiber, 277 mg sodium, 91 mg cholesterol.

Nutmeg Pots de Crème

MAKES 6 servings **PREP** 10 minutes
BAKE at 350° for 30 to 33 minutes

2   cups heavy cream
½   cup packed light-brown sugar
4   egg yolks
2   teaspoons vanilla
1   teaspoon ground nutmeg

1. Heat oven to 350°.

2. Combine cream and brown sugar in a small saucepan; bring just to boiling over medium heat, stirring to dissolve sugar.

3. Whisk together egg yolks and vanilla in a small bowl. Gradually whisk in ½ cup hot cream mixture. Gradually whisk in remaining cream, whisking gently to avoid bubbles.

4. Pour custard through a fine-mesh sieve into six 4- or 5-ounce custard cups. Sprinkle with nutmeg, dividing evenly. Place cups in a baking pan on oven rack. Pour hot water into pan to come halfway up sides of custard cups (see Baking Bath, page 178).

5. Bake in heated 350° oven until custards are nearly set in center, 30 to 33 minutes. Transfer cups to a wire rack to cool 15 minutes.

6. Serve custard warm and soft or refrigerate, covered, up to 8 hours.

PER SERVING
387 calories, 33 g fat (19 g saturated), 4 g protein,
21 g carbohydrate, 0 g fiber, 42 mg sodium,
251 mg cholesterol.

Chocolate-Walnut Bread Pudding

MAKES 12 servings **PREP** 25 minutes
BAKE at 350° for 35 to 40 minutes

6   cups cubed stale Italian bread
1   cup chopped walnuts, toasted (see page 232)
4   cups milk
¾   cup packed light-brown sugar
3   tablespoons unsalted butter
⅛   teaspoon salt
4   squares (1 ounce each) semisweet chocolate, chopped
1   square (1 ounce) unsweetened chocolate, chopped
4   eggs
2   teaspoons vanilla
    White Chocolate Sauce for serving (opposite)

1. Heat oven to 350°. Butter a shallow 2-quart baking dish. Add bread to dish; sprinkle walnuts on top.

2. Combine 2 cups milk, brown sugar, butter and salt in a medium-size pan; bring to simmering over medium heat. Stir to melt butter. Remove pan from heat. Add semisweet and unsweetened chocolates; let stand 5 minutes. Whisk until chocolate is melted and mixture is smooth.

3. Whisk together eggs, vanilla and remaining milk in a medium-size bowl. Whisk into chocolate mixture, then pour over bread in baking dish.

4. Bake pudding in heated 350° oven 35 to 40 minutes or until center is set and registers 160° on an instant-read thermometer. Serve with sauce.

PER SERVING (with 2 tablespoons sauce)
434 calories, 29 g fat (14 g saturated), 10 g protein,
38 g carbohydrate, 2 g fiber, 190 mg sodium,
118 mg cholesterol.

White Chocolate Sauce

Combine 1 cup heavy cream, 2 tablespoons granulated sugar and ⅛ teaspoon salt in a small saucepan. Bring to simmering over medium heat. Adjust heat to medium-low. Dissolve 2 teaspoons cornstarch in 1 tablespoon water in a small cup; stir into cream mixture. Simmer, stirring, until thickened, about 1 minute. Remove pan from heat. Chop 3 ounces white baking chocolate. Stir chocolate and ¼ teaspoon vanilla into cream mixture until smooth and well blended.

MAKES 1⅓ cups

PER 2 TABLESPOONS
119 calories, 10 g fat (6 g saturated), 1 g protein, 7 g carbohydrate, 0 g fiber, 39 mg sodium, 29 mg cholesterol.

Crescent Roll Bread Pudding

MAKES 12 servings **PREP** 20 minutes
STAND 30 minutes
BAKE at 350° for 1½ hours

8	egg yolks
4	whole eggs
4	cups milk
1	cup heavy cream
1	cup granulated sugar
2	teaspoons vanilla
½	teaspoon salt
2	packages (6.25 ounces each) prepared butter crescent rolls
1	cup milk chocolate chips (6 ounces)
½	cup dark seedless raisins

Whipped Cream

1	cup heavy cream
2	tablespoons confectioners' sugar
1	teaspoon vanilla

1. Whisk together egg yolks, whole eggs, milk, cream, granulated sugar, vanilla and salt in a large bowl.

2. Coat a 2½-quart glass baking dish with nonstick cooking spray. Cut rolls in half horizontally; place bottom halves in prepared pan. Sprinkle chocolate chips and raisins over rolls. Place top half on each roll. Pour egg mixture over rolls. Submerge rolls in liquid by setting a second glass dish on top. Let stand 30 minutes.

3. Heat oven to 350°.

4. Remove top baking dish. Cover roll pudding in bottom dish loosely with aluminum foil; place in a large baking pan on oven rack. Pour hot water into large pan to reach depth of 1 inch (see Baking Bath, page 178).

5. Bake in heated 350° oven 1 hour. Remove foil. Bake 30 minutes longer or until center of pudding is set and registers 160° on an instant-read thermometer. Carefully remove pudding dish from water; transfer to a wire rack.

6. Prepare whipped cream: Beat cream in a medium-size bowl on medium speed until foamy. Add confectioners' sugar and vanilla; continue to beat until soft peaks form. Serve pudding warm, at room temperature or chilled, dolloped with whipped cream.

PER SERVING
523 calories, 32 g fat (18 g saturated), 12 g protein, 50 g carbohydrate, 2 g fiber, 349 mg sodium, 300 mg cholesterol.

Double-Crust Pie Pastry

The pastry can be made ahead and refrigerated, well wrapped, for up to 2 days or frozen for up to 1 month. Thaw frozen dough in refrigerator overnight.

MAKES two 9-inch crusts **PREP** 10 minutes **REFRIGERATE** 30 minutes

2¼ cups all-purpose flour
1 teaspoon salt
½ teaspoon ground cinnamon or 1 teaspoon ground ginger plus ½ teaspoon ground white pepper (optional)
½ cup solid vegetable shortening, cut into pieces and chilled
⅓ cup butter, cut into pieces and chilled
⅓ cup plus 2 tablespoons cold water

1. (To mix pastry in a food processor, see box, below.) Whisk together flour, salt and spice if desired in a medium-size bowl.

2. Cut in shortening with a pastry blender or 2 knives used scissor fashion until mixture is consistency of coarse meal.

Cut in butter. Add water, a little at a time, tossing with a fork, until dough is moistened and holds together when pinched.

3. Turn dough out onto a sheet of plastic wrap; gently press into a ball. Cut ball in half; flatten each half into a disc. Wrap each disc with plastic wrap. Refrigerate at least 30 minutes.

PER SERVING
206 calories, 14 g fat (5 g saturated), 3 g protein, 18 g carbohydrate, 1 g fiber, 195 mg sodium, 14 mg cholesterol.

> ### FOOD PROCESSOR PIE PASTRY
>
> Combine flour, salt and spice if desired in a processor fitted with a steel blade. Pulse just to mix. Add shortening; whirl until mixture is consistency of coarse meal. Add butter and pulse again. With machine running, add water in a slow and steady stream just until mixture begins to form a ball. Proceed with step 3, above.

Apple Ginger Tarts

MAKES 12 tarts **PREP** 45 minutes
BAKE at 425° for 25 to 27 minutes

Double-Crust Pie Pastry (left), prepared with ginger and white pepper
3 **Granny Smith apples (about 1½ pounds), peeled, halved, cored and each half cut into 12 slices (for 72 slices total)**
½ **cup sugar**
2 **tablespoons all-purpose flour**
1½ **teaspoons ground ginger**
2 **tablespoons apple jelly**

1. Roll out 1 disc of pie pastry on a lightly floured surface to ¼-inch thickness. Using a 3¼-inch round cookie cutter, cut out 6 rounds, gathering and rerolling scraps if necessary. Repeat with remaining disc of dough, for a total of 12 rounds. Transfer rounds to 2 ungreased baking sheets.

2. Position oven racks in top third and lower third of oven. Heat oven to 425°.

3. Toss together apples, sugar, flour and ginger in a large bowl. Arrange 6 apple slices on each pastry round, overlapping in a fan pattern.

4. Bake in heated 425° oven 25 to 27 minutes or until pastry is golden and crisp, switching baking sheets between racks and rotating sheets front to back halfway through baking.

5. Transfer tarts to wire racks and let cool slightly. Melt apple jelly in a small saucepan over low heat; brush over tops of tarts. Serve slightly warm or at room temperature.

PER TART
285 calories, 14 g fat (5 g saturated), 3 g protein, 38 g carbohydrate, 2 g fiber, 197 mg sodium, 14 mg cholesterol.

Cran-Apple Pie

Shown on page 132.

MAKES 12 servings **PREP** 1 hour
BAKE at 425° for 15 minutes; then at 400° for 40 to 45 minutes

1	cup fresh or frozen cranberries, chopped
½	cup apple juice
½	teaspoon grated orange rind
¾	cup granulated sugar
	Double-Crust Pie Pastry (opposite), prepared with cinnamon
8	McIntosh apples (about 2½ pounds)
½	cup packed light-brown sugar
3	tablespoons cornstarch
	Pinch ground cinnamon
	Pinch ground cloves
1	egg yolk
1	tablespoon milk

1. Combine cranberries, apple juice, orange rind and 3 tablespoons granulated sugar in a small saucepan. Bring to simmering over high heat; lower heat. Simmer, stirring occasionally, 12 minutes or until consistency of cranberry sauce. Let cool.

2. Heat oven to 425°.

3. For bottom crust, roll out 1 disc of pie pastry on a floured surface into a 13-inch round. Fit into a 9-inch pie plate. Smooth pastry over bottom and up sides of plate. Trim off excess dough.

4. Peel and core apples; cut each horizontally into eight ½-inch-thick slices. Combine with ¼ cup granulated sugar, brown sugar, cornstarch, cinnamon and cloves in a large bowl. Add cooled cranberry mixture and egg yolk; stir until well mixed. Scrape into prepared crust. Spread apples, mounding high in center; do not compact them.

5. Roll out remaining disc of pastry to a 13-inch round. Place over filling. Trim dough, leaving ¾-inch overhang. Fold top crust under bottom crust. Press to seal; flute edge. Cut 10 vents in top. Brush crust with milk; sprinkle with remaining 1 tablespoon granulated sugar. Place on a baking sheet.

6. Bake in heated 425° oven 15 minutes. Lower oven temperature to 400°. Bake 40 to 45 minutes or until pastry is golden brown. Remove to a wire rack; cool at least 40 minutes.

PER SERVING
341 calories, 15 g fat (6 g saturated), 3 g protein, 51 g carbohydrate, 3 g fiber, 201 mg sodium, 32 mg cholesterol.

Upside-Down Pecan-Apple Pie

For a real treat, serve this warm with vanilla or butter-pecan ice cream.

MAKES 8 servings **PREP** 20 minutes
BAKE at 450° for 10 minutes; then at 350° for 40 to 45 minutes

6	cups peeled Granny Smith apple slices (about 2½ pounds)
3	tablespoons fresh lemon juice
2	tablespoons butter or margarine, at room temperature
⅔	cup pecan halves
1	cup packed light-brown sugar
2	refrigerated ready-to-use piecrusts
1	tablespoon all-purpose flour
½	teaspoon ground cinnamon
½	teaspoon ground nutmeg
¼	teaspoon salt

1. Heat oven to 450°.

2. Toss together apple slices and lemon juice in a large bowl until slices are well coated.

3. Spread butter over sides and bottom of a 9-inch glass pie plate. Arrange pecans, flat side up, in bottom of pie plate in a decorative pattern; press pecans into butter to hold in place.

4. Crumble ⅔ cup brown sugar evenly over bottom and sides of pie plate, covering pecans and butter. Gently cover sugar and pecans with 1 piecrust, pressing crust over sides and bottom of plate and being careful not to move pecans or tear crust.

5. Mix remaining ⅓ cup brown sugar, flour, cinnamon, nutmeg and salt in a small bowl. Add to apples; toss to mix.

6. Mound apple slices in piecrust in plate. Top with second piecrust.

Pecan-Apple Pie How-To's

Arrange pecans, flat side up, in a buttered pie plate, making a decorative pattern.

Crumble brown sugar evenly over bottom and sides of pie plate, covering pecans and butter.

Crimp edges together; flute. Prick top crust in several places with a fork. Place pie plate on a large baking sheet.

7. Bake in heated 450° oven 10 minutes. Lower oven temperature to 350°. Bake 40 to 45 minutes or until crust is golden. Let pie rest on a wire rack 5 minutes or until sugar stops bubbling around edge.

8. Invert a serving plate over pie; then invert pie plate and serving plate together. Carefully remove pie plate.

PER SERVING
424 calories, 23 g fat (2 g saturated), 1 g protein, 57 g carbohydrate, 2 g fiber, 350 mg sodium, 18 mg cholesterol.

Rich 'n' Creamy Pear Pie

MAKES 8 servings **PREP** 10 minutes
BAKE at 400° for 40 minutes

1 **refrigerated ready-to-use piecrust**
1 **egg white, lightly beaten**
1 **cup sour cream**
2 **eggs**
⅓ **cup granulated sugar**
½ **teaspoon vanilla**
3 **tablespoons light-brown sugar**
3 **tablespoons cake crumbs or graham cracker crumbs**
1 **tablespoon butter**
2 **ripe pears**
   Whipped cream for garnish (optional)

1. Unfold piecrust; fit into a 9-inch tart pan with a removable bottom. Trim overhang to fit. Brush bottom with egg white.

2. Place a baking sheet in oven. Heat oven to 400°.

3. Stir together sour cream, eggs, granulated sugar and vanilla in a small bowl. Crumble together brown sugar, crumbs and butter in another small bowl.

4. Peel, halve and core pears. Cut lengthwise into ¼-inch-thick slices. Arrange slices in piecrust in 2 concentric rings, overlapping slightly.

5. Pour sour cream mixture over pears. Sprinkle with crumb mixture.

6. Bake tart on heated baking sheet in heated 400° oven 40 minutes or until cream is set and top is lightly golden.

7. Serve warm or at room temperature, garnished with whipped cream if desired.

PER SERVING
285 calories, 16 g fat (5 g saturated), 3 g protein, 33 g carbohydrate, 1 g fiber, 194 mg sodium, 75 mg cholesterol.

Ginger Pear Pie

For a homemade crust, prepare the dough for Ginger Sugar Cookies on page 202; use half of the recipe, shaping into a disc and chilling 10 minutes. If making your own dough, skip step 2.

MAKES 8 servings **PREP** 15 minutes
BAKE at 325° for 20 to 25 minutes

Dough
9   ounces (half of 18-ounce tube) refrigerated sugar-cookie dough
¼   cup all-purpose flour
1   tablespoon mild-flavored molasses
1   teaspoon ground ginger

Filling
1   package (8 ounces) light cream cheese, at room temperature
3   tablespoons sugar
1⅛ teaspoons ground ginger
1   can (15 ounces) ginger-flavored pear halves or canned pears in heavy syrup, well drained and thinly sliced lengthwise
3   tablespoons currant jelly
Fresh mint sprig for garnish (optional)

1. Heat oven to 325°. Lightly grease bottom and sides of a 9-inch glass pie plate.
2. Prepare dough: Using a wooden spoon, work together dough, flour, molasses and ground ginger in a large bowl until well blended. (If this makes dough too soft to work with, shape it into a disc, wrap and return to refrigerator until firm, about 10 minutes.)
3. Press dough evenly over bottom and halfway up sides of prepared pie plate.

Bake in heated 325° oven 20 to 25 minutes or until center springs back when lightly touched with a fingertip. Transfer to a wire rack to cool.

4. Prepare filling: Beat together cream cheese, sugar and 1 teaspoon ground ginger in a small bowl until blended and smooth. Spread mixture over crust, leaving a ¼-inch border. Arrange pear slices decoratively on top.
5. Heat currant jelly and remaining ⅛ teaspoon ground ginger in a small saucepan over low heat until jelly is melted. Lightly brush jelly mixture evenly over pear slices. Garnish with sprig of fresh mint if desired.

PER SERVING
316 calories, 14 g fat (6 g saturated), 5 g protein, 44 g carbohydrate, 1 g fiber, 278 mg sodium, 31 mg cholesterol.

Checkerboard Strawberry Pie

MAKES 8 servings **PREP** 25 minutes
COOK 5 to 6 minutes **STAND** 2 hours
REFRIGERATE 4 hours

Chocolate Crust
1¼ cups graham cracker crumbs (about 9 whole graham crackers)
2   tablespoons unsweetened cocoa powder
2   tablespoons confectioners' sugar
5   tablespoons butter, melted

Filling
¼   cup granulated sugar
3   tablespoons cornstarch
1½ cups milk
1   cup white chocolate chips

1 teaspoon vanilla
3 drops red food coloring
1 container (12 ounces) frozen nondairy whipped topping, thawed
2 cups chopped strawberries (about 1½ pints whole strawberries)

Decoration
6 strawberries
6 striped chocolate kisses, wrapping removed

1. Prepare crust: Mix graham cracker crumbs, cocoa powder and confectioners' sugar in a medium-size bowl. Stir in melted butter until well mixed. Press mixture over bottom and up sides of a 9-inch glass pie plate. Cover and place in freezer until ready to fill.

2. Prepare filling: Mix sugar and cornstarch in a medium-size saucepan. Place over medium heat; gradually stir in milk. Cook over medium-high heat, stirring constantly, until mixture thickens and comes to boiling, about 5 minutes. Remove from heat. Add chocolate chips, vanilla and food coloring, stirring until chocolate is melted and mixture is smooth. Transfer to a large bowl; cover surface directly with plastic wrap. Let cool to room temperature, about 2 hours.

3. When cool, whisk chocolate mixture until smooth. Reserve 1 cup whipped topping and fold remainder into chocolate mixture.

4. Spread half of chocolate filling over bottom of prepared crust. Top with chopped strawberries. Spread remaining chocolate filling over strawberries. Refrigerate at least 4 hours.

5. Prepare decoration: Spoon reserved cup whipped topping into a pastry bag fitted with a large star tip. Make a grid over top of pie, piping 1 line across center and 1 line on each side of center line; repeat piping at a right angle to first 3 lines. Pipe a decorative border around edge of pie. Arrange whole strawberries in alternate squares on top of pie. Arrange kisses in remaining alternate squares.

PER SERVING
478 calories, 28 g fat (19 g saturated), 5 g protein, 54 g carbohydrate, 2 g fiber, 168 mg sodium, 30 mg cholesterol.

Strawberry-Rhubarb Pie

MAKES 8 servings PREP 10 minutes
BAKE at 400° for 50 minutes

2 refrigerated ready-to-use piecrusts
3 cups fresh or thawed rhubarb pieces (1-inch)
1 pint (2 cups) strawberries, hulled and quartered
1 cup sugar
⅓ cup cornstarch
⅛ teaspoon salt
⅛ teaspoon ground nutmeg

1. Heat oven to 400°. Unfold 1 piecrust and fit into a 9-inch glass pie plate.

2. Place rhubarb, strawberries, sugar, cornstarch, salt and nutmeg in a large bowl; stir gently to combine. Do not crush strawberries or rhubarb.

3. Unfold second piecrust on a lightly floured surface and flatten slightly with a rolling pin. Using a paring knife or cookie cutter, cut out six 1-inch strawberry shapes in a ring around center of crust. Cut out leaf shapes from the cutouts; reserve the leaves on a sheet of waxed paper.

4. Spoon strawberry filling into crust-lined pie plate. Place second piecrust on top. Fold edge of top piecrust under edge of bottom piecrust; crimp edges of crusts together to seal. Using a little water as glue, arrange dough leaves in a ring on crust, inside strawberry cutouts.

5. Bake in heated 400° oven 50 minutes or until crust is golden and filling is bubbly. If edges of crust brown too quickly, cover them with a piece of aluminum foil. Transfer pie to a wire rack and let cool completely.

PER SERVING
377 calories, 15 g fat (0 g saturated), 3 g protein, 58 g carbohydrate, 1 g fiber, 246 mg sodium, 0 mg cholesterol.

Three-Nut Pie

MAKES 10 servings PREP 30 minutes
REFRIGERATE 1 hour
BAKE at 325° for 50 minutes

Pastry
1¼ cups all-purpose flour
¼ teaspoon salt
⅓ cup solid vegetable shortening, chilled and cut into small pieces
1 tablespoon butter, chilled and cut into small pieces
3 to 4 tablespoons ice water
1 teaspoon cider vinegar

Nut Filling
¾ cup packed dark-brown sugar
¾ cup dark or light corn syrup
¼ cup (½ stick) butter
1½ teaspoons ground cinnamon
¼ teaspoon salt
⅛ teaspoon ground cloves
4 eggs
¾ cup blanched slivered almonds
½ cup chopped hazelnuts
1 cup pecan halves

1. Prepare pastry: Mix flour and salt in a medium-size bowl. Cut in shortening and butter with a pastry blender or 2 knives used scissor fashion until mixture resembles coarse meal.

2. Sprinkle ice water, 1 tablespoon at a time, and vinegar over flour mixture, mixing lightly with a fork after each addition, until pastry is just moist enough to hold together. Shape and flatten dough into a 5-inch disc. Cover with plastic wrap. Refrigerate until thoroughly chilled, about 1 hour.

3. Heat oven to 325°.

4. Roll out dough on a floured surface into an 11-inch round. Fit into a 9-inch pie plate. Fold overhanging pastry under to make an edge; press all around edge with tines of a fork.

5. Prepare filling: Heat brown sugar, corn syrup, butter, cinnamon, salt and cloves in a medium-size saucepan over medium heat until butter is melted. Remove pan from heat; whisk in eggs, one at a time. Add almonds and hazelnuts. Pour into prepared crust. Arrange pecans on filling in concentric circles, beginning at outside and working toward center.

6. Bake in heated 325° oven 50 minutes or until crust is golden brown and a knife inserted near center of filling comes out clean. Cool on a wire rack.

PER SERVING
441 calories, 27 g fat (7 g saturated), 8 g protein, 46 g carbohydrate, 3 g fiber, 177 mg sodium, 101 mg cholesterol.

Grasshopper Pie

MAKES 12 servings **PREP** 15 minutes
REFRIGERATE 2 hours or overnight

28 chocolate sandwich cookies
1   cup plus 2 to 3 tablespoons milk
1   box (3 ounces) vanilla instant pudding-and-pie-filling mix
¼   cup crème de menthe liqueur or peppermint schnapps (see note below)
2   cups frozen nondairy whipped topping, thawed

1. Place 20 cookies in a food processor or blender; whirl until finely crushed. Add 2 to 3 tablespoons milk; whirl until crumbs begin to hold together. Press mixture into a 9-inch pie plate.

2. Chop remaining 8 cookies. Beat instant pudding-and-pie-filling mix, remaining 1 cup milk and crème de menthe in a large bowl until thickened and smooth. Using a rubber spatula, fold in whipped topping. Fold chopped cookies into pudding mixture.

3. Spoon filling into crust, swirling top decoratively. Refrigerate 2 hours or overnight.

Note: If you are using a clear liqueur, you may wish to add 1 or 2 drops green food coloring to the filling.

PER SERVING
223 calories, 8 g fat (4 g saturated), 2 g protein, 32 g carbohydrate, 1 g fiber, 302 mg sodium, 3 mg cholesterol.

3. Roll out dough on a lightly floured surface into a 13-inch round. Roll dough back onto rolling pin; unroll onto an ungreased large baking sheet.

4. Halve and pit plums; cut each half into 4 slices. Toss slices in a medium-size bowl with remaining ⅓ cup brown sugar, remaining ⅓ cup pecans and flour. Mound plum mixture onto center of dough, leaving a 2-inch border. Spoon any sugar mixture left in bowl on top of filling. Fold border up over filling, working all the way around.

5. Bake in heated 375° oven 35 to 40 minutes or until filling is hot and crust is golden. Cool galette on baking sheet on a wire rack. Serve slightly warm.

PER SERVING
243 calories, 13 g fat (3 g saturated), 3 g protein, 31 g carbohydrate, 2 g fiber, 200 mg sodium, 0 mg cholesterol.

Plum Galette

MAKES 12 servings **PREP** 20 minutes
BAKE at 375° for 35 to 40 minutes

1 **box (11 ounces) piecrust mix**
⅓ **cup plus 3 tablespoons packed brown sugar**
⅔ **cup chopped pecans**
1¼ **pounds plums**
1 **tablespoon all-purpose flour**

1. Heat oven to 375°.

2. Combine piecrust mix, 3 tablespoons brown sugar and ⅓ cup pecans in a medium-size bowl. Stir in amount of water recommended on crust box for making a double-crust pie; continue stirring until ingredients come together to form a ball of dough.

Hazelnut Fruit Tart

MAKES 8 servings **PREP** 40 minutes
REFRIGERATE crust 1 hour; pastry cream 1 hour; tart 1 hour
COOK 9 to 10 minutes
BAKE at 350° for 25 minutes

Crust
1 **cup all-purpose flour**
¼ **cup sugar**
2 **tablespoons ground hazelnuts**
¼ **teaspoon salt**
¼ **cup (½ stick) butter, cut into small pieces and chilled**
1 **whole egg, lightly beaten**

Pastry Cream

2   **cups milk**
⅓   **cup sugar**
½   **vanilla bean, split in half**
4   **egg yolks**
2   **tablespoons all-purpose flour**
2   **tablespoons cornstarch**
1   **teaspoon unflavored gelatin**
2   **tablespoons hazelnut liqueur**

Topping

1   **pint strawberries, hulled and sliced (1½ cups)**
2   **kiwis, peeled and sliced**
2   **bananas, sliced**
½   **pint raspberries**
2   **tablespoons currant jelly**
2   **tablespoons ground hazelnuts**

1. Prepare crust: Mix flour, sugar, hazelnuts and salt in a large bowl. Cut in butter with a pastry blender or 2 knives used scissor fashion until mixture resembles coarse crumbs. Using a fork, blend whole egg into flour mixture just until dough comes together. Pat into bottom and up sides of an ungreased 9-inch tart pan with a removable bottom. Cover; refrigerate 1 hour (see note).

2. Heat oven to 350°.

3. Line crust with aluminum foil. Fill with dried beans or rice. Bake in heated 350° oven 15 minutes. Remove foil and beans. Bake 10 minutes longer or until crust just starts to brown. Let cool in pan on a wire rack 5 minutes. Remove sides of pan and let crust cool completely.

4. Prepare pastry cream: Mix milk and about half of sugar in a small saucepan. Scrape seeds and pulp from vanilla bean into pan; add pod. Bring to boiling over medium-high heat. Remove from heat; let steep 15 minutes. Discard bean.

5. Meanwhile, whisk egg yolks and remaining sugar in a small bowl until lemon-colored and smooth. Sift in flour and cornstarch; whisk until well blended and smooth.

6. Whisk ½ cup hot milk mixture into yolk mixture. Pour yolk mixture into milk mixture in saucepan. Bring to boiling over medium heat, whisking constantly; boil 2 minutes, whisking occasionally. Remove from heat.

7. Sprinkle gelatin over liqueur in a small bowl; let stand 1 minute to soften. Stir to dissolve gelatin; warm slightly in a microwave oven if necessary to dissolve completely. Stir gelatin mixture into egg mixture in saucepan. Strain into a small bowl. Place bowl in a larger bowl filled halfway with ice and water; cool, gently stirring occasionally, 15 minutes.

8. Place plastic wrap directly on surface of pastry cream. Refrigerate to chill thoroughly, about 1 hour (see note).

9. Prepare topping: Transfer crust to a serving plate. Spread pastry cream over bottom of crust. Arrange fruit on top. Melt jelly in a small saucepan. Cool slightly; brush over fruit. Garnish with nuts. Refrigerate at least 1 hour before serving.

Note: Crust can be prepared ahead and refrigerated up to 2 days. Pastry cream can be prepared ahead and refrigerated up to 1 day. Tart can be assembled and refrigerated a few hours before serving.

PER SERVING
357 calories, 13 g fat (6 g saturated), 8 g protein, 53 g carbohydrate, 4 g fiber, 118 mg sodium, 157 mg cholesterol.

Pecan–Sweet Potato Pie

This beautiful sweet treat, embellished with pastry holly and maple leaves, would enhance a holiday table or disappear quickly from a bake sale. Add whipped cream or vanilla ice cream, and who could resist?

MAKES 10 servings **PREP** 25 minutes
REFRIGERATE 1 hour
BAKE at 350° for 1 hour

Crust

1¾	cups all-purpose flour
1	teaspoon salt
7	tablespoons solid vegetable shortening, chilled
¼	cup cold water

Filling

1	can (15¾ ounces) cooked sweet potato, drained
4	eggs
⅓	cup packed dark-brown sugar
½	teaspoon ground allspice
½	cup dark corn syrup
⅓	cup granulated sugar
1	teaspoon vanilla
1¼	cups pecan halves

Whipped cream or vanilla ice cream for serving (optional)

1. Prepare crust: Mix flour and salt in a large bowl. Cut in shortening with a pastry blender or 2 knives used scissor fashion until mixture resembles coarse crumbs. Sprinkle cold water, 1 tablespoon at a time, over mixture, mixing lightly with a fork after each addition, until dough comes together. Loosely shape dough into a ball; cut into quarters. Shape 1 piece into a disc; wrap in plastic wrap. Shape remaining 3 pieces together into another disc; wrap. Refrigerate both discs 1 hour.

2. On a waxed-paper-lined baking sheet, roll out smaller disc of dough to ¼-inch thickness. Using a 1¾-inch holly-leaf cutter, cut about 30 leaves into dough; lift and reserve scraps. Place baking sheet with leaves in refrigerator.

3. On a lightly floured surface, roll out larger disc of dough into a 12-inch round. Fit into a 9-inch pie plate, trimming dough even with edge of plate rim. Gather all dough scraps together.

4. Remove baking sheet with holly leaves from refrigerator. Dip a pastry brush into water; brush over a small section of piecrust edge. Arrange holly leaves, overlapping, along edge, moistening overlapping portions of leaves. Continue in this manner to arrange leaves all around crust edge. Refrigerate crust.

5. Roll out gathered dough scraps on floured surface to ¼-inch thickness. Using a 1¼-inch maple-leaf cutter, cut out about 12 maple leaves. Transfer to the same baking sheet and refrigerate.

6. Heat oven to 350°.

7. Prepare filling: With a mixer on medium-high speed, beat sweet potato, 1 egg, dark-brown sugar and allspice in a medium-size bowl until smooth, 2 to 3 minutes. Scrape mixture into crust, spreading evenly.

8. Whisk together corn syrup, granulated sugar, vanilla and remaining 3 eggs in a clean medium-size bowl until well combined and smooth. Stir in pecans. Pour over sweet potato mixture in crust.

9. Arrange maple leaves decoratively on top of pecan mixture. Bake pie in heated 350° oven 1 hour or until filling is set and crust is lightly browned. Cool pie on a wire rack. Serve with whipped cream or vanilla ice cream if desired.

PER SERVING
421 calories, 21 g fat (4 g saturated), 6 g protein, 54 g carbohydrate, 3 g fiber, 300 mg sodium, 85 mg cholesterol.

Tropical Chocolate-Banana Tart

MAKES 12 servings **PREP** 30 minutes
COOK 5 minutes **REFRIGERATE** 2 hours

½ **cup sweetened flake coconut**
½ **cup macadamia nuts, chopped**
¾ **cup heavy cream**
1 **package (12 ounces) semisweet chocolate chips (2 cups)**
2 **medium ripe bananas**
¼ **cup confectioners' sugar**
2 **teaspoons lime juice**
½ **teaspoon coconut extract**
1 **package (8 ounces) cream cheese**

1. Grease a 9-inch springform pan.

2. In a medium-size skillet over medium heat, lightly toast coconut and macadamias 2 minutes.

3. Heat cream just to boiling in a small pan. Remove from heat. Stir in chocolate chips until melted and smooth. Add ½ cup coconut-macadamia mixture; reserve remainder. Set cream mixture aside until slightly thickened, 10 minutes. Pour into prepared pan. Refrigerate until firm, 1½ hours.

4. Slice bananas; arrange in pan in a single layer on top of chocolate.

5. Beat confectioners' sugar, lime juice and coconut extract into cream cheese. Spread over bananas using a rubber spatula. Sprinkle remaining coconut-macadamia mixture around top edge, making a narrow border.

6. Chill tart 30 minutes. To serve, remove sides of pan; cut tart into slices.

PER SERVING
345 calories, 26 g fat (13 g saturated), 3 g protein, 29 g carbohydrate, 1 g fiber, 72 mg sodium, 41 mg cholesterol.

1. Heat oven to 350°. Lightly grease a 9-inch springform pan.

2. Prepare dough: Using a wooden spoon, work together dough and lemon rind in a large bowl until well blended. (If this makes dough too soft to work with, shape it into a disc, wrap and return to refrigerator until firm, about 10 minutes.)

3. Press dough evenly over bottom and ½ inch up sides of prepared pan. Bake in heated 350° oven 20 minutes or until crust is golden brown and center springs back when lightly touched with a fingertip. Transfer pan to a wire rack. Using a thin metal spatula, carefully loosen crust from sides of pan. Remove sides of pan; cool crust completely on wire rack.

4. Place crust on a cake plate. Spread lemon curd over crust. Arrange raspberries, stem end down, on top.

PER SERVING
229 calories, 9 g fat (2 g saturated), 2 g protein, 40 g carbohydrate, 3 g fiber, 167 mg sodium, 10 mg cholesterol.

Lemon Curd Tart

For a homemade crust, prepare the dough for Lemon Sugar Cookies on page 202; use half of the recipe, shaping into a disc and chilling 10 minutes. If making your own dough, skip step 2.

MAKES 8 servings **PREP** 10 minutes
BAKE at 350° for 20 minutes

Dough
9   ounces (half of 18-ounce tube) refrigerated sugar-cookie dough
2   teaspoons grated lemon rind

½   cup jarred lemon curd
3   cups fresh raspberries

Chocolate and Ginger Tarts

MAKES 14 tarts **PREP** 1 hour
REFRIGERATE 3 hours **COOK** 5 minutes

Ginger Filling
¼   cup sugar
3   tablespoons cornstarch
1   teaspoon grated fresh ginger
¼   teaspoon salt
2   cups milk

Chocolate Tart Shells

1 **package (12 ounces) semisweet chocolate chips (2 cups)**
2 **tablespoons solid vegetable shortening**
2 **cups finely chopped nuts, such as walnuts**

Topping

¾ **cup semisweet chocolate chips**
1 **cup strawberries, hulled and quartered**
2 **tablespoons finely chopped candied ginger**

1. Prepare filling: Combine sugar, cornstarch, fresh ginger and salt in a medium-size saucepan. Gradually add milk, blending until smooth. Cook over medium heat, stirring constantly, until mixture thickens and comes to boiling; cook, stirring continuously, 1 minute. Pour into a small bowl. Place a piece of plastic wrap directly on surface. Refrigerate several hours or until mixture is completely chilled.

2. Meanwhile, prepare tart shells: Cut fourteen 5-inch squares of aluminum foil. Invert fourteen 10-ounce metal or glass baking dishes on a work surface. Center a foil square over bottom of each dish and press to wrap against sides. Alternatively, use 4½-inch disposable round foil pans, as is or covered with foil squares.

3. Melt chocolate and shortening in top of a double boiler over barely simmering, not boiling, water, stirring until smooth. Stir in nuts. Let mixture cool slightly, being sure it remains spreadable, about 15 minutes.

4. Using a small metal spatula, carefully spread 2 tablespoons chocolate-nut mixture over bottom and about ¼ inch down sides of each inverted foil-covered dish. Refrigerate at least 30 minutes or until firm.

5. When chocolate is firm, remove 1 chocolate-and-foil-covered dish from refrigerator; slip dish out of foil and carefully peel foil away from chocolate. Place chocolate shell, right side up, on a serving platter in refrigerator. Repeat for each shell.

6. Remove 1 shell from refrigerator. Spoon level 2 tablespoons chilled filling into it; spread until smooth. Return to refrigerator. Repeat, using all shells and filling.

7. Prepare topping: Melt chocolate chips in top of a double boiler over barely simmering, not boiling, water, stirring until smooth. Remove from heat and cool slightly.

8. Meanwhile, arrange quartered strawberries on top of filling in each tart. Sprinkle with candied ginger.

9. Pour melted chocolate into a small plastic food-storage bag. Snip off a corner of bag to make a very small opening. Pipe chocolate over tarts in a decorative pattern. Serve immediately.

PER TART
335 calories, 24 g fat (8 g saturated), 5 g protein, 33 g carbohydrate, 3 g fiber, 61 mg sodium, 5 mg cholesterol.

Strawberry Tartlets

MAKES 12 tartlets **PREP** 20 minutes
BAKE at 300° for 25 to 30 minutes
REFRIGERATE 1½ hours

Crust

1¼ **cups graham cracker crumbs
     (8 whole graham crackers)**
3   **tablespoons granulated sugar**
¼   **cup (½ stick) butter, melted**

Filling

2   **packages (8 ounces each) cream
     cheese, at room temperature**
½   **cup granulated sugar**
¼   **cup strawberry jam**
1   **tablespoon cornstarch**
2   **eggs**
2   **teaspoons strawberry extract**
1   **teaspoon vanilla extract**
1   **drop red food coloring**

Topping

¾   **cup heavy cream**
3   **tablespoons confectioners' sugar**
12 **strawberries**

1. Heat oven to 300°. Grease a standard
   12-muffin pan.

2. Prepare crust: Mix graham cracker
   crumbs, granulated sugar and butter
   in a small bowl. Press a scant
   2 tablespoons crumb mixture over
   bottom and up sides of each prepared
   muffin cup.

3. Prepare filling: Beat cream cheese
   and granulated sugar in a large bowl
   until smooth and creamy, about
   2 minutes. Add jam, cornstarch, eggs,
   strawberry and vanilla extracts and
   food coloring; beat until well
   combined. Spoon mixture into a
   plastic food-storage bag. Snip off a
   corner of bag. Squeeze filling into
   crumb crusts, dividing evenly.

4. Bake tartlets in heated 300° oven
   25 to 30 minutes or until centers are
   set. Cool in pan on a wire rack
   30 minutes. Refrigerate until
   thoroughly chilled, about 1½ hours.

5. Prepare topping: Beat cream and
   confectioners' sugar in a small bowl
   until stiff peaks form. Remove tartlets
   from cups. Spoon whipped cream on
   top of each tartlet. Leaving caps
   attached, thinly slice strawberries and
   arrange one in a fan on each tartlet.

PER TARTLET
364 calories, 25 g fat (15 g saturated), 5 g protein,
31 g carbohydrate, 1 g fiber, 207 mg sodium,
108 mg cholesterol.

Coconut-Strawberry Tartlets

MAKES 12 servings **PREP** 25 minutes
BAKE at 400° for about 12 minutes
COOK 12 to 15 minutes
REFRIGERATE 30 minutes

6   **frozen pastry tart shells (one
     10-ounce package), thawed**
1   **egg**
1   **tablespoon water**
1   **package (3½ ounces) vanilla
     pudding-and-pie-filling mix
     (not instant)**
1   **can (14 ounces) light coconut milk**
⅓   **cup sweetened flake coconut,
     coarsely chopped**
¼   **teaspoon coconut extract**
½   **cup strawberry jelly**
2   **to 3 pints small or medium
     strawberries (48 berries), hulled**

1. Heat oven to 400°.

2. On a lightly floured surface, roll out each tart shell to form a 6-inch round. Mix egg with water in a small cup. Brush edges of each tart shell lightly with egg wash. Fold edges up to form a lip. Prick center of each tart shell with a fork. Place on a baking sheet.

3. Bake in heated 400° oven about 12 minutes or until golden brown. Remove from oven and gently press down center of tart shells if puffed up. Cool on a wire rack.

4. Meanwhile, whisk together pudding-and-pie-filling mix and coconut milk in a small saucepan. Stir in flake coconut. Cook according to pudding package directions until thickened, 12 to 15 minutes. Remove from heat. Stir in coconut extract. Press plastic wrap onto surface of pudding. Refrigerate until cool to the touch, about 30 minutes.

5. Melt jelly in a small saucepan; remove from heat. Spoon pudding into tart shells, dividing equally. Place strawberries, hulled end down, over pudding. Lightly glaze strawberries with melted jelly. To serve, cut tarts in half.

PER SERVING
238 calories, 10 g fat (2 g saturated), 3 g protein, 34 g carbohydrate, 2 g fiber, 193 mg sodium, 18 mg cholesterol.

Cherry Cobbler

MAKES 8 servings **PREP** 5 minutes
BAKE at 400° for 30 minutes

2 **cans (1 pound 5 ounces each) cherry pie filling**
1½ **cups all-purpose flour**
¼ **cup plus 2 tablespoons sugar**
2 **teaspoons baking powder**
½ **teaspoon salt**
¼ **cup (½ stick) butter, cut into small pieces**
½ **cup milk**
½ **cup sliced almonds, toasted (see page 232)**
Light cream or sweetened whipped cream for serving (optional)

1. Heat oven to 400°.

2. Spread pie filling over bottom of a shallow 3-quart baking dish.

3. Sift flour, ¼ cup sugar, baking powder and salt into a medium-size bowl. Cut butter into flour mixture with a pastry blender or 2 knives used scissor fashion until mixture resembles coarse crumbs. Stir in milk until a stiff dough forms.

4. Drop dough by tablespoonfuls onto pie filling in baking dish. Sprinkle with toasted almonds and remaining 2 tablespoons sugar.

5. Bake in heated 400° oven 30 minutes or until topping is golden brown. Serve warm with cream if desired.

PER SERVING
388 calories, 10 g fat (4 g saturated), 5 g protein, 73 g carbohydrate, 2 g fiber, 251 mg sodium, 18 mg cholesterol.

1. Heat oven to 375°. Butter a 2- to 2½-quart shallow baking dish.

2. Beat together sour cream and eggs in a medium-size bowl on medium speed until smooth. On low speed, gradually beat in ¾ cup granulated sugar, flour, vanilla and almond extracts and salt until mixture is well blended and smooth.

3. Pour batter into prepared dish. Top with peach slices, overlapping to cover batter. Sprinkle top with remaining 2 tablespoons granulated sugar.

4. Bake in heated 375° oven 50 to 60 minutes or until a wooden pick inserted in center comes out clean. Dust with confectioners' sugar if desired. Serve warm.

PER SERVING
268 calories, 12 g fat (6 g saturated), 6 g protein, 36 g carbohydrate, 1 g fiber, 71 mg sodium, 126 mg cholesterol.

Peaches and Cream Unpie

MAKES 8 servings **PREP** 15 minutes
BAKE at 375° for 50 to 60 minutes

1½ cups sour cream
4   eggs
¾   cup plus 2 tablespoons granulated sugar
½   cup all-purpose flour
2   teaspoons vanilla extract
⅛   to ¼ teaspoon almond extract
    Pinch salt
5   peaches (1½ pounds), halved, pitted and cut into 2-inch-thick slices
    Confectioners' sugar for dusting (optional)

Raspberry-Peach Betty with Pecans

MAKES 8 servings **PREP** 20 minutes
BAKE at 350° for 1 hour

1½ pounds peaches, halved, peeled, pitted and cut into 2-inch-thick slices
1   pint raspberries (about 2¼ cups)
⅓   cup granulated sugar
1½ cups crushed vanilla wafer cookies (38 cookies)
½   cup chopped pecans
¼   cup packed light-brown sugar
½   cup (1 stick) butter, melted
2   tablespoons butter, cut into small pieces

1. Heat oven to 350°.
2. Toss peaches, raspberries and granulated sugar in a large bowl.
3. Combine crushed cookies, pecans and brown sugar in a medium-size bowl. Pour melted butter on top; toss until mixture is well blended and evenly moistened.
4. Sprinkle one-third of cookie mixture evenly over bottom of an ungreased 6-cup soufflé dish. Spoon half of fruit mixture on top. Sprinkle with half of remaining cookie mixture. Spoon remaining fruit on top. Sprinkle with remaining cookie mixture. Dot evenly with remaining 2 tablespoons butter.
5. Bake in heated 350° oven 1 hour or until top is golden and fruit is bubbling. Serve warm.

PER SERVING
372 calories, 24 g fat (9 g saturated), 2 g protein, 40 g carbohydrate, 4 g fiber, 75 mg sodium, 39 mg cholesterol.

Biscuit-Topped Apricot-Strawberry Bake

MAKES 8 servings **PREP** 20 minutes **BAKE** at 375° for 1 hour

Fruit
½ cup sugar
1 tablespoon cornstarch
1 tablespoon grated orange rind
1½ pints strawberries, hulled and quartered (about 3¼ cups)
3 apricots, halved, pitted and cut into eighths

Biscuit Topping
1¼ cups buttermilk baking mix
¼ cup plus 1 teaspoon sugar
1½ teaspoons grated orange rind
⅓ cup milk
2 tablespoons butter, melted

1. Heat oven to 375°.
2. Prepare fruit: With a fork, mix sugar, cornstarch and orange rind in a small bowl until well blended. Mix strawberries and apricots in a 10-inch glass pie plate. Sprinkle sugar mixture evenly over fruit; gently toss fruit to coat evenly.
3. Prepare topping: Combine baking mix, ¼ cup sugar and orange rind in a medium-size bowl until well blended. Stir in milk and melted butter with a fork until dry ingredients are moistened.
4. Using rounded tablespoonfuls, drop dough onto fruit, forming a ring about 1 inch inside edge of pie plate. Sprinkle dough with remaining 1 teaspoon sugar. Place pie plate on a baking sheet to catch any drips.
5. Bake in heated 375° oven 1 hour or until topping is browned and fruit is bubbly in center. If topping begins to brown too much, cover with foil. Let cool 30 minutes before serving.

PER SERVING
218 calories, 6 g fat (3 g saturated), 2 g protein, 39 g carbohydrate, 1 g fiber, 238 mg sodium, 9 mg cholesterol.

Mixed-Berry Cornmeal Cobbler

MAKES 8 servings **PREP** 15 minutes
BAKE at 350° for 1 hour 20 minutes

1   pint blueberries (about 2 cups)
1   pint raspberries (about 2¼ cups)
1   pint strawberries, hulled and halved
½   cup sugar
3   tablespoons cornstarch

Topping
⅓   cup sugar
¼   cup (½ stick) butter, at room temperature
1   egg
1   teaspoon vanilla
⅔   cup all-purpose flour
⅓   cup yellow cornmeal
2   teaspoons baking powder
¼   teaspoon salt
¼   cup milk

1. Heat oven to 350°.

2. Toss blueberries, raspberries, strawberries, sugar and cornstarch in a large bowl until well mixed. Spoon into an ungreased 8 x 8 x 2-inch baking dish, spreading evenly.

3. Prepare topping: In same bowl, beat together sugar and butter on medium speed until light and fluffy, about 3 minutes. Beat in egg and vanilla until well blended.

4. Mix together flour, cornmeal, baking powder and salt in a small bowl.

5. Add half of flour mixture to butter mixture. On low speed, beat just until combined. Beat in milk, then remaining flour mixture. Drop dough by large spoonfuls onto berry mixture in baking dish.

6. Bake in heated 350° oven 1 hour 20 minutes or until top is golden and fruit is bubbly. Serve warm.

PER SERVING
272 calories, 7 g fat (4 g saturated), 4 g protein, 50 g carbohydrate, 4 g fiber, 178 mg sodium, 43 mg cholesterol.

Blueberry-Nectarine Crisp

MAKES 8 servings **PREP** 10 minutes
BAKE at 375° for 50 to 60 minutes

1½ pounds nectarines, pitted and cut into eighths
1   pint blueberries (about 2 cups)
½   cup granulated sugar
4   teaspoons lemon juice
1   tablespoon cornstarch
1   cup all-purpose flour
½   cup packed light-brown sugar
½   cup (1 stick) unsalted butter, cut into small pieces

1. Heat oven to 375°.

2. Toss nectarines, blueberries, granulated sugar, lemon juice and cornstarch in a large bowl. Spoon fruit mixture into an 8 x 8 x 2-inch baking dish.

3. In same bowl, mix flour and brown sugar. With fingertips, mix butter into flour mixture until crumbly. Sprinkle over top of fruit.

4. Bake in heated 375° oven 50 to 60 minutes or until crisp is bubbly and browned.

PER SERVING
311 calories, 12 g fat (7 g saturated), 3 g protein, 50 g carbohydrate, 3 g fiber, 8 mg sodium, 31 mg cholesterol.

Brandied Apple Bundt Cake

MAKES 16 servings **PREP** 25 minutes
BAKE at 350° for about 50 minutes

Cake
3¼ cups sifted cake flour (not self-rising)
1 teaspoon baking powder
¾ teaspoon salt
½ teaspoon baking soda
½ teaspoon ground cinnamon
½ teaspoon ground nutmeg
⅛ teaspoon ground cloves
½ cup (1 stick) butter, at room temperature
1 cup sugar
3 eggs
½ cup sour cream
1 cup unsweetened applesauce
2 Golden Delicious apples (about 1 pound), peeled and diced

Syrup
½ cup sugar
⅓ cup brandy or Calvados (apple brandy)
¼ cup apple juice

Glaze
1 cup plus 2 tablespoons confectioners' sugar
2 tablespoons apple juice
Pinch ground nutmeg

1. Heat oven to 350°. Coat a 10-inch bundt pan with nonstick cooking spray.

2. Prepare cake: Sift flour, baking powder, salt, baking soda, cinnamon, nutmeg and cloves into a small bowl.

3. Beat together butter and sugar in a large bowl on medium-high speed until smooth and creamy, about 2 minutes. Add eggs, one at a time, beating well after each addition. Beat in sour cream and applesauce; mixture may look curdled. On low speed, slowly add flour mixture, beating until well blended. Gently fold in apples. Scrape batter into prepared pan, smoothing top.

4. Bake in heated 350° oven about 50 minutes or until a wooden pick inserted in center of cake comes out clean.

5. Meanwhile, prepare syrup: Mix sugar, brandy and apple juice in a small saucepan. Cook over medium-low heat until sugar dissolves, stirring occasionally; do not boil. Remove from heat.

6. Transfer cake in pan to a wire rack. Brush top of cake with half of brandy syrup. Let stand 10 minutes. Invert cake onto wire rack and remove pan; place rack over a sheet of waxed paper. Brush cake with remaining syrup; let cool completely.

7. Prepare glaze: Stir together confectioners' sugar, apple juice and nutmeg in a small bowl until smooth. Drizzle over cake. Let harden slightly.

PER SERVING
300 calories, 9 g fat (5 g saturated), 3 g protein, 51 g carbohydrate, 1 g fiber, 190 mg sodium, 59 mg cholesterol.

2. Melt butter in a medium-size saucepan over low heat. Remove pan from heat. Stir in flour, brown sugar and cinnamon until mixture forms coarse crumbs. Measure out and reserve ½ cup mixture.

3. Whisk together sour cream and baking soda in a small bowl. Whisk in vanilla and egg yolk. Stir sour cream mixture into crumb mixture in saucepan, stirring until nearly smooth. Spread batter in prepared pan. Sprinkle top with reserved ½ cup crumb mixture.

4. Bake in heated 375° oven 20 minutes or until top is golden brown and a wooden pick inserted in center comes out clean. Serve warm or at room temperature. Dust with confectioners' sugar before serving if desired.

PER SERVING
341 calories, 14 g fat (9 g saturated), 4 g protein, 51 g carbohydrate, 2 g fiber, 140 mg sodium, 73 mg cholesterol.

Cinnamon Crumb Cake

MAKES 6 servings **PREP** 15 minutes **BAKE** at 375° for 20 minutes

6 tablespoons butter
1¼ cups all-purpose flour
¾ cup packed light-brown sugar
2 teaspoons ground cinnamon
½ cup reduced-fat sour cream, plain yogurt or buttermilk
½ teaspoon baking soda
1 teaspoon vanilla
1 egg yolk
Confectioners' sugar for dusting (optional)

1. Heat oven to 375°. Coat an 8 x 8 x 2-inch square baking pan with nonstick cooking spray.

Almond-Plum Coffee Cake

MAKES 8 servings **PREP** 20 minutes **BAKE** at 350° for about 1 hour

1½ cups all-purpose flour
2 teaspoons baking powder
¼ teaspoon salt
¾ cup granulated sugar
½ cup blanched whole almonds
½ cup (1 stick) butter, at room temperature, cut into 8 pieces
2 eggs
1 teaspoon vanilla
½ cup milk
1 teaspoon grated orange rind

Topping
1¼ **pounds plums (5 to 6 plums),
    pitted and cut into eighths (3 cups)**
¼ **cup granulated sugar**
2 **tablespoons butter, cut into
    small pieces
    Confectioners' sugar for dusting
    (optional)**

1. Heat oven to 350°. Butter and flour
    a 9-inch springform pan.

2. Combine flour, baking powder and
    salt in a medium-size bowl.

3. Place sugar and almonds in a food
    processor. Whirl until finely ground.
    Add butter to processor. Whirl to
    combine. Add eggs and vanilla; whirl
    to combine.

4. Add milk to mixture in processor;
    whirl until blended. Add flour mixture;
    whirl until well blended. Add orange
    rind; whirl to blend. Spoon batter
    into prepared pan.

5. Prepare topping: Arrange plum slices
    on batter, overlapping in a decorative
    pattern. Sprinkle granulated sugar
    over plums. Dot with butter.

6. Bake in heated 350° oven about
    1 hour or until top is lightly browned
    and a wooden pick inserted in
    center comes out clean. Dust with
    confectioners' sugar if desired. Cool
    before serving.

PER SERVING
426 calories, 22 g fat (10 g saturated), 7 g protein,
54 g carbohydrate, 3 g fiber, 188 mg sodium,
94 mg cholesterol.

Blueberry Crumb Cakes

MAKES 12 jumbo-muffin-size cakes
PREP 10 minutes
BAKE at 350° for 32 minutes

5 **crisp ginger cookies**
¼ **cup chopped pecans**
1 **box (1 pound) angelfood cake mix**
1 **cup water**
1 **can (15 ounces) blueberries in
    heavy syrup, drained and rinsed**
3 **tablespoons confectioners' sugar
    for dusting**

1. Position oven rack in lower third
    of oven. Heat oven to 350°. Line
    cups in 2 jumbo 6-muffin pans with
    paper liners.

2. Crush ginger cookies. Toss with
    chopped pecans in a small bowl.

3. Stir together cake mix and water in
    a large bowl until well blended.
    Beat on medium speed 1 to 2 minutes
    or until thick and fluffy. Fold in
    drained berries.

4. Spoon batter into prepared muffin
    cups, dividing equally. Sprinkle
    tops with cookie-pecan mixture,
    dividing equally.

5. Bake cakes in heated 350° oven
    32 minutes or until they are puffed
    and tops are lightly golden and firm.
    Remove cakes from pans and transfer
    to a wire rack to cool completely.

6. Sift confectioners' sugar over top of
    cooled cakes.

PER CAKE
201 calories, 2 g fat (0 g saturated), 4 g protein,
43 g carbohydrate, 1 g fiber, 299 mg sodium,
0 mg cholesterol.

Four-Layer Spice Cake

MAKES 12 servings **PREP** 40 minutes
BAKE at 350° for 30 minutes
ASSEMBLE 30 minutes
REFRIGERATE 1 hour

2½ cups all-purpose flour
1 tablespoon baking powder
2 teaspoons ground cinnamon
1 teaspoon ground nutmeg
1 teaspoon ground ginger
½ teaspoon ground cloves
½ teaspoon salt
1 cup (2 sticks) butter, at room temperature
1¼ cups packed dark-brown sugar
4 eggs
1 teaspoon vanilla extract
1 teaspoon walnut extract
¾ cup milk
¾ cup walnuts, finely chopped

Filling
6 tablespoons dark-brown sugar
6 tablespoons water
3 tablespoons dark rum
1 teaspoon unflavored gelatin
2 cups heavy cream
1 teaspoon vanilla extract
1 cup red glacé cherries, halved

Garnishes
¼ cup red glacé cherries, halved
¼ cup walnut halves
   Fresh mint sprigs

1. Heat oven to 350°. Coat two 8-inch round layer-cake pans with nonstick cooking spray. Line bottoms with waxed paper; coat paper with spray.

2. Whisk together flour, baking powder, cinnamon, nutmeg, ginger, cloves and salt in a large bowl.

3. In another large bowl, beat butter and sugar on medium-high speed about 3 minutes or until smooth and fluffy. Add eggs, one at a time, beating well after each addition. Add vanilla and walnut extracts and beat until combined.

4. On low speed, beat flour mixture into butter mixture in 3 additions, alternating with milk and ending with flour; then beat 2 minutes. Fold in nuts. Divide batter equally between prepared pans.

5. Bake in heated 350° oven 30 minutes or until a wooden pick inserted in center of cake layers comes out clean. Cool cake layers in pans on wire racks 10 to 15 minutes. Turn out onto wire racks; remove waxed paper. Let cool completely.

6. Meanwhile, prepare filling: Stir together brown sugar and water in a small heavy saucepan. Bring to boiling over medium-high heat. Remove syrup from heat. Stir in rum.

7. Place 2 tablespoons sugar syrup in a small dish. Sprinkle gelatin over top. Let stand until softened, about 1 minute. Stir to dissolve gelatin; warm slightly in a microwave oven if necessary to completely dissolve. Set remaining syrup aside.

8. Beat cream in a medium-size bowl on medium speed until frothy. Add gelatin mixture and vanilla. Beat on high speed until soft peaks form.

9. Slice each cake layer in half horizontally for a total of 4 layers. Place 1 layer on a cake plate. Brush

generously with reserved syrup. Spread 1 cup whipped cream over top of layer. Evenly arrange about ⅓ cup glacé cherries on whipped cream, gently pressing cherries into cream. Place a second cake layer on top; brush with syrup and add whipped cream and cherries as before; repeat once more.

10. Add fourth cake layer; brush with syrup. Spread remaining whipped cream over top. Garnish with glacé cherries, walnut halves and mint sprigs. Refrigerate at least 1 hour before serving.

PER SERVING
617 calories, 38 g fat (20 g saturated), 8 g protein, 62 g carbohydrate, 2 g fiber, 259 mg sodium, 169 mg cholesterol.

Macadamia Upside-Down Cake

MAKES 8 servings **PREP** 25 minutes
BAKE at 350° for 35 minutes

¾ **cup macadamia nuts (3 ounces), chopped**
1 **can (8½ ounces) crushed pineapple, drained**
6 **tablespoons butter or margarine**
⅓ **cup packed dark-brown sugar**
¼ **cup dark corn syrup**
2 **teaspoons water**
8 **glacé cherries**
1 **cup all-purpose flour**
1 **teaspoon baking powder**
⅛ **teaspoon salt**
2 **eggs**
⅔ **cup granulated sugar**
½ **cup milk**
1½ **teaspoons vanilla**

1. Position oven rack in lower part of oven. Heat oven to 350°. Grease an 8 x 8 x 2-inch square baking pan.

2. Combine nuts and pineapple in a small bowl.

3. Melt butter in a small saucepan. Transfer 2 tablespoons melted butter to a small cup and reserve. Add brown sugar, corn syrup and water to butter remaining in saucepan. Bring to boiling; cook 30 seconds, stirring to dissolve sugar. Pour into prepared baking pan. Scatter glacé cherries over brown sugar mixture; sprinkle nut-pineapple mixture on top.

4. Stir together flour, baking powder and salt on a sheet of waxed paper.

5. Beat eggs in a large bowl on medium speed until foamy, about 30 seconds. Gradually add granulated sugar, beating constantly. Beat in flour mixture just until blended. Add milk, reserved melted butter and vanilla; beat until blended. Pour into prepared pan.

6. Bake in lower part of heated 350° oven 35 minutes or until a wooden pick inserted in center comes out clean. Immediately run a thin metal spatula around edge of pan to loosen cake. Cool cake in pan on a wire rack 15 minutes.

7. Invert cake onto rack and remove pan. Replace any nuts or cherries that have fallen off. Cool cake at least 10 minutes longer before serving, or cool completely.

PER SERVING
382 calories, 18 g fat (7 g saturated), 5 g protein, 52 g carbohydrate, 1 g fiber, 130 mg sodium, 79 mg cholesterol.

Streusel-Topped Apple Cake

MAKES 16 servings **PREP** 20 minutes
BAKE at 350° for 50 minutes

2½ cups all-purpose flour
2 teaspoons baking powder
½ teaspoon baking soda
¼ teaspoon salt
¼ teaspoon ground cinnamon
⅛ teaspoon ground nutmeg
⅛ teaspoon ground cardamom
½ cup (1 stick) butter, at room temperature
1¼ cups granulated sugar
3 eggs
1 container (8 ounces) apple-cinnamon low-fat yogurt
⅓ cup apple juice
1 teaspoon vanilla
2 Granny Smith apples (1 pound), peeled, cored and coarsely chopped
½ cup chopped walnuts (optional)

Topping
¾ cup all-purpose flour
⅓ cup packed light-brown sugar
½ teaspoon ground cinnamon
⅓ cup butter, at room temperature
¼ cup chopped walnuts (optional)

1. Heat oven to 350°. Coat a 13 x 9 x 2-inch baking pan with nonstick cooking spray.

2. Whisk flour, baking powder, baking soda, salt, cinnamon, nutmeg and cardamom in a small bowl.

3. Beat butter and granulated sugar in a large bowl on medium-high speed until smooth and creamy, 2 minutes. Beat in eggs, one at a time, beating well after each addition. Mix yogurt, apple juice and vanilla in a small bowl.

4. On low speed, beat flour mixture into butter mixture in 3 additions, alternating with yogurt mixture and ending with flour mixture. Stir in apples and, if desired, walnuts. Spread batter in prepared pan.

5. Prepare topping: Mix flour, brown sugar and cinnamon in a small bowl. With fingertips, work butter into flour mixture until pea-size pieces form. Add nuts if desired. Sprinkle over batter.

6. Bake in heated 350° oven 50 minutes or until a wooden pick inserted in center comes out clean. Transfer pan to a wire rack to cool. Serve slightly warm.

PER SERVING
300 calories, 11 g fat (6 g saturated), 5 g protein, 46 g carbohydrate, 1 g fiber, 146 mg sodium, 66 mg cholesterol.

New York–Style Cheesecake

MAKES 16 servings PREP 20 minutes
BAKE at 325° for 1 hour 45 minutes
REFRIGERATE 6 hours or overnight

Crust

1⅔ cups graham cracker crumbs (about 12 whole graham crackers)
2 tablespoons granulated sugar
2 tablespoons light-brown sugar
¼ teaspoon ground cinnamon
3 tablespoons butter, melted

Filling

2 packages (8 ounces each) cream cheese, at room temperature
1 cup granulated sugar
¼ cup all-purpose flour
¼ cup heavy cream
4 eggs, at room temperature
1 teaspoon vanilla
½ teaspoon grated orange rind
½ teaspoon grated lemon rind
¼ teaspoon salt

Topping

1 cup sour cream
2 tablespoons granulated sugar
½ teaspoon vanilla

1. Heat oven to 325°. Wrap outside of a 9-inch springform pan with aluminum foil.

2. Prepare crust: Combine graham cracker crumbs, granulated sugar, brown sugar, cinnamon and butter in a small bowl until well blended. Press crumb mixture over bottom and halfway up sides of prepared pan.

3. Prepare filling: Beat together cream cheese, sugar and flour in a large bowl on medium speed until smooth and creamy, about 2 minutes. Add cream; beat 30 seconds. Add eggs, one at a time, beating well after each addition. Beat in vanilla, orange rind, lemon rind and salt until well combined. Scrape filling into crust in pan (it will come above crust sides); smooth top.

4. Place springform pan in a large baking pan on oven rack. Pour hot water into large pan to come halfway up sides of springform (see Baking Bath, page 178). Bake in heated 325° oven 1 hour 30 minutes or until center is set.

5. Remove springform pan from water; leave baking pan in oven and leave oven on.

6. Prepare topping: Stir together sour cream, granulated sugar and vanilla in a small bowl. Pour over cake top; spread evenly. Return springform pan to baking pan with water in oven. Bake another 15 minutes or until topping is set.

7. Remove springform pan from water; remove foil. Run a thin knife around inside of pan. Let cake cool in springform pan on a wire rack. Refrigerate, covered, 6 hours or overnight. Remove sides of pan to serve cake.

PER SERVING
392 calories, 28 g fat (17 g saturated), 7 g protein, 28 g carbohydrate, 0 g fiber, 284 mg sodium, 133 mg cholesterol.

Italian Ricotta Cheesecake

MAKES 16 servings **PREP** 20 minutes
BAKE at 325° for 1 hour 15 minutes
REFRIGERATE 6 hours or overnight

Crust

2	tablespoons butter, at room temperature
1	whole egg
2	tablespoons sugar
¼	teaspoon vanilla
⅛	teaspoon lemon extract
1	cup all-purpose flour
¾	teaspoon baking powder
¼	teaspoon salt
3	tablespoons pine nuts, toasted (see page 232)
1	egg white, lightly beaten

Filling

1¼	pounds ricotta cheese
1	cup sugar
5	eggs
4	teaspoons all-purpose flour
1	teaspoon vanilla
½	teaspoon grated lemon rind

Topping

2	tablespoons apricot jam
9	tablespoons pine nuts, toasted (see page 232)

1. Heat oven to 325°. Wrap outside of a 9-inch springform pan with aluminum foil.

2. Prepare crust: Beat butter, whole egg and sugar in a medium-size bowl until combined, 2 minutes. Beat in vanilla and lemon extract. Sift flour, baking powder and salt onto a piece of waxed paper. Beat flour mixture into egg mixture until a dough forms.

3. Shape dough into a disc and place between 2 sheets of waxed paper. Roll out into a 10-inch round crust. Peel off top sheet of paper; invert crust into prepared pan. Without stretching, press crust onto bottom and sides of pan; peel off remaining paper. If there are holes in crust, press closed with fingers.

4. Scatter nuts over crust; lightly press nuts into surface. Brush crust with a small amount of egg white; discard remainder of white.

5. Prepare filling: Beat together ricotta, sugar, eggs, flour, vanilla and lemon rind in a medium-size bowl until well combined, about 2 minutes. Pour into crust in pan.

6. Place springform pan in a large baking pan on oven rack. Pour hot water into large pan to come halfway up sides of springform (see Baking Bath, page 178). Bake in heated 325° oven 1 hour 15 minutes or until center is set. If top of filling begins to brown too much, cover loosely with aluminum foil.

7. Remove springform pan from water; remove foil. Run a thin knife around inside of pan. Let cake cool in springform pan on a wire rack. Refrigerate, covered, 6 hours or overnight.

8. Prepare topping: Remove sides of pan. Melt jam in a small saucepan. Brush around top edge of cake, making a 1-inch border. Sprinkle border with nuts.

PER SERVING
234 calories, 12 g fat (5 g saturated), 9 g protein, 25 g carbohydrate, 1 g fiber, 110 mg sodium, 102 mg cholesterol.

Amaretto Light Cheesecake

MAKES 16 servings **PREP** 20 minutes
BAKE at 325° for 1 hour
REFRIGERATE 4 hours or overnight

11	reduced-fat chocolate sandwich cookies, crushed (about 1 cup)
2	tablespoons chopped pecans
3	tablespoons butter, melted
8	ounces low-fat (1%) cottage cheese
2	packages (8 ounces each) ⅓-less-fat cream cheese, at room temperature
¾	cup sugar
¼	teaspoon salt
2	tablespoons amaretto liqueur
2	tablespoons cornstarch
2	teaspoons vanilla extract
1	teaspoon almond extract
3	whole eggs
6	egg whites
1½	cups fresh raspberries

1. Heat oven to 325°. Wrap outside of a 9-inch springform pan with aluminum foil.

2. Mix cookies, pecans and butter in a small bowl. Pat over bottom of prepared pan.

3. Whirl cottage cheese in a food processor to puree. Add cream cheese, sugar and salt; whirl to combine. Add amaretto, cornstarch, vanilla and almond extracts; whirl 1 minute. Transfer to a large bowl. Add whole eggs and egg whites, one at a time, beating after each addition. Pour filling over cookie crust in pan.

4. Place springform pan in a large baking pan on oven rack. Pour hot water into large pan to come halfway up sides of springform (see Baking Bath, page 178). Bake in heated 325° oven 1 hour or until center is set.

5. Remove springform pan from water; remove foil. Run a thin knife around inside of pan. Let cake cool in springform pan on a wire rack. Refrigerate, covered, 4 hours or overnight.

6. Remove sides of pan. Arrange berries on cake.

PER SERVING
211 calories, 10 g fat (5 g saturated), 8 g protein, 23 g carbohydrate, 2 g fiber, 251 mg sodium, 62 mg cholesterol.

Chocolate Cheesecake

MAKES 16 servings **PREP** 20 minutes
BAKE at 325° for 1 hour 10 minutes
REFRIGERATE 6 hours or overnight

Chocolate Crust

1¼ cups chocolate wafer cookie crumbs (about 28 cookies)
¼ cup slivered blanched almonds, ground
¼ cup (½ stick) butter, melted
2 tablespoons sugar
¼ teaspoon salt

Filling

1 package (12 ounces) semisweet chocolate chips (2 cups)
1½ pounds cream cheese, at room temperature
¾ cup sugar
1 tablespoon cornstarch
4 eggs, at room temperature
1 cup sour cream
1 teaspoon vanilla

Garnishes

½ cup sliced almonds
½ cup heavy cream
1 tablespoon packaged premelted unsweetened chocolate
½ teaspoon vanilla

1. Heat oven to 325°. Wrap outside of a 9-inch springform pan with aluminum foil.

2. Prepare crust: Mix cookie crumbs, almonds, butter, sugar and salt in a medium-size bowl. Pat evenly over bottom of prepared pan.

3. Prepare filling: Melt chocolate chips in top of a double boiler over barely simmering, not boiling, water. Beat cream cheese, sugar and cornstarch in a large bowl until creamy, 2 minutes.

Add eggs, one at a time, beating well after each addition. Beat in melted chocolate, sour cream and vanilla. Pour filling over crust in pan.

4. Place springform pan in a large baking pan on oven rack. Pour hot water into large pan to come halfway up sides of springform. Bake in heated 325° oven 1 hour 10 minutes or until center is set.

5. Remove springform pan from water; remove foil. Run a thin knife around inside of pan. Let cake cool in springform pan on a wire rack. Refrigerate, uncovered, 6 hours or overnight.

6. Add garnishes: Remove sides of pan. Sprinkle a few sliced almonds onto center of cake top. Cover cake sides with remaining almonds, pressing lightly to adhere. Beat heavy cream, unsweetened chocolate and vanilla in a medium-size bowl until stiff peaks form; spoon into a pastry bag fitted with a medium-size tip. Pipe rosettes around top edge of cake, spacing them about 1 inch apart.

PER SERVING
462 calories, 35 g fat (19 g saturated), 8 g protein, 35 g carbohydrate, 2 g fiber, 236 mg sodium, 124 mg cholesterol.

Baking Bath

Add hot water to baking pan, filling to halfway up sides of foil-wrapped springform pan.

Orange–Poppy Seed Bundt Cake

MAKES 16 servings **PREP** 30 minutes
BAKE at 350° for 40 to 45 minutes

3   cups cake flour (not self-rising)
2   teaspoons baking powder
⅛   teaspoon salt
1   cup (2 sticks) butter, at room temperature
1½ cups granulated sugar
5   eggs
2   teaspoons vanilla extract
½   teaspoon orange extract
2   teaspoons grated orange rind
1   cup orange juice
2   tablespoons poppy seeds

Glaze
2   cups confectioners' sugar
2½ tablespoons orange juice
1½ teaspoons grated orange rind

Garnish (optional)
2   unsprayed fresh roses, separated into petals
    Powdered egg whites mixed to equal to 1 egg white (see page 232)
2   tablespoons superfine sugar

1. Heat oven to 350°. Coat a 10-inch (12-cup) bundt pan with nonstick cooking spray.

2. Whisk together flour, baking powder and salt in a large bowl.

3. Beat butter and granulated sugar in a second large bowl on medium-high speed until smooth, about 3 minutes. Add eggs, one at a time, beating well after each addition. Beat in vanilla and orange extracts and orange rind until combined.

4. On low speed, beat flour mixture into egg mixture in 3 additions, alternating with orange juice and ending with

flour mixture. Beat on medium-high speed 2 minutes or until well blended. Stir in poppy seeds. Pour batter into prepared pan.

5. Bake in heated 350° oven 40 to 45 minutes or until a wooden pick inserted in center of cake comes out clean. Cool in pan on a wire rack 15 minutes. Turn out cake onto rack and cool completely.

6. Prepare glaze: Beat confectioners' sugar, orange juice and orange rind in a medium-size bowl on medium speed until smooth. Drizzle over cooled cake. Let stand until set.

7. Prepare garnish if using: Lightly brush rose petals on both sides with egg white. Sprinkle both sides with superfine sugar. Place petals on a wire rack in a cool place to dry, about 1 hour. Arrange on cake.

PER SERVING
336 calories, 14 g fat (8 g saturated), 4 g protein, 50 g carbohydrate, 1 g fiber, 88 mg sodium, 98 mg cholesterol.

Basketweave Cake

MAKES 16 servings
PREP 30 minutes plus decorating time
BAKE at 350° for 25 minutes
REFRIGERATE 1 hour

Cake
2¼ cups all-purpose flour
1 tablespoon baking powder
½ teaspoon salt
¼ cup (½ stick) butter, at room temperature
1½ cups granulated sugar
4 eggs
2 teaspoons vanilla
1¼ cups milk

Vanilla and Chocolate Frostings
½ cup (1 stick) butter, at room temperature
½ cup solid vegetable shortening
2 boxes (1 pound each) confectioners' sugar
10 tablespoons milk, plus more if needed
2 teaspoons vanilla
6 squares (1 ounce each) unsweetened chocolate, melted and slightly cooled

Decorations
**Assorted prepared candy flowers and leaves (see note, opposite)
Yellow candy-coated almonds**

1. Prepare cake: Heat oven to 350°. Coat two 8 x 8 x 2-inch square cake pans with nonstick cooking spray. Line bottoms with waxed paper; coat paper with spray.

2. Whisk together flour, baking powder and salt in a large bowl.

3. Beat butter in a large bowl on medium speed 1 minute or until creamy. Add granulated sugar; beat 2 minutes or until fluffy. Add eggs, one at a time, beating after each addition. Beat in vanilla.

4. On low speed, beat flour mixture into butter mixture in 3 additions, alternating with milk and ending with flour mixture. Beat 2 minutes on medium speed. Divide batter equally between prepared cake pans.

5. Bake in heated 350° oven 25 minutes or until a wooden pick inserted in center of cake layers comes out clean. Cool cake layers in pans on wire racks 10 minutes. Turn out onto wire racks; remove waxed paper. Let cakes cool completely.

6. Meanwhile, prepare frostings: Beat butter and shortening in a large bowl on medium speed until blended, about 1 minute. Add confectioners' sugar, milk and vanilla; beat on low speed until blended. Beat on medium-high 1 minute. Transfer ¼ cup frosting to a small bowl; cover with plastic wrap.

7. On low speed, beat melted chocolate into larger amount of frosting until smooth. Add additional milk if needed for a good spreading consistency. Cover with plastic wrap.

Decorate

1. Place 1 cake layer on a cake plate. Spread ½ cup chocolate frosting over top. Place second layer on top of first. Spread reserved white vanilla frosting over top. Using ¼ cup chocolate frosting, spread a thin layer over sides of cake.

2. Fit a pastry bag with a coupler and basketweave tip. Fill bag halfway with chocolate frosting. To make a basketweave pattern, begin by piping a vertical band up one side of cake. At top, pipe a short horizontal band across and to the right of this vertical band. Leave a space the width of a band, and pipe another horizontal band beneath it. Repeat until you reach bottom of cake. Pipe another vertical band adjacent to first vertical band and over ends of horizontal bands. To fill in the open spaces, bury tip under first vertical band and pipe short horizontal bands across second vertical band. Continue in this manner to cover sides of cake. Refill bag as needed.

3. With same pastry bag, make a zigzag pattern around top edge of cake where chocolate frosting meets white frosting.

4. Decorate top with flowers and leaves. Use frosting as glue.

5. For bumblebees, press almonds onto top of cake. Fit a small writing tip onto pastry bag with chocolate frosting. Draw bumblebee stripes, wings, antennae and stinger over each almond. Refrigerate cake 1 hour to set.

Note: To make your own decorative flowers and leaves, prepare Royal Icing, page 206. Use soft gel food coloring to tint small amounts in various colors. Refer to Rosebud Cake, page 183, for a method of flower and leaf making.

PER SERVING (without flower decorations)
584 calories, 23 g fat (12 g saturated), 6 g protein, 93 g carbohydrate, 2 g fiber, 171 mg sodium, 80 mg cholesterol.

Foolproof Basketweave

Fill in intervals with short horizontal bands; begin at the first vertical band and pipe across the second.

Rosebud Cake

Follow our detailed instructions to make this glorious cake, shown on page 133.

MAKES 16 servings
PREP 35 minutes plus decorating time
BAKE at 350° for 30 to 32 minutes

Cake

3	cups all-purpose flour
4	teaspoons baking powder
½	teaspoon salt
¾	cup (1½ sticks) butter, at room temperature
2	cups granulated sugar
5	eggs
1	teaspoon vanilla
½	teaspoon lemon extract
1¼	cups water

Frosting and Filling

¾	cup (1½ sticks) butter, at room temperature
2	boxes (1 pound each) confectioners' sugar
¼	cup milk, plus more if needed
¼	cup fresh lemon juice
2	teaspoons vanilla extract
½	cup strawberry preserves

Royal Icing (page 206)
Leaf green and fuchsia soft gel paste food coloring

1. Prepare cake: Heat oven to 350°. Coat three 9-inch round layer-cake pans with nonstick cooking spray. Line bottoms with waxed paper; coat paper with spray.

2. Whisk together flour, baking powder and salt in a large bowl.

3. Beat butter in a large bowl on medium speed about 1 minute or until creamy. Add granulated sugar; beat 2 minutes or until fluffy. Add eggs, one at a time, beating well after each addition. Add vanilla and lemon extracts; beat 1 minute.

4. On low speed, beat flour mixture into butter mixture in 3 additions, alternating with water and ending with flour mixture. On medium-high, beat 3 minutes. Divide batter equally among pans.

5. Bake in heated 350° oven 30 to 32 minutes or until a wooden pick inserted in center of cake layers comes out clean. Cool cake layers in pans on wire racks 10 minutes. Turn out onto wire racks; remove waxed paper. Let cool completely. Trim layers with a serrated knife to level if necessary.

6. Meanwhile, prepare frosting and filling: Beat butter in a large bowl on medium speed until fluffy, 1 minute. Add confectioners' sugar, milk, lemon juice and vanilla; beat on low speed until well blended. Beat 1 minute. Add additional milk if necessary for a spreading consistency. For filling, mix 1 cup frosting and strawberry preserves in a small bowl; cover and set aside. Press plastic wrap onto surface of frosting; set aside.

Leaves, Roses and Rosebuds

1. Divide Royal Icing between 2 small bowls. Tint 1 bowl leaf green and 1 bowl fuchsia. Press plastic wrap onto surface of icing and keep covered until ready to use.

2. Line 3 baking sheets with waxed paper.

3. Fit a medium-size pastry bag with a coupler and plain medium leaf tip; fill bag halfway with green icing. Pipe about 30 small leaves onto paper on 1 baking sheet. Cover end of tip with moist paper toweling and plastic wrap until ready to pipe vines.

4. Fit another medium-size pastry bag with a coupler and plain medium rose tip. Fill halfway with fuchsia icing. Using a flower nail with a small square of waxed paper (attached with a drop of icing) for each rose, pipe about 12 large roses. To begin, pipe a small cone in center. Then pipe a stand-up petal around cone. Continue, piping about 4 concentric stand-up petals around center. Transfer each rose on its paper square to paper on second baking sheet. Replenish bag with icing as needed.

5. Pipe about 20 rosebuds onto third baking sheet. Let leaves, roses and rosebuds dry completely.

Decorate

1. Place ½ cup white frosting in a pastry bag fitted with a large round tip. Measure out ½ cup frosting for piping around bottom of cake; cover and reserve. Keep remainder of frosting in bowl covered until ready to frost top and sides of cake.

2. Place 1 cake layer on a cake plate. Using white frosting in bag, pipe a border around top edge of layer. Spread half of strawberry filling inside white border. Place second cake layer on top; pipe a border and spread remaining filling in same way. Place remaining cake layer on top.

3. Frost top and sides of cake with remaining white frosting in mixing bowl.

4. Using a wooden pick, gently outline a trailing vine pattern on top and sides of cake. Place a small round tip on pastry bag with green icing. Pipe vines over pattern on cake.

5. Carefully remove leaves and rosebuds from waxed paper. Attach over vines, using a dab of green icing for glue. Remove roses from paper and glue onto cake with green icing. Spoon reserved ½ cup white frosting into bag fitted with a large round tip. Pipe a border around bottom of cake. Refrigerate at least 1 hour to set.

PER SERVING (without flower decorations)
607 calories, 19 g fat (11 g saturated), 5 g protein, 106 g carbohydrate, 1 g fiber, 191 mg sodium, 114 mg cholesterol.

Glorious Roses

Pipe a small icing cone in center of flower nail. Then for first petal, pipe a stand-up ring of icing around cone.

Continue, piping about 4 concentric stand-up petals around center.

Ribbons and Bows Cake

MAKES 16 servings
PREP 30 minutes plus decorating time
BAKE at 350° for 25 to 30 minutes
REFRIGERATE 1 hour

Cake

3½ cups cake flour (not self-rising)
1¼ teaspoons baking soda
½ teaspoon salt
1 cup solid vegetable shortening
2 cups granulated sugar
1 teaspoon vanilla
3 tablespoons peach schnapps
1 cup buttermilk
½ cup diced canned peaches (4 peach halves in heavy syrup, drained)
6 egg whites
1 teaspoon cream of tartar

Frosting

½ cup (1 stick) unsalted butter, at room temperature
½ cup solid vegetable shortening, at room temperature
2 boxes (1 pound each) confectioners' sugar
6 tablespoons milk, plus more if needed
1 tablespoon plus 1 teaspoon peach schnapps
Green, yellow and red soft gel paste food coloring

1. Prepare cake: Heat oven to 350°. Coat three 8-inch round layer-cake pans with nonstick cooking spray. Line bottoms with waxed paper; coat paper with spray.

2. Whisk together flour, baking soda and salt in a large bowl.

3. Beat shortening in a large bowl on medium speed, gradually adding 1½ cups granulated sugar, vanilla and schnapps; beat mixture 1 minute.

4. On low speed, beat flour mixture into shortening mixture in 3 additions, alternating with buttermilk and ending with flour mixture. Beat 2 minutes on medium-high speed. With a rubber spatula, gently fold in peaches.

5. Beat egg whites in a medium-size bowl on medium speed until foamy. Add cream of tartar; beat on high speed until soft peaks form. Gradually beat in remaining ½ cup granulated sugar until stiff, glossy peaks form.

6. Stir about one-quarter of beaten egg whites into cake batter to lighten. Carefully fold in remaining egg whites. Divide batter equally among prepared pans.

7. Bake in heated 350° oven 25 to 30 minutes or until a wooden pick inserted into center of cake layers comes out clean. Cool cake layers in pans on wire racks 10 minutes. Turn out onto wire racks; remove waxed paper. Let cool completely.

8. Meanwhile, prepare frosting: Beat together butter and vegetable shortening in a large bowl on medium speed until blended, about 1 minute. Add confectioners' sugar, milk and schnapps; beat on low speed until mixture is well blended. Scrape down sides of bowl with a rubber spatula. Beat on high speed 1 minute or until frosting is very smooth and spreadable. Add additional milk if necessary for good spreading consistency.

9. Spoon ½ cup frosting into a pastry bag fitted with a small star tip. Cover tip with plastic wrap until ready to use. Tint 1 cup frosting medium green. Place in another pastry bag fitted with a plain medium-size rose tip. Cover tip until ready to use. Tint remainder of frosting peach, using 3 parts yellow to 1 part red food coloring.

Decorate

1. Place 1 cake layer on a cake plate. Spread ½ cup peach frosting over top. Place another cake layer on top of first. Spread ½ cup peach frosting over top. Top with third cake layer. Frost top and sides of cake with remaining peach frosting.

2. For ribbon garland, use a wooden pick to make 6 equidistant marks around top edge of cake. Using pastry bag filled with green frosting, pipe a shallow swag on side of cake between 2 marks; below it, pipe a second swag between same marks. Repeat to pipe double swags between remaining marks.

3. Continuing with bag of green frosting, pipe a bow at each mark (where double swags meet); use a figure-8 motion for bow loops, then use a downward motion to give each bow 2 tails.

4. Using pastry bag filled with white frosting, pipe a ring of stars along top edge of cake. Pipe a second ring of stars around base at cake plate. Refrigerate 1 hour to set.

PER SERVING
660 calories, 26 g fat (9 g saturated), 4 g protein, 105 g carbohydrate, 1 g fiber, 208 mg sodium, 17 mg cholesterol.

Festive Ribbons and Bows

Use a figure-8 motion to pipe bow loops between each set of double swags.

Citrus Roll

A light, pretty cake with a peppy, refreshing taste, this is a good choice to serve at the end of a rich meal.

MAKES 10 servings **PREP** 15 minutes
BAKE at 400° for 8 to 10 minutes

Cake

¼ **cup all-purpose flour**
½ **teaspoon baking powder**
4 **eggs, separated**
¼ **teaspoon salt**
⅓ **cup granulated sugar**
½ **teaspoon lemon extract**

Filling

1 **cup frozen light nondairy whipped topping, thawed**
⅓ **cup jarred lemon curd**
1 **can (11 ounces) Mandarin orange segments, drained and patted dry**

Confectioners' sugar for dusting (optional)
Fresh mint sprigs for garnish (optional)

1. Prepare cake: Heat oven to 400°. Coat a 15½ x 10½ x 1-inch jelly-roll pan with nonstick cooking spray. Line bottom of pan with aluminum foil, leaving a 2-inch overhang on short ends. Lightly coat foil with nonstick cooking spray.

2. Sift flour and baking powder onto a sheet of waxed paper.

3. Beat egg whites and salt in a large bowl until whites are fluffy. Gradually beat in sugar until firm, but not dry, peaks form. Beat egg yolks and lemon extract in a medium-size bowl until mixture is thick and lemon-colored, about 3 minutes.

4. Gently fold ½ cup beaten egg whites into egg yolks to lighten. Fold in remaining whites and flour mixture until no streaks of white remain. Spread batter in prepared pan, making sure batter is even all around edges.

5. Bake in heated 400° oven 8 to 10 minutes or until top is golden and cake springs back when lightly pressed with a fingertip.

6. Place a 16-inch-long sheet of aluminum foil on a wire rack. Coat foil with nonstick cooking spray. Loosen cake around edges with a thin knife; invert cake onto foil. Remove pan; peel top layer of foil from cake. Let cake cool.

7. Prepare filling: Gently fold together whipped topping and lemon curd in a small bowl. Set aside 5 Mandarin orange sections; coarsely chop remainder. Fold chopped oranges into lemon curd mixture.

8. Transfer foil with cake to a flat surface. Spread filling evenly over entire cake. Using foil as an aid, roll up cake from a short end. Discard foil. Place cake, seam side down, on a serving platter. If desired, sift confectioners' sugar over top of cake and garnish with reserved Mandarin oranges and mint sprigs.

PER SERVING
118 calories, 4 g fat (1 g saturated), 3 g protein, 19 g carbohydrate, 0 g fiber, 107 mg sodium, 85 mg cholesterol.

Strawberry Jelly Roll

MAKES 10 servings **PREP** 30 minutes
BAKE at 375° for about 12 minutes
REFRIGERATE at least 1 hour

Cake

8	**egg whites**
½	**teaspoon cream of tartar**
¾	**cup granulated sugar**
¼	**cup vegetable oil**
1	**teaspoon vanilla**
¾	**cup sifted self-rising cake flour**
3	**tablespoons confectioners' sugar**

Filling

1	**container (8 ounces) strawberry-flavor cream cheese, at room temperature**
¼	**cup sour cream**
¼	**cup strawberry jam**
1½	**cups chopped strawberries (1 pint)**

Garnishes (optional)

**Confectioners' sugar
Whole strawberries**

1. Prepare cake: Heat oven to 375°. Coat a 15½ x 10½ x 1-inch jelly-roll pan with nonstick cooking spray. Line bottom of pan with waxed paper; lightly coat paper with nonstick cooking spray.

2. Beat egg whites and cream of tartar in a large bowl until foamy. Gradually add ¼ cup granulated sugar and beat until soft peaks form.

3. Beat together oil and remaining ½ cup granulated sugar in a second large bowl until well mixed, about 1 minute. Beat in vanilla.

4. Stir cake flour into oil mixture. Gently fold in one-quarter of egg whites until completely blended, then gently fold in remaining egg whites. Spread batter evenly in prepared pan.

5. Bake in heated 375° oven about 12 minutes or until top is very lightly browned and springs back when lightly pressed with a fingertip.

6. Loosen cake around edges with a thin knife. Sprinkle top with confectioners' sugar. Cover with a clean kitchen towel. Top with a slightly larger baking sheet; invert. Remove pan, then waxed paper. Starting from a short end, roll up cake and towel together. Place seam side down on a wire rack to cool.

7. Prepare filling: Stir together cream cheese, sour cream and jam in a medium-size bowl. Gently fold in strawberries.

8. Unroll cake. Spread filling over cake, leaving a ½-inch border all around edges of cake. Carefully reroll cake. Refrigerate at least 1 hour.

9. Place cake, seam side down, on a serving platter. Trim ends of cake. If desired, sprinkle roll evenly with confectioners' sugar and garnish with strawberries.

PER SERVING
265 calories, 13 g fat (5 g saturated), 5 g protein, 32 g carbohydrate, 0 g fiber, 214 mg sodium, 20 mg cholesterol.

Cake-Rolling Hints

Starting from a short end, roll up cake and towel together.

Six-Layer Cake with Chocolate Ganache Frosting

When sliced, this tall and festively trimmed cake reveals its colorful layers.

MAKES 16 servings
PREP 45 minutes plus decorating time
BAKE at 350° for 20 minutes
REFRIGERATE 1 hour

Cake

2¼   cups all-purpose flour
1   tablespoon baking powder
½   teaspoon salt
¼   cup (½ stick) butter, at room temperature
1½   cups granulated sugar
4   eggs
2   teaspoons vanilla
1¼   cups plus 2 tablespoons milk
       Pink soft gel paste food coloring
2   tablespoons unsweetened cocoa powder

Filling

1   cup heavy cream
1   teaspoon vanilla
3   tablespoons granulated sugar

Ganache Frosting

1½   cups heavy cream
12   squares (1 ounce each) semisweet chocolate, chopped

Marshmallow Collar

¾   cup marshmallow cream
1¼   cups confectioners' sugar
       Cornstarch for dusting

1   tablespoon confectioners' sugar for dusting

1. Prepare cake: Heat oven to 350°. Coat three 8-inch round layer-cake pans with nonstick cooking spray. Line bottoms with waxed paper; coat paper with spray.

2. Whisk together flour, baking powder and salt in a large bowl.

3. Beat butter in a large bowl on medium speed until smooth and creamy, about 1 minute. Add granulated sugar and beat until light and fluffy, about 2 minutes. Add eggs, one at a time, beating well after each addition. Add vanilla and beat 1 minute.

4. On low speed, beat flour mixture into butter mixture in 3 additions, alternating with 1¼ cups milk and ending with flour mixture. Beat on medium speed 2 minutes.

5. Pour 1½ cups batter into 1 prepared pan. Pour 1½ cups batter into a small bowl; tint pink and pour into second prepared pan. In a small measuring cup, mix together remaining 2 tablespoons milk and cocoa powder until dissolved. Beat into remaining batter. Pour into remaining prepared pan.

6. Bake in heated 350° oven about 20 minutes or until a wooden pick inserted in center of cake layers comes out clean. Cool cake layers in pans on wire racks about 10 minutes. Turn out onto wire racks; remove waxed paper. Let cool completely.

7. Prepare filling: Beat cream in a medium-size bowl on medium-high speed until foamy. Add vanilla and granulated sugar, 1 tablespoon at a time, beating until medium-stiff peaks form. Cover bowl and refrigerate filling until ready to use.

8. Prepare ganache frosting: Heat cream in a medium-size saucepan to boiling. Pour over chopped chocolate in a heatproof bowl; stir until chocolate is melted and smooth. Beat on medium speed until cool and fluffy, 5 to 7 minutes; do not overbeat, or frosting will be difficult to pipe. Cover; set aside.

9. Place wooden picks around sides of 1 cake layer, measuring halfway up side. Using picks as a guide, slice cake in half horizontally. Repeat with other 2 cake layers to make a total of 6 layers.

10. Place 1 chocolate cake layer on a cake plate; spread ⅓ cup filling over top. Place a pink layer on top; spread with ⅓ cup filling. Place a vanilla layer on top; spread with ⅓ cup filling. Repeat with remaining 3 cake layers and filling, ending with a vanilla cake layer, no filling on top.

Decorate

1. Cover sides of cake with ganache frosting. Using a pastry comb, make a decorative pattern on frosting. Spread a thin layer of ganache over top of cake. Spoon remaining ganache into a pastry bag fitted with a coupler and ⅜-inch plain round tip.

2. Prepare marshmallow collar: Stir marshmallow cream and 1 cup confectioners' sugar in a medium-size bowl with a wooden spoon until a thick mass forms. Knead in bowl until mass comes together. Turn out onto a work surface; knead until smooth, working in more confectioners' sugar.

3. Dust work surface and a rolling pin with cornstarch. Shape marshmallow mixture into a disc. Roll out to ⅛-inch thickness. Cut into 1½-inch-wide strips.

4. Crimp each strip as you would a piecrust, forming a ruffle. Arrange ruffled strips around top of cake, slightly overhanging edge.

5. Using pastry bag with ganache, pipe teardrops over top of cake; space teardrops tightly and cover surface in an orderly pattern.

6. Replace ⅜-inch tip with a small round tip. Pipe a ring of small beads around base of cake.

7. Using a small sieve, carefully dust confectioners' sugar evenly over ganache teardrops, being careful not to dust marshmallow collar. Refrigerate cake at least 1 hour before serving.

PER SERVING
506 calories, 26 g fat (11 g saturated), 6 g protein, 63 g carbohydrate, 1 g fiber, 183 mg sodium, 115 mg cholesterol.

Double-Chocolate Fudge Cake

MAKES 12 servings **PREP** 20 minutes
COOK about 15 minutes **BAKE** at 350° for
30 minutes **REFRIGERATE** 30 minutes

Cake

4	squares (1 ounce each) unsweetened chocolate, chopped
2	cups all-purpose flour
2	teaspoons baking powder
½	teaspoon baking soda
½	teaspoon salt
¾	cup (1½ sticks) butter or margarine, at room temperature
1½	cups packed light-brown sugar
2	eggs
1	teaspoon vanilla
1	cup plus 2 tablespoons milk

Creamy Fudge Frosting

4	egg yolks
2	cups granulated sugar
1	cup milk
2	tablespoons butter or margarine
8	squares (1 ounce each) unsweetened chocolate, chopped
2	teaspoons vanilla

Garnish

¼	cup semisweet chocolate chips
24	whole blanched almonds

1. Prepare cake: Heat oven to 350°. Coat two 8-inch round layer-cake pans with nonstick cooking spray.

2. Melt chocolate in top of a double boiler over barely simmering, not boiling, water; stir until smooth.

3. Sift flour, baking powder, baking soda and salt into a medium-size bowl.

4. Beat butter in a large bowl until creamy. Beat in brown sugar. Add eggs to butter mixture, one at a time, beating after each addition. Add vanilla and melted chocolate. Sift flour mixture into butter mixture in 3 additions, alternating with milk and ending with flour mixture, beating after each addition. Pour into prepared pans, dividing equally.

5. Bake in heated 350° oven 30 minutes or until a wooden pick inserted in center of cake layers comes out clean. Cool cake layers in pans on wire racks 10 minutes. Loosen edges with a knife; turn out onto racks. Cool completely.

6. Prepare frosting: Beat egg yolks in a medium-size bowl until thick and lemon-colored. Gradually beat in 1 cup granulated sugar until very light in color, 5 to 7 minutes. Beat in milk.

7. Transfer mixture to a medium-size saucepan and add butter and remaining 1 cup granulated sugar. Slowly bring to boiling over medium heat, whisking occasionally, 12 to 15 minutes. Boil, whisking, 1 minute. Remove from heat. Using a wooden spoon, stir in chocolate until melted; add vanilla. Transfer to a medium-size bowl. Refrigerate 30 minutes or until spreading consistency.

8. Beat frosting on medium speed until light and fluffy, about 4 minutes. Immediately frost cake, using 1 cup to sandwich layers, 1½ cups for sides and ½ cup for top.

9. Prepare garnish: Melt chocolate in top of a double boiler over barely simmering, not boiling, water, stirring until smooth. Dip one end of each almond into chocolate and then stand it, dipped side down, at edge of cake, forming a ring.

PER SERVING
631 calories, 36 g fat (20 g saturated), 9 g protein, 80 g carbohydrate, 5 g fiber, 253 mg sodium, 149 mg cholesterol.

Strawberry Cupcakes

MAKES 18 cupcakes PREP 15 minutes
COOK 8 to 10 minutes STAND 1 hour
BAKE at 350° for 18 to 20 minutes

1½ cups chopped strawberries (about
    1 pint whole strawberries)
1¼ cups granulated sugar
1   teaspoon grated lemon rind
2   cups cake flour (not self-rising)
1   teaspoon baking powder
½   teaspoon baking soda
¼   teaspoon salt
½   cup (1 stick) butter, at room
    temperature
3   eggs
1   teaspoon vanilla
¾   cup buttermilk

Frosting
¼   cup (½ stick) butter, at room
    temperature
1¾ cups confectioners' sugar
2   tablespoons milk
¼   teaspoon vanilla

Garnishes (optional)
9   strawberries, halved or quartered
¼   cup strawberry jelly, melted

1. Heat oven to 350°. Line 18 cups
   in 2 standard 12-muffin pans with
   paper liners.

2. Mix chopped strawberries, ¼ cup
   granulated sugar and lemon rind in a
   medium-size saucepan. Cook over
   medium heat, stirring occasionally,
   8 to 10 minutes or until sugar is
   dissolved and mixture is thickened.
   Spoon into a small bowl; let cool
   completely, about 1 hour.

3. Mix flour, baking powder, baking
   soda and salt in a large bowl.

4. Beat together butter and remaining
   1 cup granulated sugar in a medium-
   size bowl on low speed until fluffy,
   about 2 minutes. Add eggs, one
   at a time, beating after each addition.
   Beat in vanilla.

5. On low speed, beat flour mixture
   into butter mixture in 3 additions,
   alternating with buttermilk and
   ending with flour mixture. Swirl in
   cooled strawberry mixture to create a
   marble pattern. Divide batter equally
   among prepared muffin cups.

6. Bake in heated 350° oven 18 to
   20 minutes or until cupcakes spring
   back when lightly pressed with a
   fingertip. Let cool in pans on a wire
   rack 5 to 10 minutes. Turn out
   cupcakes onto rack to cool completely.

7. Prepare frosting: Beat together butter,
   confectioners' sugar, milk and vanilla
   in a medium-size bowl on low speed
   until smooth, about 3 minutes. Cover
   bowl with plastic wrap.

8. Prepare garnish if using: Place cut
   strawberries on a large plate.
   Liberally brush melted jelly over
   each piece.

9. Frost top of cupcakes. Top each with
   glazed strawberries if desired.

PER CUPCAKE
226 calories, 9 g fat (5 g saturated), 3 g protein,
35 g carbohydrate, 0 g fiber, 109 mg sodium,
57 mg cholesterol.

Sunshine Cupcakes

Here are three flowery ways to decorate cupcakes. Each frosting option will cover a dozen cupcakes; if you want to make just a few of each flower, read all the decorating directions and further divide the frosting before adding coloring.

MAKES 12 cupcakes **PREP** 25 minutes plus decorating time **BAKE** at 350° for 30 minutes **FREEZE** frosting flowers 30 minutes (except zinnias)

2¾ cups cake flour (not self-rising)
2 teaspoons baking powder
½ teaspoon baking soda
¼ teaspoon salt
1 cup sour cream
¼ cup milk
2 tablespoons frozen orange juice concentrate
2 tablespoons fresh lemon juice
1 tablespoon grated lemon rind
1 tablespoon grated orange rind
1 cup (2 sticks) unsalted butter
1¼ cups granulated sugar
4 eggs

Frosting

½ cup (1 stick) unsalted butter
½ cup solid vegetable shortening
2 boxes (1 pound each) confectioners' sugar
⅔ cup milk
1 teaspoon orange extract
Assorted soft gel paste colors
Blue and yellow decorating candies for flower centers

1. Heat oven to 350°. Line 2 jumbo 6-muffin pans with paper liners.

2. Sift flour, baking powder, baking soda and salt into a medium-size bowl.

Mix sour cream, milk, orange juice concentrate, lemon juice, lemon rind and orange rind in a small bowl.

3. Beat butter and granulated sugar in a large bowl on medium speed until light and fluffy, 3 minutes. Beat in eggs, one at a time. On low, beat in flour mixture in 3 additions, alternating with sour cream mixture and ending with flour. Spoon ½ to ⅔ cup batter into each muffin cup.

4. Bake in heated 350° oven 30 minutes or until a wooden pick inserted in centers comes out clean. Remove cupcakes from pan; cool on a wire rack.

5. Prepare frosting: Beat butter, shortening, confectioners' sugar, milk and orange extract on low speed in a large bowl until smooth, 3 minutes. Use to make forget-me-nots, yellow apple blossoms or zinnias, as described below.

Zinnias

Tint 2 cups frosting yellow; 2 cups blue; 1 cup green. Fit a large pastry bag with a large leaf tip; holding bag in one hand, scoop yellow frosting onto one side of bag. Fill other side with blue frosting. Gently squeeze until both colors are visible through tip. Fit a second bag with a medium leaf tip; fill with green frosting. Cover cupcakes with a thin layer of white frosting. Using green frosting, pipe leaves around perimeter of each cupcake top, arranging leaves so tips point out. Using yellow-and-blue-filled bag, pipe a ring of petals just inside and on top of leaves. Repeat to pipe petals in overlapping concentric rings, leaving a 1-inch center opening. Fill flower center with candies.

Yellow Apple Blossoms

Tint 3¾ cups frosting yellow; ½ cup light blue to match candy centers; ¾ cup green. Fit a large pastry bag with a large petal tip; fill with yellow frosting. Fit a small bag with a small round tip; fill with blue frosting. Fit a second small bag with a small leaf tip; fill with green frosting. Follow directions (below) for forget-me-nots to make, freeze and arrange 72 to 96 blossoms (6 to 8 per cupcake), but pipe a dot of blue frosting in flower center and then attach a blue candy.

Forget-Me-Nots

1. Tint 2 cups frosting pink; 2 cups purple; 1 cup green. Fill a pastry bag fitted with a coupler with pink frosting; fill a second bag fitted with a coupler with purple. Fit a small bag with a small leaf tip; fill with green frosting. Cut out 120 two-inch waxed-paper squares. Attach a small petal tip to coupler for pink frosting. Attach waxed paper to a flower nail with frosting. Hold bag with right hand at 45° angle, with wide end of tip toward center of square. Squeeze bag lightly; move tip toward edge of paper for first petal. Turn nail counterclockwise; relax pressure. Bring tip back to starting point. Stop squeezing, lifting tip away. Repeat, forming 3 or 4 more petals. Press a yellow candy onto flower center. Transfer flower on paper to a baking sheet. Repeat to make 59 more flowers. Repeat with purple frosting to make 60 flowers.

2. Place baking sheet with flowers in freezer until blossoms are firm,

30 minutes. Cover cupcakes with a thin layer of remaining ½ cup white frosting. Remove frozen flowers from waxed paper and arrange on cupcakes. Use green frosting to fill openings between flowers with leaves: Hold tip at 45° angle, with small opening pointing up. Gently squeeze, pulling tip away from surface. Stop squeezing; release.

PER CUPCAKE (without decoration**)**
318 calories, 21 g fat (13 g saturated), 5 g protein, 43 g carbohydrate, 0 g fiber, 201 mg sodium, 122 mg cholesterol.

Bittersweet Chocolate Cakes

MAKES 36 cakes **PREP** 30 minutes
BAKE at 350° for 15 minutes per batch

2   cups all-purpose flour
⅔   cup unsweetened cocoa powder
1½   teaspoons ground cinnamon
1   teaspoon baking powder
1   teaspoon baking soda
½   teaspoon salt
¼   teaspoon ground nutmeg
1   cup (2 sticks) butter, at room
     temperature
1½   cups packed light-brown sugar
3   eggs
2   teaspoons vanilla
1½   cups sour cream
5   squares (1 ounce each) bittersweet
     chocolate, chopped
1   cup almonds, chopped

Ganache Frosting
2¼   cups heavy cream
1   pound 2 ounces bittersweet
     chocolate, chopped

     **Sliced almonds for garnish
     (optional)**

1. Heat oven to 350°. Coat a standard
    12-muffin pan with nonstick cooking
    spray (see note, below).

2. Whisk together flour, cocoa powder,
    cinnamon, baking powder, baking
    soda, salt and nutmeg in a large bowl.

3. In a second large bowl, beat butter on
    medium speed until smooth, 1 minute.
    Gradually beat in brown sugar,
    then beat mixture on medium-high
    3 minutes or until fluffy. Add eggs,
    one at a time, beating well after each
    addition. Beat in vanilla.

4. On low speed, beat flour mixture
    into butter mixture in 3 additions,
    alternating with sour cream and
    ending with flour mixture; beat
    2 minutes. Fold in chocolate and
    almonds. Divide one-third of batter
    among muffin cups, filling each
    halfway; set remaining batter aside.

5. Bake in heated 350° oven 15 minutes
    or until tops spring back when lightly
    pressed with a fingertip. Cool cakes
    in pan on a wire rack 10 minutes.
    Turn out cakes onto rack; cool.

6. Recoat pan with spray and repeat
    with another third of batter; repeat
    again with remaining batter.

7. Prepare ganache frosting: Bring
    cream to boiling in a small saucepan
    over medium-high heat. Place
    chocolate in a small bowl. Pour
    cream over chocolate; stir until
    chocolate is melted and mixture
    is smooth.

8. Place wire racks over a jelly-roll pan.
    Place cakes, top side down, on racks.
    Pour about 2 tablespoons ganache
    evenly over each cake, covering
    completely; smooth ganache with a
    small spatula.

9. Garnish top of each cake with 2 or
    3 almond slices if desired. Refrigerate
    1 hour or until ganache is firm.

*Note: For larger cakes, use a jumbo
6-muffin pan. Bake in 2 batches,
25 minutes each. For ganache, use
1½ cups heavy cream and 12 ounces
bittersweet chocolate. Makes 12.*

PER CAKE
310 calories, 21 g fat (12 g saturated), 4 g protein,
27 g carbohydrate, 3 g fiber, 100 mg sodium,
57 mg cholesterol.

Peppermint Profiteroles

MAKES 12 profiteroles **PREP** 20 minutes
COOK 5 minutes
BAKE at 400° for 35 to 40 minutes

1   cup water
½   cup (1 stick) butter
1   teaspoon sugar
¼   teaspoon salt
1   cup all-purpose flour
4   eggs
2   pints vanilla ice cream
½   teaspoon peppermint extract
4   tablespoons crushed candy canes
    (about three 5½-inch candy canes)
    **Red and green chocolate coating
    discs for drizzling**

1. Heat oven to 400°.

2. In a medium-size saucepan, bring water, butter, sugar and salt to boiling over high heat. Add flour all at once; stir with a wooden spoon until mixture forms a ball that pulls away from sides of pan. Cook another 2 minutes, stirring constantly.

3. Remove pan from heat. Add eggs, one at a time, beating well with a wooden spoon after each addition. When all eggs have been added, continue to beat until dough is shiny.

4. Scrape dough into a large pastry bag without a tip. Pipe 12 puffs, about 2 inches in diameter, onto an ungreased baking sheet, spacing them about 2 inches apart.

5. Bake in heated 400° oven 35 to 40 minutes or until puffed and golden. Turn oven off. Let puffs stand in oven 10 minutes with door slightly ajar. Transfer puffs from baking sheet to a wire rack to cool completely.

6. Place ice cream in a medium-size bowl; let soften. Stir in peppermint extract and crushed candy canes. Cover; return to freezer.

7. Cut cooled puffs in half horizontally; remove any wet dough from centers. Using a 2½-inch ice cream scoop, place a scoop of peppermint ice cream on each puff bottom. Place a puff top on each ice cream ball. Place puffs on a baking sheet, cover with aluminum foil and place in freezer.

8. Melt red and green chocolate discs separately in small saucepans over low heat. Using a fork, drizzle some of each color over each profiterole. Return to freezer to harden before serving.

PER PROFITEROLE
232 calories, 14 g fat (8 g saturated), 5 g protein, 22 g carbohydrate, 0 g fiber, 107 mg sodium, 111 mg cholesterol.

Festive Napoleons

MAKES 6 Napoleons **PREP** 30 minutes
BAKE at 375° for 8 to 10 minutes

7 sheets (about 18 x 13 inches each) phyllo dough, thawed if frozen
2 tablespoons butter, melted
1 package (8 ounces) ⅓-less-fat cream cheese
½ cup sour cream
6 envelopes sugar substitute or equivalent to ¼ cup sugar
½ teaspoon vanilla
1 tablespoon reduced-sugar raspberry jam
3 kiwis, peeled, sliced ¼ inch thick
1 pint raspberries, halved
1½ teaspoons confectioners' sugar

1. Heat oven to 375°. Coat 2 baking sheets with nonstick cooking spray.

2. Unfold phyllo sheets on a work surface. Cover with plastic wrap and a clean dish towel. Keeping unused sheets covered as you work to prevent drying out, remove 1 sheet from stack and lay flat. Brush lightly with butter. Repeat with remaining phyllo sheets, buttering each and stacking; leave top sheet unbuttered. Cut stacked sheets lengthwise into thirds, then crosswise into sixths, making 18 rectangles. Place on prepared baking sheets.

3. Bake in heated 375° oven 8 to 10 minutes or until lightly colored. Transfer phyllo rectangles from baking sheet to a wire rack to cool.

4. Meanwhile, beat cream cheese, sour cream, sugar substitute and vanilla in a medium-size bowl until light and fluffy. Stir in jam.

5. Spread 1 rounded tablespoon cream cheese mixture over each of 12 phyllo rectangles. Arrange kiwi slices on 6 cheese-topped rectangles; arrange raspberries on remaining cheese-topped rectangles.

6. Place a raspberry rectangle on top of each kiwi rectangle, then top each with a plain rectangle. Dust tops with confectioners' sugar.

PER NAPOLEON
293 calories, 18 g fat (11 g saturated), 7 g protein, 26 g carbohydrate, 4 g fiber, 281 mg sodium, 46 mg cholesterol.

Chocolate Chip Napoleons

Prepare Festive Napoleons, omitting jam, kiwi, berries and confectioners' sugar and stirring in 2 tablespoons mini chocolate chips in step 4. Melt 2 ounces semisweet chocolate; drizzle on top of assembled pastries.

PER NAPOLEON
275 calories, 19 g fat (12 g saturated), 7 g protein, 18 g carbohydrate, 1 g fiber, 280 mg sodium, 46 mg cholesterol.

Mandarin Orange Napoleons

Prepare Festive Napoleons, substituting ¼ teaspoon almond extract for jam and one 11-ounce can Mandarin orange segments for kiwi and berries. Drain oranges before arranging on cheese-topped rectangles.

PER NAPOLEON
259 calories, 17 g fat (11 g saturated), 7 g protein, 18 g carbohydrate, 1 g fiber, 282 mg sodium, 46 mg cholesterol.

Apple-Raisin-Nut Triangles

To speed preparation, make these pastries 8 at a time, assembling the second batch while the first is in the oven. If you wish, make them ahead and freeze until ready to serve; see note, below.

MAKES 16 triangles **PREP** 30 minutes
COOK 8 minutes
BAKE at 375° for 10 to 14 minutes

2   **Granny Smith apples (about
     14 ounces total), peeled, cored
     and diced (about 3 cups)**
½   **cup dark raisins, coarsely chopped**
½   **cup packed light-brown sugar**
2   **tablespoons butter, cut into
     ½-inch pieces**
¼   **teaspoon ground cinnamon**
¼   **teaspoon ground nutmeg**
⅛   **teaspoon ground cardamom**
¼   **cup chopped walnuts**
16 **sheets phyllo dough (from 1-pound
     package), thawed if frozen
     Confectioners' sugar for dusting**

1. Toss together apples, raisins, brown sugar, butter, cinnamon, nutmeg and cardamom in a medium-size saucepan. Cook mixture over medium-high heat 8 minutes or until bubbly and thickened. Remove from heat. Stir in walnuts. Let mixture cool.

2. Heat oven to 375°.

3. Unfold phyllo sheets on a work surface. Cover with plastic wrap and a clean dish towel. Keeping unused sheets covered as you work to prevent them from drying out, remove 1 sheet from stack and lay flat. Coat with nonstick cooking spray. Top with a second sheet. Coat second sheet with spray. Repeat with 2 more sheets, coating each.

4. Cut stack of 4 sheets crosswise into 4 equal strips. Arrange strips so narrow ends are facing you. Place 1 heaping tablespoonful apple mixture near bottom of 1 strip. Fold bottom right-hand corner diagonally over filling to form a triangle. Continue folding triangle to end of strip. Press edge to seal onto triangle. Lightly coat with cooking spray. Place on an ungreased baking sheet. Repeat to fill remaining 3 strips.

5. Repeat steps 3 and 4 to make 12 more filled triangles.

6. Bake triangles in heated 375° oven 10 to 14 minutes or until golden brown. Transfer to a wire rack to cool slightly. Dust with confectioners' sugar. Serve warm.

Note: The triangles can be prepared through step 5 and frozen up to 1 month. Place them, unbaked, on a waxed-paper-lined baking sheet or in layers between sheets of waxed paper. Place in freezer until frozen solid. Transfer to a plastic food-storage bag. Bake frozen triangles on a baking sheet in a heated 375° oven about 16 minutes or until lightly golden.

PER TRIANGLE
134 calories, 4 g fat (1 g saturated), 2 g protein, 24 g carbohydrate, 1 g fiber, 97 mg sodium, 4 mg cholesterol.

Raspberry Brownies

MAKES 32 brownies **PREP** 20 minutes
FREEZE 20 minutes
BAKE at 350° for 45 minutes

- 1   cup (2 sticks) butter
- 4   squares (1 ounce each)
       unsweetened chocolate, chopped
- 4   eggs
- 1½   cups granulated sugar
- 2   tablespoons raspberry liqueur
- 1   teaspoon vanilla
- ½   teaspoon salt
- 1   cup all-purpose flour
- 1½   cups coarsely chopped walnuts
- ½   cup semisweet mini chocolate chips
- 1   cup raspberry preserves
       Confectioners' sugar for dusting
       (optional)

1. Heat oven to 350°. Coat a 13 x 9 x 2-inch baking pan with nonstick cooking spray.

2. Melt together butter and chocolate in top of a double boiler over barely simmering, not boiling, water, stirring until smooth. Set aside to cool.

3. Beat eggs and granulated sugar in a large bowl until well combined, about 1 minute. Beat in 1 tablespoon liqueur, vanilla and salt. Stir in chocolate mixture. Stir in flour in 3 additions. Fold in walnuts and chocolate chips. Spread half of batter over bottom of prepared pan.

4. Mix together preserves and remaining 1 tablespoon liqueur in a small bowl. Spread over batter in pan. Place in freezer about 20 minutes or until preserves are firm.

5. Spread remaining batter over top of preserves.

6. Bake in heated 350° oven 45 minutes or until a wooden pick inserted in center comes out clean. Cool in pan on a wire rack 15 minutes. Cut into 32 bars. Let cool completely.

7. Dust brownies with confectioners' sugar if desired.

PER BROWNIE
203 calories, 13 g fat (6 g saturated), 3 g protein, 23 g carbohydrate, 1 g fiber, 47 mg sodium, 42 mg cholesterol.

Fudgy Brownies

Enjoy these alone, or use to make one of the delicious desserts at right.

MAKES 24 brownies **PREP** 25 minutes
BAKE at 350° for 20 minutes

¾   cup (1½ sticks) unsalted butter
4   squares (1 ounce each)
     unsweetened chocolate, chopped
4   eggs
2   cups sugar
1   teaspoon vanilla
¼   teaspoon salt
1¼ cups all-purpose flour
1   cup walnuts, coarsely chopped

1. Heat oven to 350°. Line bottom of a 15½ x 10½ x 1-inch jelly-roll pan with aluminum foil. Coat foil with nonstick cooking spray.

2. Melt butter and chocolate in top of a double boiler over barely simmering, not boiling, water, stirring until smooth.

3. Beat eggs, sugar, vanilla and salt in a large bowl on high speed 3 minutes or until thick. Fold in chocolate, then flour and nuts. Spread in prepared pan.

4. Bake in heated 350° oven 20 minutes or until a wooden pick inserted in center comes out with fudgy crumbs attached; do not overbake. Cool in pan on a wire rack. Loosen around edges; invert onto rack. Peel off foil.

5. Invert cake onto a cutting board. Cut into 24 squares.

PER BROWNIE
208 calories, 12 g fat (6 g saturated), 4 g protein, 24 g carbohydrate, 1 g fiber, 35 mg sodium, 51 mg cholesterol.

Black Forest Brownie Sundae

For each serving desired, place a brownie on a dessert plate. Top with ½ cup frozen yogurt; drizzle with ¼ cup canned cherry pie filling and topping. For 8 servings, use 1 container (1 quart) frozen yogurt and 1 can (21 ounces) pie filling.

PER SUNDAE
387 calories, 14 g fat (7 g saturated), 8 g protein, 62 g carbohydrate, 2 g fiber, 100 mg sodium, 57 mg cholesterol.

Brownie Parfaits

For each serving desired, arrange alternating layers of vanilla pudding and 1 crumbled brownie in a parfait dish. For 4 servings, use 1 package (3½ ounces) instant pudding-and-pie-filling mix, prepared according to package directions.

PER PARFAIT
372 calories, 17 g fat (3 g saturated), 8 g protein, 52 g carbohydrate, 1 g fiber, 510 mg sodium, 67 mg cholesterol.

Truffle Brownie Royale

These are equally delicious served warm, at room temperature or chilled—so take your preference.

MAKES 24 bars or diamonds
PREP 10 minutes
BAKE at 350° for 26 to 30 minutes

¼ **cup (½ stick) butter, cut into 6 pieces**
9 **squares (1 ounce each) bittersweet chocolate, chopped, or 1½ cups bittersweet chocolate chips**
½ **cup plus ⅓ cup sugar**
3 **eggs**
1 **cup all-purpose flour**
¾ **cup heavy cream**
2 **ounces white baking chocolate for decorating (optional)**

1. Heat oven to 350°.

2. Heat together butter and 3 ounces (about ½ cup) bittersweet chocolate in a medium-size saucepan over medium-low heat, stirring, until nearly melted. Remove saucepan from heat; stir until mixture is completely melted. Stir in ½ cup sugar. Working quickly to prevent curdling, whisk in 1 egg. Stir in flour to make a smooth batter. Spread batter evenly in an ungreased 9 x 9 x 2-inch square baking pan. Set aside in refrigerator.

3. In same saucepan, combine cream and remaining ⅓ cup sugar. Bring to boiling over medium-high heat. Meanwhile, place remaining 6 ounces (about 1 cup) bittersweet chocolate in a small bowl. Pour hot cream mixture over chocolate; let stand 2 minutes, then stir until chocolate is melted and smooth. Whisk in remaining 2 eggs until mixture is smooth. Spread chocolate mixture evenly over batter in pan.

4. Bake in heated 350° oven until top center of cake is soft but no longer liquid, 26 to 30 minutes. Let cool in pan on a wire rack at least 10 minutes. Cut into 24 bars or diamonds.

5. If decoration is desired, microwave white chocolate in a small microwave-safe bowl at 100% power 1 minute; stir until smooth. Scrape into a small plastic food-storage bag. Snip off a small corner of bag; drizzle chocolate over brownies. Let stand until firm.

Note: Bars can be refrigerated, covered, for up to 5 days or frozen up to 1 month.

PER BROWNIE
171 calories, 10 g fat (6 g saturated), 2 g protein, 19 g carbohydrate, 1 g fiber, 14 mg sodium, 43 mg cholesterol.

Blueberry Bars

MAKES 30 bars **PREP** 15 minutes
BAKE crust at 350° for 12 to 15 minutes; bars at 300° for 25 to 30 minutes

Cookie Crust
1¼ **cups all-purpose flour**
¼ **cup sugar**
2 **eggs**
¼ **cup (½ stick) butter, at room temperature**
1 **teaspoon vanilla**

Filling

2 packages (8 ounces each) cream cheese, at room temperature
½ cup sugar
1 tablespoon cornstarch
2 eggs
1 teaspoon vanilla
1 can (21 ounces) blueberry pie filling or topping

1. Heat oven to 350°. Coat a 13 x 9 x 2-inch baking dish with nonstick cooking spray.

2. Prepare crust: Mix flour and sugar in a large bowl. Add eggs, butter and vanilla; beat until a dough forms. Press dough over bottom of prepared dish.

3. Bake in heated 350° oven 12 to 15 minutes or until crust is firm. Transfer dish to a wire rack and let cool slightly.

4. Meanwhile, lower oven temperature to 300°.

5. Prepare filling: Beat cream cheese and sugar in a medium-size bowl until smooth and creamy, about 2 minutes. Add cornstarch, eggs and vanilla; beat 2 minutes or until well combined. Spread filling evenly over crust.

6. Bake in heated 300° oven 25 to 30 minutes or until center is set. Transfer to a wire rack and let cool.

7. Spread pie filling evenly on top of cream cheese filling. Cut into 30 bars.

PER BAR
137 calories, 8 g fat (5 g saturated), 3 g protein, 15 g carbohydrate, 0 g fiber, 59 mg sodium, 49 mg cholesterol.

Sugar Cookies Plus

Pop this refrigerated dough in the fridge or freezer for cookies at the ready. Turn the page for a photo and seven flavorful variations.

MAKES 5 dozen cookies **PREP** 20 minutes
REFRIGERATE 2 hours
BAKE at 350° for 10 to 12 minutes

1½ cups all-purpose flour
1½ teaspoons baking powder
¼ teaspoon salt
1 cup sugar
½ cup (1 stick) butter, at room temperature
1 egg
1 teaspoon vanilla

1. Combine flour, baking powder and salt in a small bowl.

2. With a mixer on medium speed, beat sugar, butter, egg and vanilla in a large bowl until smooth and creamy, 2 minutes. Using a wooden spoon, stir in flour mixture. Shape into a 15-inch-long log; wrap in plastic wrap and refrigerate at least 2 hours or up to 3 days. (For longer storage, dough may be frozen up to 3 months. When ready to use, thaw it in refrigerator.)

3. Heat oven to 350°.

4. Cut dough into ¼-inch-thick slices. Place on ungreased baking sheets, reshaping into rounds if necessary.

5. Bake in heated 350° oven 10 to 12 minutes or until cookies are lightly golden around edges. Cool cookies slightly on baking sheets, then transfer to wire racks to cool completely.

PER COOKIE
39 calories, 2 g fat (1 g saturated), 0 g protein, 6 g carbohydrate, 0 g fiber, 21 mg sodium, 8 mg cholesterol.

Thumbprint Cookies

Prepare Sugar Cookie dough through step 2. Heat oven to 350°. Cut log into ½-inch-thick slices. Roll each slice into a ball. (If sliced dough is too stiff to work with, let soften at room temperature about 10 minutes.) Place on ungreased baking sheets, spacing about 2 inches apart. Indent center of each ball by pressing with your thumb. Spoon about ½ teaspoon any flavor jam into each indentation. Bake 12 to 14 minutes or until lightly golden around edges.

MAKES about 30 cookies

PER COOKIE
88 calories, 3 g fat (2 g saturated), 1 g protein, 14 g carbohydrate, 0 g fiber, 42 mg sodium, 15 mg cholesterol.

Lemon Sugar Cookies

Prepare Sugar Cookie dough steps 1 and 2, beating 4 teaspoons grated lemon rind into butter mixture. Heat oven to 350°. Cut log into ¼-inch-thick slices. Place on ungreased baking sheets. Sprinkle about 3 tablespoons decorating sugar over slices, dividing equally. Bake 8 to 10 minutes or until cookies are golden around edges.

MAKES about 60 cookies or crusts for 2 Lemon Curd Tarts, page 162

PER COOKIE
43 calories, 2 g fat (1 g saturated), 0 g protein, 7 g carbohydrate, 0 g fiber, 21 mg sodium, 8 mg cholesterol.

Almond Sugar Cookies

Toast ¾ cup slivered almonds (see page 232); cool. Grind nuts (you should have ¾ cup). Prepare Sugar Cookie dough steps 1 and 2, adding ½ cup ground nuts

to dry ingredients (reserve remaining nuts) and beating ½ teaspoon almond extract into butter mixture. Heat oven to 350°. Cut log into ¼-inch-thick slices. Place on ungreased baking sheets. Sprinkle ⅛ to ¼ teaspoon reserved ground nuts over each slice. Bake 8 to 10 minutes or until cookies are golden around edges.

MAKES about 60 cookies or the cookie base for Windowpane Linzer Cookies, page 209

PER COOKIE
47 calories, 2 g fat (1 g saturated), 1 g protein, 6 g carbohydrate, 0 g fiber, 21 mg sodium, 8 mg cholesterol.

Ginger Sugar Cookies

Prepare Sugar Cookie dough steps 1 and 2, adding another ¼ cup flour and 1 teaspoon ground ginger to dry ingredients and beating 1 tablespoon mild molasses into butter mixture. Heat oven to 350°. Cut log into ¼-inch-thick slices. Place on ungreased baking sheets. Lightly dip tines of a fork into some flour; firmly press a crisscross design onto each slice. Bake for 8 to 10 minutes or until cookies are slightly darkened around edges.

MAKES about 40 cookies or crusts for 2 Ginger Pear Pies, page 154

PER COOKIE
63 calories, 3 g fat (2 g saturated), 1 g protein, 10 g carbohydrate, 0 g fiber, 31 mg sodium, 12 mg cholesterol.

Chocolate Chip Sugar Cookies

Prepare Sugar Cookie dough steps 1 and 2, stirring 1 cup chocolate chips into mixed dough and shaping dough into a 10-inch-long log. Heat oven to 350°.

Cut log into ½-inch-thick slices. Place on an ungreased baking sheet. Bake 12 to 15 minutes or until cookies are lightly golden around edges.

MAKES about 20 cookies or crusts for 2 Golden Baked Alaskas, page 136

PER COOKIE
158 calories, 8 g fat (4 g saturated), 2 g protein, 23 g carbohydrate, 1 g fiber, 63 mg sodium, 23 mg cholesterol.

Mocha Sugar Cookies

Prepare Sugar Cookie dough steps 1 and 2, adding ¼ cup unsweetened cocoa powder and an additional ¼ teaspoon salt to dry ingredients and stirring 1 teaspoon instant espresso powder into egg before beating it into butter mixture. Heat oven to 350°. Cut log into ¼-inch-thick slices. Place on ungreased baking sheets. Bake 8 to 10 minutes or until slightly darkened around edges.

When cookies are cool, melt 3 ounces semisweet chocolate; spoon into a small plastic bag. Snip off a corner of bag and drizzle chocolate over 30 cookies. In the same way, melt and drizzle 3 ounces white baking chocolate over remaining 30 cookies.

MAKES 60 cookies or dough for Tiramisu, page 147

PER COOKIE
55 calories, 3 g fat (2 g saturated), 1 g protein, 7 g carbohydrate, 0 g fiber, 32 mg sodium, 8 mg cholesterol.

Choco-Chocolate Chip Cookies

Prepare Sugar Cookie dough steps 1 and 2, adding ¼ cup unsweetened cocoa powder to dry ingredients and stirring ½ cup mini chocolate chips and ½ cup finely chopped unsalted

dry-roasted peanuts into mixed dough. Heat oven to 350°. Cut log into ½-inch-thick slices. Place on ungreased baking sheets. Measure 2 tablespoons granulated sugar onto a piece of waxed paper. For each cookie, dampen bottom of a small glass with water and dip into sugar; press down on cookie to flatten to about 2 inches in diameter. Bake 12 to 15 minutes or until cookies are slightly darkened around edges.

When cookies are cool, mix 1¼ cups creamy peanut butter with ½ cup confectioners' sugar. Spread half of cookies with 2 teaspoons mixture. Sandwich with remaining cookies.

MAKES 15 sandwich cookies

PER COOKIE
363 calories, 22 g fat (7 g saturated), 9 g protein, 38 g carbohydrate, 3 g fiber, 182 mg sodium, 31 mg cholesterol.

Petits Fours

MAKES 8 dozen petits fours
PREP 30 minutes
BAKE at 350° for 15 to 20 minutes
STAND 1 hour (to harden frosting)

¾   **cup cake flour (not self-rising)**
1   **teaspoon baking powder**
½   **teaspoon salt**
5   **eggs, separated**
⅔   **cup granulated sugar**
1   **teaspoon vanilla**
1   **jar (13 ounces) apple jelly**
2   **tablespoons water**

Glaze
3   **boxes (1 pound each)
    confectioners' sugar**
¾   **cup plus 3 tablespoons water
    Pink soft gel paste food color**

**Candied flowers for garnish
(optional)**

1. Heat oven to 350°. Grease a 15½ x
   10½ x 1-inch jelly-roll pan. Line with
   waxed paper; grease paper.

2. Whisk together flour, baking powder
   and salt in a small bowl.

3. Beat egg yolks, ⅓ cup granulated
   sugar and vanilla in a large bowl on
   medium-high speed until thick and
   lemon-colored, about 1 minute.

4. On low speed, beat flour mixture
   into egg yolk mixture.

5. With clean beaters, beat egg whites
   in a medium-size bowl on high speed
   until foamy. Slowly add remaining
   ⅓ cup granulated sugar, beating until
   stiff peaks form. Stir ½ cup beaten egg
   whites into egg yolk mixture. Fold
   remaining egg whites into mixture.
   Scrape batter into prepared pan,
   spreading evenly.

6. Bake in heated 350° oven 15 to
   20 minutes or until lightly golden
   and firm. Cool on a wire rack
   10 minutes. Invert onto rack. Peel
   off waxed paper.

7. Mix apple jelly with 2 tablespoons
   water in a small saucepan; melt over
   low heat. Brush part of jelly over
   top of cake.

8. Cut cake lengthwise into eight
   1¼-inch-wide strips. Cut each strip
   crosswise into twelve 1¼-inch squares.
   Brush cut sides with remaining jelly.
   Place on a wire rack over waxed paper.

9. Prepare glaze: Mix confectioners'
   sugar and ¾ cup water in a medium-
   size bowl. Add another 3 tablespoons
   water if needed to create a coating
   consistency. Using 2 forks, lift and dip
   half of cake pieces into glaze, one at a
   time; return to rack. Decorate with
   candied flowers if desired.

10. Tint remaining glaze with pink food
    color. Dip remaining cake pieces into
    glaze. Decorate as desired.

11. Let glaze harden at room temperature
    1 hour.

PER PETIT FOUR
79 calories, 1 g fat (0 g saturated), 0 g protein,
19 g carbohydrate, 0 g fiber, 20 mg sodium,
1 mg cholesterol.

Petits Fours Pointers

Using 2 forks,
lower a cake
square completely
into glaze; lift
and transfer to a
wire rack.

Chocolate-Orange Bites

MAKES 4 dozen cookies **PREP** 30 minutes
BAKE at 350° for 30 minutes
REFRIGERATE at least 1½ hours

- **2   cups all-purpose flour**
- **½   cup sugar**
- **¼   teaspoon salt**
- **1   cup (2 sticks) butter, chilled and cut into small pieces**
- **1   cup orange juice**
- **1   envelope unflavored gelatin**
- **1   box (3.4 ounces) instant vanilla pudding-and-pie-filling mix**
- **1   tablespoon grated orange rind**
- **½   cup orange marmalade**
- **½   cup heavy cream**
- **5   squares (1 ounce each) semisweet chocolate, finely chopped**
- **½   teaspoon vanilla**
      Candied flowers for garnish (optional)

1. Heat oven to 350°. Line a 13 x 9 x 2-inch baking dish with aluminum foil, extending foil over sides.

2. Mix flour, sugar and salt in a large bowl. Cut butter into flour mixture with a pastry blender or 2 knives used scissor fashion until mixture resembles coarse crumbs. Press into bottom of prepared dish.

3. Bake in heated 350° oven 30 minutes or until edges are lightly browned. Let cool in dish on a wire rack 30 minutes.

4. Place ½ cup orange juice in a glass measure. Sprinkle gelatin over top. Let stand until softened, about 5 minutes. Microwave at 100% power 20 seconds. Stir to dissolve gelatin. (Or heat mixture in a small saucepan.) Let cool slightly.

5. Whisk together pudding-and-pie-filling mix, remaining ½ cup orange juice and orange rind in a medium-size bowl. Stir in gelatin mixture.

6. Remove pastry from baking dish and place on a baking sheet. Spread marmalade in a thin layer over pastry. Top with pudding mixture in an even layer. Refrigerate at least 30 minutes.

7. Bring cream to boiling in a small heavy saucepan. Remove from heat. Stir in chocolate until melted and mixture is smooth. Stir in vanilla. Let cool slightly. Pour over pudding layer; make a decorative pattern with a pastry comb or fork. Refrigerate at least 1 hour. Cut into 48 diamond-shaped pieces. Garnish each piece with a candied flower if desired.

PER COOKIE
104 calories, 6 g fat (3 g saturated), 1 g protein, 13 g carbohydrate, 0 g fiber, 44 mg sodium, 14 mg cholesterol.

Almond Flower Cookies

MAKES about 16 cookies
PREP 30 minutes plus decorating time
REFRIGERATE 1 hour
BAKE at 350° for 12 to 15 minutes

2½ cups all-purpose flour
½ teaspoon salt
½ teaspoon baking soda
1 cup (2 sticks) unsalted butter,
   at room temperature
¾ cup sugar
1 egg
1 teaspoon lemon extract
1 teaspoon vanilla extract
1 cup finely ground blanched
   almonds
3 cups Royal Icing (left)
   Liquid or soft gel paste food colors
1 jar (11 ounces) lemon curd
3 teaspoons white nonpareil candies

1. Combine flour, salt and baking soda
   in a small bowl. Beat butter and sugar
   in a large bowl on medium speed until
   creamy. Beat egg, lemon extract and
   vanilla extract into butter mixture until
   fluffy, 1 minute. Stir in flour mixture
   and ground almonds. Divide dough in
   half. Flatten each half into a disc; wrap
   in plastic wrap. Refrigerate 1 hour.

2. Heat oven to 350°.

3. On a lightly floured surface, using a
   floured rolling pin, roll 1 disc of
   dough to ¼-inch thickness. With a
   floured 3¼-inch fluted round cookie
   cutter, cut out as many cookies as
   possible. Place cookies, 1 inch apart,
   on ungreased baking sheets. With a
   floured 1-inch round cookie cutter,
   cut out center from half of cookies.
   Gather scraps and center cutouts;
   rewrap and reserve.

Royal Icing

In a medium-size bowl, whisk
together 1 pound confectioners'
sugar and 3 tablespoons meringue
powder or egg white powder (see
page 232) until well combined.
On medium speed, gradually beat
in 6 tablespoons warm water. Beat
until peaks form and icing is thick
enough to pipe, about 10 minutes.
Press plastic wrap onto surface;
keep covered until ready to use.

MAKES about 3 cups. Divide the
ingredients by thirds to make 1 or
2 cups icing.

PER TABLESPOON
37 calories, 0 g fat (0 g saturated), 0 g protein,
9 g carbohydrate, 0 g fiber, 0 mg sodium,
0 mg cholesterol.

4. Repeat rolling and cutting with second disc of dough. Gather scraps and cutouts; reroll together with reserved scraps. Cut out more cookies, making a total of 32 cookies, 16 with centers cut out.

5. Bake in heated 350° oven 12 to 15 minutes or until lightly browned. Transfer cookies to wire racks to cool.

6. Place one-quarter of icing in a pastry bag fitted with a small round tip. Divide remaining icing among 3 bowls and tint with food colors as desired for flowers.

7. Spread colored icing over cookies with cut-out centers. Allow to dry. With white icing, pipe an outline of 2 concentric rings of "petals" on top of each iced cookie. Let dry completely. Spread 1 tablespoon lemon curd over each undecorated cookie; top with an iced cookie, pressing lightly together. Fill each center cutout with ¼ teaspoon nonpareils.

PER COOKIE (with filling and icing)
431 calories, 17 g fat (8 g saturated), 6 g protein, 69 g carbohydrate, 2 g fiber, 151 mg sodium, 44 mg cholesterol.

Peanut Butter Cookies

MAKES 32 cookies **PREP** 5 minutes
BAKE at 350° for 15 minutes

1	**tube (18 ounces) refrigerated sugar-cookie dough**
½	**cup creamy peanut butter**
½	**cup semisweet mini chocolate chips**
½	**cup peanut butter chips**
½	**cup peanuts, coarsely chopped**

1. Heat oven to 350°.

2. Beat together cookie dough and peanut butter in a large bowl until blended and smooth. Stir or knead in chocolate chips, peanut butter chips and peanuts until evenly distributed.

3. Drop dough by heaping tablespoonfuls onto ungreased baking sheets. Bake in heated 350° oven 15 minutes. Cool cookies slightly on baking sheets, then transfer to wire racks to cool completely.

PER COOKIE
140 calories, 8 g fat (2 g saturated), 3 g protein, 15 g carbohydrate, 1 g fiber, 110 mg sodium, 5 mg cholesterol.

Heart-Shaped Sandwich Cookies

MAKES sixty 2-inch cookies (40 single, 20 sandwiches) and twenty 1-inch single cookies **PREP** 20 minutes **REFRIGERATE** 1 hour 40 minutes **BAKE** at 350° for 5 to 8 minutes per batch

Cookies

3   **cups all-purpose flour**
2   **teaspoons baking powder**
¼   **teaspoon salt**
1   **cup (2 sticks) butter**
1   **cup granulated sugar**
3   **egg yolks**
1   **teaspoon vanilla**

Icing

1   **box (1 pound) confectioners' sugar**
3   **tablespoons egg white powder (see page 232)**
6   **to 7 tablespoons water**
    Pink and violet soft gel paste food colors

    Mini white sugar balls or red heart candies (optional)
¼   **cup raspberry jam**

1. Prepare cookies: Mix flour, baking powder and salt in a medium-size bowl.

2. Beat butter and granulated sugar in a large bowl on medium speed until creamy, 3 minutes. Beat in egg yolks and vanilla. On low speed, beat in flour mixture in 3 batches to form a stiff dough. Divide dough in half. Flatten each half into a disc; wrap in plastic wrap. Refrigerate 1 hour.

3. Heat oven to 350°. Grease 2 baking sheets.

4. On a floured work surface, roll 1 disc of dough to ⅛-inch thickness. Using a 2-inch heart-shaped cutter and gathering dough scraps and rerolling as necessary, cut out a total of 40 cookies; place on prepared baking sheets. Refrigerate 20 minutes.

5. Bake in heated 350° oven 8 minutes; do not allow to brown. Cool cookies slightly on baking sheets, then transfer to wire racks to cool completely.

6. Roll out remaining disc of dough. Working as before, cut out 40 cookies; use a 1-inch heart-shaped cutter to cut center from 20 cookies. Place all large cutouts on 1 baking sheet; place small cutouts on a second baking sheet. Refrigerate 20 minutes.

7. Bake in heated 350° oven—small cookies 5 to 6 minutes, large cookies 8 minutes. Cool as above.

8. Prepare icing: Beat confectioners' sugar, egg white powder and water in a medium-size bowl until glazing consistency, 8 minutes. Divide into thirds. Tint one third pink, one third violet and leave one third untinted.

9. Set aside twenty 2-inch heart cookies to use as sandwich bases. Decorate remaining cookies using icings and, if desired, sugar balls or heart candies. Spread 1 teaspoon jam on each reserved cookie; top with a heart-frame cookie.

PER 2-INCH SINGLE COOKIE
72 calories, 3 g fat (2 g saturated), 1 g protein, 12 g carbohydrate, 0 g fiber, 17 mg sodium, 14 mg cholesterol.

Windowpane Linzer Cookies

For a homemade cookie dough, use the dough for Almond Sugar Cookies on page 202, shaping into a disc and chilling 10 minutes. If making your own dough, skip step 2. You can toast and grind the almonds for dough and topping at the same time.

MAKES 2½ dozen cookies **PREP** 30 minutes
BAKE at 350° for 15 minutes

Dough

1   **tube (18 ounces) refrigerated sugar-cookie dough**
⅔   **cup blanched slivered almonds, toasted (see page 232) and finely ground**
¼   **to ½ teaspoon almond extract**

Topping

½   **cup orange marmalade**
½   **cup seedless strawberry jam**
⅓   **cup blanched slivered almonds, toasted and finely ground**

1. Heat oven to 350°. Lightly grease bottom and sides of a 15½ x 10½ x 1-inch jelly-roll pan.

2. Prepare dough: Using a wooden spoon, work together cookie dough, ground almonds and almond extract in a large bowl until well blended. (If this makes dough too soft to work with, shape it into a disc, wrap and return to refrigerator until firm, about 10 minutes.)

3. Press dough over bottom and about ½ inch up sides of prepared pan. Bake in heated 350° oven 15 minutes or until cookie is golden brown. Transfer pan to a wire rack to cool completely.

4. Add topping: Leaving a ½-inch border all around, cover top of cookie with bands of marmalade and jam; spread bands parallel to short ends and alternate 3 bands of marmalade with 2 of jam. Use about 2½ tablespoons for each band and make each 2 to 2½ inches wide.

5. Lightly sprinkle some ground almonds along lines where marmalade and jam bands meet. Then sprinkle on remaining almonds in 4 lines, evenly spaced and parallel to long edges of pan, creating a total of 30 rectangles. To serve, cut into rectangular cookies along almond lines.

PER COOKIE
130 calories, 6 g fat (1 g saturated), 2 g protein, 19 g carbohydrate, 1 g fiber, 85 mg sodium, 5 mg cholesterol.

Mini Cookie Roll-Ups

MAKES 15 roll-ups **PREP** 25 minutes
REFRIGERATE 30 minutes
BAKE at 350° for 8 to 10 minutes

Filling

1	**teaspoon unflavored gelatin**
2	**tablespoons cold water**
1	**container (15 ounces) ricotta cheese**
⅓	**cup confectioners' sugar**
½	**cup finely chopped glacé mix (candied fruit)**
1	**teaspoon vanilla**

Roll-Ups

½	**cup granulated sugar**
3	**tablespoons all-purpose flour**
3	**tablespoons quick-cooking oats**
2	**tablespoons ground walnuts**
⅛	**teaspoon salt**
2	**tablespoons butter, melted**
1	**tablespoon grated lemon rind**
½	**teaspoon lemon extract**
3	**egg whites, lightly beaten**

Confectioners' sugar for garnish (optional)
Grated lemon rind for garnish (optional)

1. Prepare filling: Sprinkle gelatin over cold water in a small microwave-safe bowl. Let stand until gelatin softens, about 5 minutes. Microwave at 100% power 20 seconds. Remove bowl from microwave. Let stand 1 minute, stirring to dissolve gelatin. (Or heat in a very small saucepan over low heat.)

2. Combine ricotta cheese, confectioners' sugar, glacé mix and vanilla in a medium-size bowl. Stir in gelatin mixture. Cover with plastic wrap; refrigerate until firm, at least 30 minutes.

3. Meanwhile, prepare roll-ups: Heat oven to 350°. Coat 2 baking sheets with nonstick cooking spray.

4. Combine sugar, flour, oats, walnuts and salt in a medium-size bowl. Mix butter, lemon rind, lemon extract and egg whites in a small bowl. Gradually stir egg white mixture into flour mixture until blended.

5. Spoon 1 tablespoon batter onto a prepared baking sheet; spread into a 4-inch-diameter round using a spatula. Repeat to make a total of 15 rounds.

6. Bake in heated 350° oven 8 to 10 minutes or until rounds are slightly flexible. Remove from oven. Lift 1 round from baking sheet and, using both hands, roll it into a cylinder; place it on a wire rack. Repeat with remaining rounds; if they begin to stiffen, reheat in oven 30 seconds to soften. Let roll-ups cool until crisp.

7. Just before serving, spoon filling into a pastry bag fitted with a medium round tip. Carefully fill each roll-up. If desired, dust with confectioners' sugar and garnish with lemon rind.

PER ROLL-UP
126 calories, 6 g fat (3 g saturated), 5 g protein, 14 g carbohydrate, 0 g fiber, 56 mg sodium, 18 mg cholesterol.

Roll-Up Prep Steps

Gently roll each warm cookie between your fingers to make a cylinder.

Chocolate Spritz Cookies

MAKES about 7½ dozen cookies
PREP 10 minutes **REFRIGERATE** 10 minutes
BAKE at 375° for 5 to 7 minutes per batch

- 2 **cups all-purpose flour**
- ½ **cup unsweetened cocoa powder**
- ½ **teaspoon salt**
- 1 **cup (2 sticks) unsalted butter, at room temperature**
- 1 **cup confectioners' sugar**
- 1 **egg yolk**
- 1 **box (6 ounces) white baking chocolate, chopped**
- 2 **tablespoons vegetable oil**

1. Sift flour, cocoa powder and salt into a medium-size bowl.

2. Beat together butter and sugar in a large bowl on medium speed until smooth and creamy. Beat in egg yolk.

3. On low speed, beat flour mixture into butter mixture until well combined. Cover; refrigerate 10 minutes.

4. Heat oven to 375°. Grease several baking sheets.

5. Spoon some of dough into a cookie press fitted with a bar-plate tip. Keep remaining dough refrigerated. Press dough onto a prepared baking sheet, making strips about the length of baking sheet and spaced 1 inch apart. Cut each strip into 2-inch lengths.

6. Bake in heated 375° oven 5 to 7 minutes or until firm. Remove from oven. With a pancake turner, immediately remove cookies from baking sheet to wire racks to cool.

7. Continue with remaining dough, pressing out, cutting and baking.

8. Line a clean baking sheet with waxed paper. Heat chocolate and oil in a small saucepan over low heat until melted. Dip both ends of each cookie in chocolate; place on paper. Let set.

PER COOKIE
47 calories, 3 g fat (2 g saturated), 1 g protein, 5 g carbohydrate, 0 g fiber, 14 mg sodium, 8 mg cholesterol.

Candy Cutouts

MAKES about 100 candies **PREP** 45 minutes
REFRIGERATE about 50 minutes

**12 ounces semisweet chocolate chips
   or squares, chopped
¼ cup solid vegetable shortening
2 jars (7½ ounces each)
   marshmallow cream
5 cups confectioners' sugar
¼ cup grated orange rind
2 teaspoons orange extract
⅛ teaspoon salt
   White baking chocolate for garnish
   (optional)**

1. Line bottom of a 15½ x 10½ x 1-inch jelly-roll pan with aluminum foil.

2. Melt half of semisweet chocolate and 2 tablespoons shortening in top of a double boiler over barely simmering, not boiling, water, stirring until smooth. Pour into prepared pan; spread evenly with a long metal spatula. Refrigerate about 20 minutes or until firm.

3. Tape waxed paper to bottom of a second 15½ x 10½ x 1-inch jelly-roll pan. Invert chocolate onto paper. Peel off foil. Refrigerate until ready to use.

4. Combine marshmallow cream, 4¼ cups confectioners' sugar, orange rind, orange extract and salt in a medium-size bowl. Stir with a wooden spoon until a thick mass forms; knead mixture with hands if necessary to incorporate ingredients.

5. Lightly dust a work surface with a little of remaining ¾ cup confectioners' sugar. Turn marshmallow mixture out onto prepared surface. Knead until smooth, 2 to 3 minutes.

6. Tape waxed paper to bottom of first jelly-roll pan. Lightly dust paper and a rolling pin with remaining confectioners' sugar. Roll out marshmallow mixture to ⅛- to ¼-inch thickness, covering bottom of prepared pan.

7. Remove pan with chocolate from refrigerator. Let stand to soften slightly, about 5 minutes. Carefully invert marshmallow layer on top of chocolate; peel off waxed paper. Refrigerate 15 minutes.

8. Melt remaining semisweet chocolate and remaining 2 tablespoons shortening in top of a double boiler over barely simmering, not boiling, water, stirring until smooth. Remove pan with chocolate and marshmallow layers from refrigerator. Pour melted chocolate on top, spreading smoothly over entire surface with a spatula. Refrigerate 15 to 20 minutes or until firm.

9. Using any desired 1½- to 2-inch mini cookie cutters, cut chocolate-marshmallow layers into shapes. Or cut into 1-inch squares.

10. If white chocolate details are desired, melt white chocolate in top of a double boiler over barely simmering, not boiling, water, stirring until smooth. Remove from heat and cool slightly. Pour into a small plastic food-storage bag. Snip off a corner of bag to make a very small opening. Pipe chocolate over cutouts to add features or decorative patterns. Refrigerate until ready to serve.

PER CANDY
55 calories, 2 g fat (1 g saturated), 0 g protein,
11 g carbohydrate, 0 g fiber, 5 mg sodium,
0 mg cholesterol.

Easter Eggs

Each of the three coatings given here will cover one batch of candy eggs. Take your choice.

MAKES about 10 large or 20 small eggs
PREP 45 minutes **COOK** 5 minutes
REFRIGERATE 30 minutes

Candy Eggs
⅓ **cup butter or margarine**
1 **package (about 3 ounces) chocolate pudding-and-pie-filling mix (not instant)**
¼ **cup milk**
⅛ **teaspoon almond extract**
1¾ **cups confectioners' sugar**
½ **cup finely ground blanched almonds**

Chocolate Coatings
1 **package (12 ounces) milk chocolate chips (2 cups) plus 6 tablespoons solid vegetable shortening**
1 **package (12 ounces) semisweet chocolate chips (2 cups) plus ¼ cup solid vegetable shortening**
1 **pound white baking chocolate plus ½ cup solid vegetable shortening**

1. Prepare eggs: Melt butter in a saucepan over medium-low heat. Stir in pudding-and-pie-filling mix until smooth. Gradually add milk, stirring constantly until mixture is thickened and creamy, about 5 minutes. Remove from heat. Stir in almond extract. Spoon into a large bowl. Place plastic wrap directly on surface of pudding. Allow to reach room temperature, stirring occasionally, about 20 minutes.

2. Beat in confectioners' sugar with a wooden spoon until smooth (mixture will be stiff). Stir in almonds. Cover; refrigerate 30 minutes or until mixture holds its shape.

3. Using 2 level measuring tablespoonfuls pudding mixture for each large candy or 1 level tablespoonful for each small candy, form mixture into egg shapes. Place on a small baking sheet. Cover loosely with plastic wrap. Refrigerate 1 hour or until eggs are firm.

4. Prepare your choice of chocolate coating: Melt together chocolate and shortening in top of a double boiler over barely simmering, not boiling, water, stirring until smooth. Pour into a small bowl. Let cool 5 minutes.

5. Line a baking sheet with waxed paper. Reshaping eggs if necessary, place them, one at a time, in chocolate coating; use a fork to roll each until completely coated. Lift egg with fork, let excess chocolate drip back into bowl and transfer egg to prepared baking sheet. Touch up coating with a small metal spatula if necessary.

6. Let eggs stand at room temperature until firm. If they became soft during dipping, place in refrigerator until firm.

7. Repeat dipping process to coat eggs in another layer of chocolate. Let firm completely on baking sheet. Loosen from waxed paper with a thin spatula.

PER SMALL CANDY
(with milk chocolate coating)
153 calories, 9 g fat (4 g saturated), 2 g protein,
18 g carbohydrate, 0 g fiber, 23 mg sodium,
11 mg cholesterol.

Lollipops

MAKES 24 lollipops **PREP** 10 minutes
COOK about 40 minutes

**Assorted candies for decorations
(cinnamon red-hots, hearts and
flowers)**
2   **cups sugar**
1   **cup water**
¾   **cup light corn syrup**
½   **teaspoon cinnamon extract**
24 **lollipop sticks**

1. Lightly coat twenty-four 2-inch
   heart-shaped lollipop molds with
   nonstick cooking spray. Arrange red-
   hots, hearts and flowers in molds.

2. Heat sugar, water and corn syrup in
   a heavy saucepan over medium heat,
   stirring, until sugar dissolves, about
   5 to 7 minutes.

3. Clip a candy thermometer to side
   of saucepan. Continue to cook over
   medium-high heat, without stirring,
   until thermometer registers 300°,
   about 30 to 35 minutes. Remove pan
   from heat. Stir in extract.

4. Working quickly, ladle half of liquid
   into 12 molds, dividing equally. Press
   lollipop sticks into centers. Repeat
   with remaining liquid, remaining
   molds and remaining sticks. Cool
   completely. Loosen lollipops from
   molds and remove.

PER LOLLIPOP
86 calories, 0 g fat (0 g saturated), 0 g protein,
22 g carbohydrate, 0 g fiber, 11 mg sodium,
0 mg cholesterol.

Lollipop Know-How

Working quickly,
ladle hot mixture
into prepared
molds filled with
candies.

Chocolate Berry Truffles

MAKES about 2 dozen truffles
PREP 1 hour **REFRIGERATE** 1 hour

1 **package (6 ounces) semisweet chocolate chips (1 cup)**
3 **tablespoons butter**
2 **tablespoons heavy cream**
1 **tablespoon raspberry-flavored liqueur or red wine**
½ **cup finely ground shelled pistachios, walnuts or chocolate cookies**
   Fresh raspberries (optional)

1. Melt chocolate chips in top of a double boiler over barely simmering, not boiling, water. Add butter, stirring until melted. Add cream and liqueur, stirring until blended and smooth.

2. Pour chocolate mixture into a small bowl. Let stand at room temperature, stirring frequently, 45 minutes or until thick enough to pipe through a pastry bag.

3. Line a large baking sheet with aluminum foil. Sprinkle with nuts or cookies. Fit a pastry bag with a large star tip. Fill with chocolate mixture. Pipe 1½-inch rosettes onto prepared baking sheet. If using raspberries, place one in center of each rosette. Refrigerate 1 hour or until firm enough to pick up.

4. Gently loosen truffles from baking sheet, using a thin metal spatula if necessary. Transfer to a serving plate, or store in a single layer in a tightly sealed container 1 to 2 days.

PER TRUFFLE
68 calories, 5 g fat (3 g saturated), 1 g protein,
5 g carbohydrate, 1 g fiber, 2 mg sodium,
6 mg cholesterol.

Almond-Stuffed Strawberries

Shown on page 211.

MAKES 12 servings **PREP** 15 minutes
REFRIGERATE 10 minutes

12 **strawberries, rinsed**
¾ **cup semisweet chocolate chips**
1 **package (3 ounces) cream cheese**
2 **tablespoons honey**
¼ **teaspoon almond extract**
1 **tablespoon chopped almonds**

1. Using a paring knife, halve berries lengthwise, cutting through the leafy cap as well. Using knife tip, remove center core from each half; dry berries on a layer of paper toweling.

2. Place chocolate chips in a small microwave-safe bowl. Microwave at 100% power 1 minute to melt; stir.

3. Line a baking sheet with waxed paper. Hold each berry half by its cap and dip halfway into chocolate; place on lined baking sheet. Refrigerate 10 minutes.

4. Beat together cream cheese, honey and almond extract in a small bowl. Spoon into a pastry bag fitted with a small tip. Pipe mixture into berries. Sprinkle with nuts.

PER SERVING (2 halves)
100 calories, 6 g fat (3 g saturated), 1 g protein,
12 g carbohydrate, 1 g fiber, 23 mg sodium,
8 mg cholesterol.

Caramel Apples

MAKES 8 apples **PREP** 30 minutes
COOK 15 minutes
REFRIGERATE about 1¼ hours

8   **small to medium McIntosh apples
    (about 3½ pounds)**
8   **long cinnamon sticks or flat
    wooden sticks**
2   **packages (14 ounces each) creamy
    caramels (98 candies total)**
2   **tablespoons water**
¾   **cup shelled pistachios, coarsely
    chopped**
½   **cup semisweet chocolate chips
    (3 ounces)**

1. Lightly coat a large baking sheet with
    nonstick cooking spray.

2. Remove stems from apples; wash and
    dry apples. Insert a cinnamon stick
    into stem end of each apple.

3. Unwrap caramels and place in a
    medium-size heavy saucepan. Add
    water; heat over medium-low heat,
    stirring occasionally, until caramels
    are melted and smooth.

4. Working quickly and keeping caramel
    over low heat, dip apples into caramel,
    turning to coat completely; remove
    and gently shake, letting excess caramel
    drip back into pan. Pat pistachios
    onto top of apple and 1 inch down
    sides; place on prepared baking sheet.
    Refrigerate 10 minutes or until
    caramel is cool.

5. Meanwhile, melt chocolate in top of a
    double boiler over barely simmering,
    not boiling, water, stirring until
    smooth. Transfer melted chocolate to
    a small plastic food storage bag. Snip
    off a small corner. Drizzle melted
    chocolate onto each apple, making a
    decorative pattern on area not
    covered with nuts. Refrigerate until
    chocolate hardens, about 1 hour.

6. Serve apples in decorative muffin cup
    liners if desired.

PER APPLE
580 calories, 17 g fat (9 g saturated), 7 g protein,
108 g carbohydrate, 6 g fiber, 243 mg sodium,
7 mg cholesterol.

Coconut Rum Balls (page 226); Chocolate Chip Rugelach

Chocolate Chip Rugelach

MAKES 32 rugelach **PREP** 15 minutes
REFRIGERATE 4 hours or overnight
BAKE at 350° for 20 to 25 minutes.

1   cup (2 sticks) unsalted butter, at room temperature
¼   cup granulated sugar
1   package (8 ounces) cream cheese, at room temperature
2   egg yolks
1   teaspoon vanilla
¼   teaspoon salt
2   to 2½ cups all-purpose flour
½   cup cherry jam or jelly
1   cup dried cherries
½   cup semisweet mini chocolate chips
¼   cup milk for brushing
3   tablespoons coarse sugar for sprinkling

1. With a mixer on medium-low speed, beat butter and granulated sugar in a medium-size bowl until creamy. Beat in cream cheese, egg yolks, vanilla and salt, about 1 minute. Stir in flour until smooth, using enough flour to make a stiff dough. Divide dough into quarters; shape each piece into a disc and wrap in plastic wrap; refrigerate at least 4 hours or overnight.

2. Position oven rack in top third of oven. Heat oven to 350°. Grease a large baking sheet.

3. On a well-floured surface, roll out 1 disc of dough into an 8-inch round. Spread with 2 tablespoons jam. Sprinkle with ¼ cup dried cherries and 2 tablespoons chocolate chips.

4. Cut dough into 8 equal pie-shaped wedges. Starting at outside edge, roll up each triangle, enclosing filling. Transfer to prepared baking sheet, spacing 1 inch apart. Repeat to make 24 more rugelach, using remaining dough and remaining filling ingredients.

5. Brush each rugelach very lightly with milk. Sprinkle with coarse sugar. Bake in top third of heated 350° oven until lightly browned, 20 to 25 minutes. Transfer rugelach to a wire rack to cool completely.

PER RUGELACH
161 calories, 9 g fat (6 g saturated), 2 g protein, 17 g carbohydrate, 1 g fiber, 44 mg sodium, 37 mg cholesterol.

Jam-Filled Cookies

MAKES 3½ dozen cookies
PREP 30 minutes **REFRIGERATE** 1 hour
BAKE at 350° for 8 to 10 minutes

2   **cups all-purpose flour**
¼   **teaspoon baking powder**
¼   **teaspoon salt**
½   **cup (1 stick) unsalted butter,
    at room temperature**
¾   **cup confectioners' sugar**
1   **egg**
1   **teaspoon vanilla**
¼   **cup seedless raspberry jam**
¼   **cup strawberry preserves
    Confectioners' sugar for dusting**

1. Combine flour, baking powder and
    salt in a medium-size bowl. With a
    mixer on low speed, beat together
    butter, confectioners' sugar, egg and
    vanilla in a large bowl until well
    mixed. On low speed, beat in flour
    mixture until blended. Divide dough
    in half; shape each piece into a disc
    and wrap in plastic wrap; refrigerate
    1 hour or until firm.

2. Heat oven to 350°. Coat a baking
    sheet with nonstick cooking spray.

3. Place a sheet of waxed paper on a
    work surface; dust with flour. Roll
    out 1 piece of dough on floured
    waxed paper to ¼-inch thickness.
    Using a 1¾-inch scalloped round
    cutter, cut out cookies. Using a
    ¾-inch plain round cutter, cut a hole
    in center of half of cookies. Repeat
    with second piece of dough. Gather
    hole cutouts and dough scraps; reroll
    and cut out more cookies. You should
    have a total of about 84 cookies.
    Using a wide metal spatula, transfer
    cookies from waxed paper to prepared
    baking sheet.

4. Bake cookies in heated 350° oven
    8 to 10 minutes or until very lightly
    browned around edges. Transfer
    cookies from baking sheet to a wire
    rack to cool.

5. Spread a scant ½ teaspoon jam on
    each solid cookie, using raspberry
    jam for half of the cookies and
    strawberry preserves for other half.
    Dust cookies with hole in center
    with confectioners' sugar; place one
    on each jam-topped cookie.

PER COOKIE
61 calories, 2 g fat (1 g saturated), 1 g protein,
9 g carbohydrate, 0 g fiber, 19 mg sodium,
11 mg cholesterol.

Raspberry-Swirl Lemon Bars

MAKES 32 bars **PREP** 20 minutes
BAKE crust at 350° for 35 minutes;
bars for 35 minutes

Crust

1   **cup (2 sticks) butter, melted**
¼   **cup granulated sugar**
¼   **cup packed light-brown sugar**
2   **teaspoons vanilla**
⅛   **teaspoon salt**
2   **cups all-purpose flour**

Lemon Filling

2   **cups granulated sugar**
⅓   **cup plus 1 tablespoon all-purpose
    flour**
6   **eggs**
½   **cup lemon juice (about 4 lemons)**
2   **teaspoons grated lemon rind**

Raspberry Topping

5 ounces (half of 10-ounce package) frozen raspberries in syrup, thawed

1 tablespoon granulated sugar

1. Heat oven to 350°. Line a 13 x 9 x 2-inch baking pan with aluminum foil.

2. Prepare crust: Using a fork, stir together butter, granulated and brown sugars, vanilla and salt in a medium-size bowl. Gradually stir in flour until smooth. Press dough onto bottom of prepared pan.

3. Bake in heated 350° oven 35 minutes or until edges just start to brown. Transfer crust to a wire rack to cool; leave oven on.

4. Meanwhile, prepare filling: Whisk together granulated sugar and flour in a large bowl. Whisk in eggs until smooth. Stir in lemon juice and lemon rind.

5. Prepare topping: Place raspberries and granulated sugar in a food processor; whirl until smooth. Pour into a glass measuring cup.

6. Spread filling over crust. Pour raspberry mixture in 5 parallel lines across width of pan, using 1 tablespoon for each. Working from one end of pan to the other in alternating directions, gently pull tip of a table knife through raspberry lines, creating a scallop design. Refrigerate remaining raspberry topping for another use.

7. Bake in heated 350° oven 35 minutes or until filling is set. Cool in pan on a wire rack. Cut into 32 bars.

PER BAR
164 calories, 7 g fat (4 g saturated), 2 g protein, 24 g carbohydrate, 0 g fiber, 23 mg sodium, 55 mg cholesterol.

Almond Pine-Nut Cookies

Shown on pages 6 and 220.

MAKES 28 cookies **PREP** 20 minutes
BAKE at 325° for 15 minutes

7 ounces almond paste (marzipan), cut into small pieces
⅓ cup sugar
2 egg whites
½ teaspoon vanilla extract
½ teaspoon orange extract
3 tablespoons all-purpose flour
½ cup pine nuts

1. Position oven rack in top third of oven. Heat oven to 325°. Line 2 baking sheets with parchment paper or aluminum foil. If using foil, coat with nonstick cooking spray.

2. With mixer on low speed, beat together marzipan, sugar and 1 egg white in a medium-size bowl until smooth. Beat in second egg white, then vanilla and orange extracts. Stir in flour until a stiff dough forms.

3. Drop dough by heaping teaspoonfuls onto prepared baking sheets, spacing 2 inches apart. Cover each cookie with pine nuts, using ½ teaspoon for each.

4. Bake in top third of heated 325° oven until edges are golden, about 15 minutes. Cool cookies on baking sheets on wire racks.

PER COOKIE
60 calories, 3 g fat (0 g saturated), 2 g protein, 7 g carbohydrate, 1 g fiber, 5 mg sodium, 0 mg cholesterol.

Chocolate-Dipped Almond Biscotti

MAKES 2 dozen biscotti **PREP** 20 minutes
BAKE almonds at 375° for 4 to 5 minutes;
biscotti at 375° for 15 to 18 minutes;
then at 325° for 15 to 20 minutes

1	cup blanched slivered almonds
1¼	cups all-purpose flour
1	teaspoon baking powder
¼	teaspoon salt
6	tablespoons butter, at room temperature
½	cup sugar
1	whole egg
1	egg yolk
½	teaspoon vanilla extract
¼	teaspoon almond extract
1	teaspoon grated orange rind
8	squares (1 ounce each) bittersweet chocolate, chopped

1. Heat oven to 375°. Spread almonds evenly on a baking sheet.

2. Bake in heated 375° oven 4 to 5 minutes or until lightly browned. Let cool, then coarsely chop. Leave oven on.

3. Whisk together flour, baking powder and salt in a small bowl. Beat butter and sugar in a medium-size bowl until creamy. Beat in whole egg, egg yolk, vanilla and almond extracts and orange rind. Stir flour mixture into butter mixture. Stir in chopped almonds.

4. Scrape dough onto an ungreased baking sheet. Shape into an 11 x 4-inch log. If dough is too soft to hold its shape, refrigerate until firm.

5. Bake in heated 375° oven 15 to 18 minutes or until lightly browned. Remove log to a cutting board. Lower oven temperature to 325°.

6. Let log stand until cool enough to handle, about 10 minutes.

7. Using a serrated knife, cut log crosswise on a slight angle into ½-inch-thick slices. Gently transfer slices to a clean ungreased baking sheet, cut side down.

8. Bake in heated 325° oven 15 to 20 minutes or until golden. Transfer biscotti to a wire rack to cool completely.

9. Line a baking sheet with waxed paper. Melt chocolate in top of a double boiler over barely simmering, not boiling, water, stirring until smooth. Remove pan from above water. One at a time, dip one end of each biscotti into chocolate and then place on lined baking sheet. Let stand in a cool place until chocolate is firm.

PER BISCOTTI
150 calories, 9 g fat (4 g saturated), 3 g protein,
16 g carbohydrate, 1 g fiber, 44 mg sodium,
26 mg cholesterol.

Gingerbread Cookies

MAKES sixteen 3½-inch cookies
PREP 20 minutes **REFRIGERATE** 1 hour
BAKE at 350° for about 15 minutes

2½ **cups all-purpose flour**
2 **teaspoons ground ginger**
1 **teaspoon ground cinnamon**
½ **teaspoon salt**
¼ **teaspoon ground cloves**
14 **tablespoons (1¾ sticks) unsalted butter, at room temperature**
1 **cup packed dark-brown sugar**
2 **egg yolks**
1 **teaspoon vanilla**

Icing and Decorations
2½ **cups confectioners' sugar**
¼ **cup orange juice**
½ **teaspoon orange extract**
  Assorted soft gel paste food colors
  Assorted candies, such as licorice whips, fruit leather and gumdrops

1. Sift together flour, ginger, cinnamon, salt and cloves in a medium-size bowl.

2. With a mixer on low speed, beat butter and brown sugar in a large bowl until smooth and creamy. Beat in egg yolks and vanilla. Stir flour mixture into butter mixture just until blended. Divide dough in half; shape each piece into a disc and wrap in plastic wrap. Refrigerate until firm enough to roll, about 1 hour.

3. Heat oven to 350°. Line a large baking sheet with parchment paper or aluminum foil.

4. On a well-floured surface, roll out 1 disc of dough to ⅛-inch thickness.

5. Using any desired 3½-inch cookie cutter, cut out cookies. Using a wide metal spatula, carefully transfer cookies to prepared baking sheet, spacing 1 inch apart. Gather dough scraps; if too soft to reroll, refrigerate until firm, about 10 minutes. Reroll scraps and cut out more cookies.

6. Bake cookies in heated 350° oven until golden brown, about 15 minutes. Cool cookies completely on baking sheet on a wire rack.

7. Prepare icing: Whisk together confectioners' sugar, orange juice and orange extract in a medium-size bowl. Divide into several batches; tint each batch as desired with food color. If icing is too thick, add a drop or two of water or milk to thin to a good piping consistency. If icing is too thin, add ¼ to ½ cup confectioners' sugar to thicken.

8. Transfer icings to pastry bags fitted with writing tips. Pipe decorations onto cookies as desired.

9. Use icing to attach candies to cookies. Let stand until icing is completely dry.

PER ICED COOKIE (without decorations)
284 calories, 11 g fat (6 g saturated), 3 g protein, 45 g carbohydrate, 1 g fiber, 81 mg sodium, 54 mg cholesterol.

Fruitcake Bars

MAKES 24 bars **PREP** 20 minutes
STAND 4 hours or overnight
BAKE at 350° for 20 to 25 minutes

1   **cup chopped dried pears
    (about 5½ ounces)**
1   **cup raisins**
1   **cup chopped dried figs
    (about 5½ ounces)**
½   **cup dark rum**
¾   **cup all-purpose flour**
½   **teaspoon baking powder**
½   **teaspoon salt**
½   **teaspoon ground ginger**
¼   **teaspoon ground nutmeg**
½   **cup (1 stick) unsalted butter,
    at room temperature**
⅓   **cup packed dark-brown sugar**
2   **eggs**
2   **teaspoons grated orange rind**
1¼ **cups chopped walnuts**

Rum Buttercream Frosting
1   **box (1 pound) confectioners' sugar**
½   **cup (1 stick) unsalted butter, at
    room temperature**
3   **tablespoons dark rum (see note)**
⅛   **teaspoon salt**

1   **tube red decorating icing**
1   **tube green decorating icing**

1. Combine pears, raisins, figs and rum
    in a heavy-duty plastic food-storage
    bag. Seal bag; let stand at least 4 hours
    or overnight.

2. Heat oven to 350°. Line bottom and
    sides of a 13 x 9 x 2-inch baking
    pan with aluminum foil, leaving an
    overhang on short ends. Butter and
    flour foil.

3. Whisk together flour, baking powder,
    salt, ginger and nutmeg in a medium-
    size bowl. With a mixer on medium
    speed, beat butter and brown sugar
    in a large bowl until smooth and
    creamy, about 2 minutes. Add eggs,
    one at a time, beating well after
    each addition. Beat in orange rind.
    Gradually beat flour mixture into
    butter mixture. Stir in walnuts and
    fruit mixture. Spoon batter into
    prepared pan, smoothing top.

4. Bake in heated 350° oven 20 to
    25 minutes or until a wooden pick
    inserted in center comes out clean.
    Transfer pan to a wire rack and let
    cool completely.

5. Prepare frosting: With mixer on low
    speed, beat confectioners' sugar,
    butter, rum and salt in a large bowl
    until blended. Increase speed to
    medium and beat until mixture is a
    good spreading consistency, about
    2 minutes.

6. Lift foil from pan to remove cake;
    transfer cake to a work surface.
    Spread frosting over top of cake. Cut
    cake into 24 bars. Decorate bars with
    squiggly lines of red and green icing.

*Note: For frosting, you can substitute
3 tablespoons orange juice and 1 teaspoon
grated orange rind for the rum.*

PER BAR
237 calories, 8 g fat (5 g saturated), 2 g protein,
40 g carbohydrate, 2 g fiber, 54 mg sodium,
38 mg cholesterol.

Black-and-White Fudge Brownies

MAKES 16 brownies **PREP** 20 minutes
BAKE at 325° for 35 to 40 minutes

¼ **cup (½ stick) butter or margarine, at room temperature**
1 **package (6 ounces) semisweet chocolate chips (1 cup)**
4 **ounces white baking chocolate, chopped**
¼ **cup solid vegetable shortening**
2 **eggs**
1 **cup sugar**
½ **teaspoon vanilla**
¼ **teaspoon salt**
1 **cup all-purpose flour**

Garnish (optional)
16 **whole blanched almonds**
   Melted semisweet chocolate

1. Heat oven to 325°. Coat an 8 x 8 x 2-inch square baking pan with nonstick cooking spray.

2. Combine butter and ½ cup chocolate chips in a small metal bowl. Set over simmering water and stir until melted. Set aside to cool slightly.

3. Combine white chocolate and shortening in another metal bowl. Melt over simmering water as in step 2. Set aside to cool slightly.

4. With mixer on medium speed, beat together 1 egg, ½ cup sugar, vanilla and ⅛ teaspoon salt in a medium-size bowl until foamy, about 30 seconds. Stir in dark chocolate mixture and ½ cup flour until well blended. Stir in remaining ½ cup chocolate chips.

5. In a second medium-size bowl, beat remaining egg, remaining ½ cup sugar and remaining ⅛ teaspoon salt until foamy, about 30 seconds. Stir in white chocolate mixture and remaining ½ cup flour.

6. Alternating dark and white chocolate mixtures, drop heaping tablespoonfuls of batter into prepared baking pan. Swirl gently with a knife to marbleize.

7. Bake in heated 325° oven 35 to 40 minutes or until a wooden pick inserted in center comes out clean. Cool in pan on a wire rack. Cut into 16 squares.

8. If garnish is desired, dip almonds, one at a time, into melted chocolate and immediately press onto top of brownies.

PER BROWNIE
231 calories, 13 g fat (6 g saturated), 3 g protein, 29 g carbohydrate, 1 g fiber, 54 mg sodium, 36 mg cholesterol.

Berry-Pistachio Swirl Cookies

MAKES 3 dozen cookies **PREP** 20 minutes
REFRIGERATE 2 hours
BAKE at 375° for 10 to 12 minutes

½ **cup (1 stick) unsalted butter, at room temperature**
½ **cup sugar**
1 **egg**
1 **teaspoon vanilla**
1¾ **cups all-purpose flour**
½ **teaspoon baking powder**
¼ **teaspoon salt**
⅓ **cup finely ground shelled pistachios (1½ ounces)**
10 **drops green food coloring**
2 **tablespoons raspberry jam**
10 **drops red food coloring**

PACK 'EM UP

Soft drop, bar and fruit cookies are among the best travelers; choose them to mail to far-flung family and friends.

- Use a metal container or decorative tin. Line the container with waxed paper or aluminum foil.

- Wrap cookies airtight. Wrap 2 drop cookies back to back, wrap bar cookies individually.

- Nest cookies securely in container, packing them close together to minimize shifting. Use crumpled foil or waxed paper as filler. The container should be so full that you have to use a little pressure to tape it shut. Place the container in a sturdy shipping box, cushioning it so it fits tightly.

1. With a mixer on low speed, beat butter and sugar in a large bowl until smooth and creamy. Whisk egg and vanilla in a small bowl until frothy.

2. Sift together flour, baking powder and salt in a medium-size bowl. Stir flour mixture into butter mixture until a stiff dough forms.

3. Transfer half of dough to a medium-size bowl; stir in pistachios and green food coloring until blended. Stir together jam and red food coloring in a small bowl; stir into other half of dough.

4. Place green dough on a sheet of plastic wrap. Pat into an 11 x 8-inch rectangle. Place red dough on another sheet of plastic wrap. With well-floured hands, pat dough into an 11 x 8-inch rectangle. Invert red dough onto green dough; peel off plastic wrap from red dough. Starting from a long side, roll up dough, jelly-roll fashion; wrap in plastic wrap. Refrigerate at least 2 hours or until firm.

5. Heat oven to 375°. Lightly coat a large baking sheet with nonstick cooking spray.

6. Unwrap dough. Using a thin sharp knife, cut rolled dough into ¼-inch-thick slices. Place on prepared baking sheet, spacing 1 inch apart.

7. Bake in heated 375° oven 10 to 12 minutes or until edges just begin to color. Be careful not to overbake. Cool cookies on baking sheet on a wire rack 5 minutes. Transfer cookies to wire rack to cool completely.

PER COOKIE
64 calories, 3 g fat (2 g saturated), 1 g protein, 9 g carbohydrate, 0 g fiber, 24 mg sodium, 13 mg cholesterol.

Lime Squares

MAKES 16 squares **PREP** 20 minutes
BAKE at 350° for about 40 minutes

Pastry Crust

7 tablespoons unsalted butter,
   at room temperature
⅓ cup sugar
1 teaspoon grated lime rind
½ teaspoon vanilla
¼ teaspoon salt
1 cup all-purpose flour

Lime Topping

⅔ cup sugar
5 tablespoons fresh lime juice
2 eggs
2½ tablespoons all-purpose flour
2 teaspoons grated lime rind
2 teaspoons grated lemon rind
½ teaspoon baking powder
1 to 2 drops green food coloring

8 maraschino cherries, drained
   and halved
   Green decorating icing in tube
   or candy mint leaves

1. Heat oven to 350°. Line a 9 x 9 x
    2-inch square baking pan with
    aluminum foil, leaving an overhang
    on 2 opposite sides. Butter foil lightly
    or coat with nonstick cooking spray.

2. Prepare crust: With a mixer on low
    speed, beat butter and sugar in a
    medium-size bowl until smooth and
    creamy. Beat in lime rind, vanilla and
    salt. Beat in flour just until combined
    and a crumbly dough forms.

3. Dip your fingers in flour to coat well.
    Pat dough evenly over bottom of
    prepared pan. Prick dough all over
    with a fork.

4. Bake in heated 350° oven until
    golden, 18 to 20 minutes.

5. Meanwhile, prepare topping: Stir
    together sugar, lime juice, eggs, flour,
    lime rind, lemon rind, baking powder
    and food coloring in a medium-size
    bowl until very smooth.

6. Remove pan with crust from oven;
    leave oven on. Pour topping over
    crust. Return to oven and bake until
    topping is set, 15 to 20 minutes.
    Transfer pan to a wire rack and let
    cool completely.

7. Lift foil out of pan to remove lime
    square. Using a sharp knife, cut into
    16 squares or diamonds. Decorate
    each piece with a maraschino cherry
    half. Pipe on a green icing leaf or add
    a candy mint leaf.

PER SQUARE
142 calories, 6 g fat (3 g saturated), 2 g protein,
22 g carbohydrate, 0 g fiber, 57 mg sodium,
40 mg cholesterol.

Coconut Rum Balls

Shown on page 217.

MAKES 2 dozen rum balls
PREP 10 minutes **STAND** 30 minutes
before baking; then 24 hours after baking
BAKE at 325° for 18 minutes

1   package (7 ounces) sweetened
    flake coconut
6   tablespoons apricot jam
¼   cup dark rum
¼   teaspoon almond extract
1   cup finely crushed vanilla wafers
    (about 30 cookies)

1. Heat oven to 325°.

2. Spread out coconut evenly on a
    baking sheet. Bake in heated 325°
    oven until golden, about 18 minutes,
    stirring 2 to 3 times during baking.
    Let cool.

3. Stir together jam, rum and almond
    extract in a medium-size bowl. Stir
    in crushed vanilla wafers and 2 cups
    coconut. Cover; let stand 30 minutes.

4. Meanwhile, place remaining coconut
    in a plastic food-storage bag on a flat
    surface; crush coconut with a rolling
    pin. Spread coconut on a sheet of
    waxed paper.

5. Using damp hands, shape cookie
    mixture into 1-inch balls. Roll in
    coconut. Place rum balls on a platter.
    Let air-dry 24 hours.

PER RUM BALL
82 calories, 4 g fat (3 g saturated), 1 g protein,
11 g carbohydrate, 1 g fiber, 42 mg sodium,
0 mg cholesterol.

Chocolate-Hazelnut Crunch Bars

Shown on page 133.

MAKES 16 bars **PREP** 10 minutes
BAKE at 350° for 20 to 22 minutes

½   cup (1 stick) unsalted butter,
    cut into 10 pieces
½   cup packed light-brown sugar
1¼ cups all-purpose flour
⅓   cup plus ¼ cup finely chopped
    hazelnuts
½   cup jarred chocolate-hazelnut spread

1. Heat oven to 350°.

2. Heat butter and brown sugar in a
    medium-size saucepan over medium-
    high heat, stirring, until melted,
    smooth and bubbly. Remove saucepan
    from heat. Stir in flour, then ⅓ cup
    hazelnuts to make a stiff dough.
    Spread and press dough into an
    8 x 8 x 2-inch square baking pan.

3. Bake in heated 350° oven 20 to
    22 minutes or until top is golden
    brown and edges are firm. Cool in
    pan on a wire rack 10 minutes.

4. Spread chocolate-hazelnut spread
    evenly on top of cookie base. Sprinkle
    with remaining ¼ cup hazelnuts. Cut
    cookie into 16 bars. Serve at room
    temperature or refrigerate, covered,
    and serve chilled.

PER BAR
179 calories, 11 g fat (4 g saturated), 2 g protein,
20 g carbohydrate, 1 g fiber, 11 mg sodium,
16 mg cholesterol.

Christmas Stollen

MAKES 3 stollen (8 servings each)
PREP 30 minutes **RISE** 2½ to 3 hours
BAKE at 350° for 35 minutes

¾ **cup milk**
½ **cup water**
½ **cup (1 stick) butter, cut into pats**
4¼ **cups bread flour**
½ **cup granulated sugar**
2 **teaspoons salt**
2 **envelopes active dry yeast**
1 **egg**
¾ **cup candied fruit**
¾ **cup nuts, such as almonds, pecans and/or walnuts, chopped**
½ **cup raisins**
1 **teaspoon grated lemon rind**
1 **teaspoon grated orange rind**
¾ **teaspoon ground mace**

Topping
2 **tablespoons butter, melted**
¼ **cup granulated sugar**
3 **tablespoons confectioners' sugar**

1. Heat milk, water and butter in a small saucepan over medium heat until temperature of mixture registers 120° on an instant-read thermometer.

2. Whisk together 1¼ cups flour, sugar, salt and yeast in a large bowl. Add warm milk mixture; beat on medium speed 2 minutes. Add egg and 1 cup flour; beat on high speed 2 minutes. Stir in remaining 2 cups flour until batter is stiff. Transfer to a greased large bowl; turn to coat. Cover with plastic wrap. Let rise in a warm place until doubled in volume, 1½ hours.

3. Combine candied fruit, nuts, raisins, lemon rind, orange rind and mace in a small bowl. Turn out dough onto a lightly floured surface. Knead fruit mixture into dough.

4. Divide dough into thirds. Shape each third into a loaf, first rolling it into a 10 x 8-inch oval, then folding oval in half lengthwise and curving each end slightly. Transfer each to a greased baking sheet. Cover with plastic wrap; let rise in warm place until doubled in volume, 1 to 1½ hours.

5. Heat oven to 350°.

6. Bake stollen 35 minutes or until bottom of loaves sounds hollow when tapped. Transfer loaves from baking sheet to wire racks to cool 1 hour.

7. Add topping: Brush loaves with melted butter. Sprinkle with granulated sugar. Dust tops with confectioners' sugar.

PER SERVING
219 calories, 8 g fat (3 g saturated), 5 g protein, 33 g carbohydrate, 1 g fiber, 207 mg sodium, 23 mg cholesterol.

Christmas Wreath Cake

Make the almond paste pine cone decorations ahead, when you make the pine needles, or wait and make them while the cake is baking. Shown on page 232.

MAKES 16 servings
PREP 45 minutes plus decorating time
DRY pine needles 5 hours or overnight
BAKE at 350° for 30 to 35 minutes
COOK meringue 15 to 20 minutes

Pine Needles and Pine Cones

- 1 box (1 pound) confectioners' sugar
- 3 tablespoons meringue powder (see page 232)
- ½ teaspoon cream of tartar
- 6 to 8 tablespoons warm water
  Leaf green soft gel paste food color
- 3 teaspoons almond paste (marzipan)
- ¼ cup sliced almonds (not blanched)

Cake

- 2¼ cups cake flour (not self-rising)
- ⅓ cup unsweetened cocoa powder
- 2 teaspoons baking powder
- ½ teaspoon baking soda
- ½ teaspoon salt
- 3 squares (1 ounce each) unsweetened chocolate, chopped
- ¾ cup (1½ sticks) butter, at room temperature
- 1½ cups granulated sugar
- 3 eggs
- 1 teaspoon vanilla
- 1¼ cups milk

Italian Meringue

- 2 cups granulated sugar
- ½ cup water
- 8 egg whites, at room temperature
- 2 teaspoons vanilla
- ⅛ teaspoon salt

Decorations

- 1 tablespoon red-dot candies
- 1 strawberry fruit leather

Pine Needles and Pine Cones

1. With a mixer on low speed, beat confectioners' sugar, meringue powder, cream of tartar and warm water in a small bowl until combined. Increase speed to high and beat 10 minutes or until thick and glossy. Beat in food color until icing is desired shade. Place plastic wrap directly on surface of icing until ready to use.

2. Line 3 large baking sheets with waxed paper. Fit a medium-size pastry bag with a coupler and plain writing tip. Fill with half of green icing. Pipe pine needle clusters in various sizes onto lined baking sheets. For each cluster, pipe 4 or 5 individual needles, about 1 inch long, joining them at 1 end; pipe back and forth without lifting tip so each needle is a double thickness for added strength. Refill bag and repeat with remaining icing. Let pine needles dry at room temperature 5 hours or overnight.

3. Form 1 teaspoon marzipan into a pine cone shape, about 1 inch long; press against work surface to flatten back. Press sliced almonds, pointed end down, into marzipan pine cone, forming overlapping layers. Cover with plastic wrap; set aside. Repeat with remaining marzipan and almonds.

Cake and Italian Meringue

1. Prepare cake: Heat oven to 350°. Coat two 9-inch round layer-cake pans with nonstick cooking spray. Line bottom of pans with waxed paper; coat paper with spray.

2. Mix flour, cocoa powder, baking powder, baking soda and salt in a small bowl.

3. Melt chocolate in top of a double boiler over barely simmering, not boiling, water, stirring until smooth. Remove pan from above water and allow to cool.

4. Meanwhile, with a mixer on medium-high speed, beat together butter and granulated sugar in a large bowl 2 to 3 minutes or until smooth and creamy. Add eggs, one at a time, beating well after each addition. Add vanilla and chocolate; beat until combined.

5. On low speed, beat flour mixture into butter mixture in 3 additions, alternating with milk and ending with flour; beat on medium speed 2 to 3 minutes or until well blended. Scrape batter into prepared pans, dividing equally.

6. Bake in heated 350° oven 30 to 35 minutes or until a wooden pick inserted in center of cake layers comes out clean. Cool cake layers in pans on wire racks 10 minutes. Run a thin knife around inside of pans. Turn out layers onto wire racks to cool completely. Trim with a serrated knife to level if necessary.

7. Prepare meringue: Heat granulated sugar and water in small heavy-bottomed saucepan over medium-high heat until syrup registers 242° on a candy thermometer, about 15 to 20 minutes; brush down sides of pan with a wet pastry brush to prevent sugar crystals from forming. Remove from heat.

8. Place egg whites in a deep bowl in a stand mixer fitted with a whisk attachment. Beat on medium-high speed about 15 seconds. Carefully pour hot syrup down sides of bowl into whites without hitting whisk; beat on medium-high speed 5 minutes or until very thick. Add vanilla and salt; beat on high speed 2 to 3 minutes or until glossy peaks form.

Decorate

1. To anchor cake, place a small dollop of meringue in middle of a cake plate. Place 1 cake layer on plate. Spread 1½ cups meringue over top of cake. Place remaining cake layer on top. Frost top and sides of cake with remaining meringue.

2. With a small metal spatula, very gently pry pine needles off waxed paper. Arrange them in a random pattern around edge of cake top to form a wreath. (The pine needles are very fragile and many will break as you handle them; don't worry, this will make the wreath look more authentic.)

3. Unwrap pine cones. Arrange pine cones and red-dot candies randomly on wreath.

4. Form a decorative bow with a strip of strawberry fruit leather and place on wreath.

PER SERVING
589 calories, 23 g fat (9 g saturated), 11 g protein, 92 g carbohydrate, 4 g fiber, 245 mg sodium, 66 mg cholesterol.

Santa Claus Cake

MAKES 20 servings
PREP 35 minutes plus decorating time
BAKE at 350° for 35 to 40 minutes

2   cups all-purpose flour
1   tablespoon baking powder
½   teaspoon salt
1¼ cups granulated sugar
½   cup solid vegetable shortening
4   egg whites
2   tablespoons vanilla extract
1   cup milk
½   cup drained maraschino cherries,
    chopped

Frosting
½   cup (1 stick) butter, at room
    temperature
½   cup solid vegetable shortening

2   boxes (1 pound each)
    confectioners' sugar
2   teaspoons peppermint extract
2   teaspoons vanilla extract
6   to 7 tablespoons heavy cream

Decorations
    Pink and red soft gel paste
    food colors
2   medium blue gumdrops
1   red jelly bean
1   large red gumdrop

1. Heat oven to 350°. Coat a large
    heart-shaped cake pan (9½ x 8½ x
    2½ inches) with nonstick cooking
    spray. Line bottom with waxed paper;
    coat paper with spray.

2. Whisk together flour, baking powder
    and salt in a large bowl.

3. In another large bowl, beat together
    granulated sugar and shortening
    on medium-high speed until well
    combined, about 2 minutes. Beat in
    egg whites until combined. Add
    vanilla; beat 1 minute.

4. On low speed, beat flour mixture into
    shortening mixture in 3 additions,
    alternating with milk and ending with
    flour mixture. Fold in cherries. Pour
    batter into prepared pan.

5. Bake in heated 350° oven 35 to
    40 minutes or until cake springs back
    when lightly pressed with a fingertip.
    Let cake cool in pan on a wire rack
    15 minutes. Turn out cake onto rack
    and let cool completely.

6. Prepare frosting: On low speed, beat
    butter, shortening, confectioners'
    sugar, peppermint and vanilla extracts
    and 6 tablespoons cream in a medium-
    size bowl until smooth. Add another
    1 tablespoon cream if needed to make
    a good consistency for spreading
    and piping.

Decorate

1. Tint ¾ cup frosting light pink. Place cooled cake on a cake plate. Spread pink frosting in a thin coat over top of cake.

2. Spread about ¼ cup white frosting in a thin coat on sides of cake.

3. Position cake with pointed end facing away from you. Using a wooden pick, mark a placement line across cake top for base of Santa's hat, about 3½ to 4 inches from point. Also outline an area about 2½ inches in diameter in middle of cake, where face will be framed by hair and beard.

4. Tint ¼ cup frosting red. Place in a small pastry bag fitted with a coupler and small star tip. Pipe onto pointed end of cake for hat.

5. Place remaining white frosting in a large pastry bag fitted with a coupler and a small shell tip. Pipe white frosting in a tight zigzag across base of hat, making a ruffle.

6. Using a "C" motion, pipe swirls of white frosting to make hair and beard around face area and on sides of cake. Then pipe a white pom-pom on hat point.

7. Place blue gumdrops on face for eyes. Place red jelly bean on face for nose. Slice large red gumdrop in half crosswise; place, cut sides up, on face for cheeks.

8. Pipe on a white moustache. Pipe on a red mouth.

PER SERVING (without candy decorations)
437 calories, 17 g fat (7 g saturated), 3 g protein, 69 g carbohydrate, 0 g fiber, 135 mg sodium, 20 mg cholesterol.

Ricotta Party Tarts

MAKES 12 tarts **PREP** 10 minutes
BAKE at 375° for 35 minutes

1   container (15 ounces) part-skim ricotta cheese
⅔   cup nonfat half-and-half
¼   cup nonfat cream cheese
1   egg
1   teaspoon grated lemon rind
1   teaspoon vanilla
½   cup sugar
⅓   cup all-purpose flour
     Pinch ground nutmeg
2   packages (4 ounces each) graham cracker tart shells (12 shells total)
     Frozen nondairy whipped topping, thawed, for garnish (optional)
     Fresh raspberries for garnish (optional)

1. Heat oven to 375°.

2. Beat together ricotta, half-and-half and cream cheese in a large bowl on low speed until smooth, about 1 minute. Add egg, lemon rind and vanilla; beat until blended. Beat in sugar, flour and nutmeg.

3. Arrange 12 tart shells on a baking sheet. Divide cheese filling equally among tart shells.

4. Bake in heated 375° oven 30 minutes or until an instant-read thermometer inserted in filling registers 160°.

5. Transfer tarts to a wire rack to cool. (Filling will deflate when removed from oven.) If desired, garnish each tart with a dollop of whipped topping and a few raspberries.

PER TART
238 calories, 9 g fat (3 g saturated), 8 g protein, 30 g carbohydrate, 0 g fiber, 270 mg sodium, 30 mg cholesterol.

Christmas Wreath Cake (page 228)

Beyond Basics

Here are some tips you will find helpful when making recipes from this book.

TOASTING NUTS

Toast nuts in a small dry skillet over medium-high heat, stirring, until lightly browned and fragrant, about 3 minutes. Transfer to a plate to cool.

TOASTING COCONUT

Toast coconut in a small dry skillet over medium heat, stirring occasionally and shaking skillet from time to time, until light brown, about 1 minute.

TOASTING SESAME SEEDS

Spread sesame seeds in a small dry skillet and toast over medium heat until fragrant and lightly colored, about 2 minutes.

ABOUT POWDERED EGG WHITES

Meringue powder and egg white powder are available in select supermarkets, gourmet shops and health-food stores. Because of health concerns about eating raw eggs, be sure to use either meringue powder or egg white powder for uncooked icings or other no-cook recipes calling for egg whites.

Index

*Numerals set in bold type
indicate photographs.*

Photography credits

Antonis Achilleos: page 206

David Bishop: page 45

Steve Cohen: pages 7 (left), 51, 67, 68, 74, 84, 85, 94, 153

Brian Hagiwara: pages 3 (top), 6, 7 (top), 9, 14, 16, 34, 36, 38, 49, 55, 75, 88, 103, 126, 127, 128, 132, 133, 144, 146, 152 (top), 160, 166, 170, 174, 179, 180, 184, 189, 193, 195, 198, 205, 208, 211, 214, 216, 217, 220, 223, 225, 227, 230, 232

Rita Maas: pages 116, 117, 118, 177

Steven Mark Needham: pages 3 (left), 7 (bottom), 39, 81, 97, 103

Dean Powell: pages 24 (bottom), 40 (all), 48 (all), 53, 93 (all), 105, 135 (all), 137, 152, (middle and bottom), 178, 181, 183 (all), 185, 187, 204, 210, 214 (bottom)

Carin and David Riley: pages 9 (top), 23, 46, 122

Shaffer/Smith: Michael Kraus: page 2

Mark Thomas: pages 3 (right), 7 (right), 8, 13, 22, 23, 24, 30, 32, 59, 101, 102, 108, 111, 121, 123, 133, 136, 140, 155, 158, 162, 203, 207